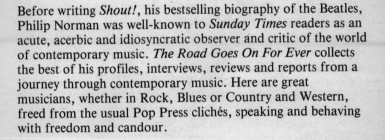

Before writing *Shout!*, his bestselling biography of the Beatles, Philip Norman was well-known to *Sunday Times* readers as an acute, acerbic and idiosyncratic observer and critic of the world of contemporary music. *The Road Goes On For Ever* collects the best of his profiles, interviews, reviews and reports from a journey through contemporary music. Here are great musicians, whether in Rock, Blues or Country and Western, freed from the usual Pop Press clichés, speaking and behaving with freedom and candour.

'Thank goodness for Philip Norman . . . such an observant writer, so precise about the physical marks of ambition and failure, that even his most ephemeral pieces are still resonant.'
Simon Frith, New Statesman

Also by Philip Norman

SHOUT! The True Story of the Beatles
THE SKATER'S WALTZ (a novel)

and published by Corgi Books

The Road Goes on Forever

Portraits From a Journey Through Contemporary Music

Philip Norman

CORGI BOOKS

THE ROAD GOES ON FOREVER

A CORGI BOOK 0 552 99051 5

Originally published in Great Britain by Elm Tree
Books/Hamish Hamilton Ltd.

PRINTING HISTORY
Elm Tree/Hamish Hamilton edition published 1982
Corgi edition published 1984

This book is set in 10/11 pt Mallard

Corgi Books are published by
Transworld Publishers Ltd.,
Century House, 61–63 Uxbridge Road,
Ealing, London W5 5SA

Made and printed in Great Britain by
Cox & Wyman Ltd., Reading, Berks.

Contents

Acknowledgements

All the following pieces were published in the London *Sunday Times* or its companion daily *The Times*. I am grateful to the respective editors for permission to collect them here. Still more indebted am I to Godfrey Smith and Magnus Linklater, my two former editors at *The Sunday Times Magazine*, without whose encouragement and indulgence I would never have made these travels nor attempted these portraits.

I, and my publishers, would also like to thank *The Sunday Times* for permission to use the following copyright photographs: the Everly Brothers and Champion Jack Dupree (photos by Alain Le Garsmeur); the more recent Beach Boys (Sally Soames); Marianne Faithfull (Donald McCullin); Fleetwood Mac and Dolly Parton (David Montgomery); Sting (Michael Ward); Suzi Quatro (Red Saunders); Stevie Wonder and Sleepy John Estes (David Reed); Ivy Benson (Frank Hermann); Fats Domino (Brian Wharton).

Thanks also to the following for the other photographs in the book:

Adrian Boot (Bob Marley); Camera Press Ltd (Johny Cash – photo by John Whitman; Bob Dylan – photo by Nobby Clark; and Barry White – photo by Les Wilson); John Hillelson Agency Ltd (Yoko Ono – photo by Allan Tannenbaum/Sygma); Keystone Press Ltd (John and Yoko, the younger Beach Boys and Ringo Starr); Popperphoto (the recent Elvis Presley) the Press Association (Bill Haley); RCA Records (the young Elvis Presley); David Redfern (the Rolling Stones – photo by Richard E. Aaron; Eric Clapton, Ray Charles, James Brown, Debbie Harry, Alice Cooper, John Lennon, Chuck Berry); Riva Records (Rod Stewart); Universal Pictorial Press Ltd (Bryan Ferry).

Part One
Rock, Pop and Country

What Makes the Stones Keep Rolling

The John F. Kennedy Stadium, Philadelphia, is a bleak circle
of red-tinted stone, with colonnades and sub-Gothic arch-
ways recalling some nineteenth century British colonial fort.
This afternoon, September 25, 1981, the fort has long since
surrendered to the mutineers. On the outside, nothing
remains but the cars with which America's young can so
quickly become an army mobilising. Decrepit 'gas-guzzlers,'
garish Dodge pickups, graffiti-plastered Volkswagen buses
surround JFK Stadium for approximately five square miles,
cooking gently in the pale sunshine, watched over by battal-
ions of mistrustful police. On the inner approaches, officers
in crash helmets sit astride undersized horses whose manure
is the unexpected element in a deep, shifting carpet of cans,
bottles, food wrapping and foot-crunched paper cups.

Within the castellated walls an audience of 90,000 awaits
the first concert in the Rolling Stones' twentieth anniversary
American tour. The crowd fills even this immense baseball
arena, sloping down thick on all sides to the stage erected at
its far-distant western curve. The stage, slung between scaffolding towers, is draped with pale pink and purple and
moored in place by bunches of multi-coloured balloons. It is
also – as it has been for several hours – devoid of any activity.
The crowd bears this vigil, not merely with patience but with
enjoyment. Overhead, a small plane drones in circles, towing
letters that form an incomprehensible message. Helicopters,
informing police or radio stations, hover down low, casting
shadows like giant bees over the seething, shirtless multitude.

The Stones wait to perform in a walled garden implanted at

11

the inner end of the players' tunnel. Canvas screens, painted in vague psychedelic colours, surmounted at intervals by Japanese masks on poles, have been insecurely fastened around two trailer caravans and a square of bright green artificial turf. In the centre stand three white tables with sun umbrellas, such as one might see outside any London suburban pub.

Mick Jagger, in a bright yellow jacket and American football player's kneebreeches, trots briskly round the garden's perimeter. At intervals he stops, touches his toes, spreads his legs, flexes his trunk and works his shoulder muscles from the elbow. He is 38 and, from a distance, almost eerily unchanged. His body remains as slight and self-aware as a girl's before puberty. Hair, still growing thick, still teased into feminine lovelocks, edges the same wide-set eyes, retroussé nose and broad, full, endlessly ambiguous mouth.

The face is heavily made up, to hide the wrinkles and deep cheek-grooves that predominate now in Jagger's photographs. Likewise, his body keeps its girlishness only by incessant hard physical exercise. This past month, while rehearsing with the Stones, Jagger has run seven miles daily, played squash and exercised with weights and barbells. His circuit-training continues until the moment he starts to sing. How it would astonish the colonels and chief constables who used to say that what these damned Rolling Stones needed was a good, stiff dose of P.T.

Only two of the four remaining Stones have so far arrived in the garden. Bill Wyman, the bass guitarist, and Charlie Watts, the drummer, stand around in the postures of what must be an eternal drinks party. Wyman, whose pallid scowl so long epitomised the menace of the Stones, nowadays looks positively benign. Watts, grey-haired, in a pastel-striped sweater, wanders back and forth a little distractedly. His face, always dourly soulful, has assumed the expression of a man with some safe, cherished skill, like pottery. 'We should have been on at 2.15,' he murmurs. 'I hate keeping people waiting.'

A stir in the exterior compound announces that the last two

12

Stones are finally here. Keith Richards and Ronnie Wood come in together accompanied by a retinue of girls bearing rugs, half-empty liquor bottles and small, bedraggled cigarettes. The effect, on that pastoral pantomine set, is of matching Demon Kings. Wood, spiky-haired, in earrings, bangles and a red leather jerkin, staggers along on heels as high as a wartime tart's. Richards, corpse-pale, unshaven, worn as thin by excess as Jagger is by exertion, wears little but his scuffed boots, white scarf, dirty jeans, and his pale translucent skin. As he comes, he flicks off the top of a beer bottle with his thumb. Those in the garden know better than to offer him a glass.

Bill Wyman looks at his watch, then starts towards one of the painted caravan doors. 'It's like going off with the family to the seaside,' he says. 'You have to make sure and have a wee first. We *are* on stage for two hours.'

Even Wyman, the Stones' own archivist, is unsure on what precise date their twentieth anniversary falls. He remembers only that it was in December 1962, a cold, snowy day, when he hauled his bass guitar and amplifier into the Weatherby Arms, Chelsea, to audition with a Rhythm and Blues group whose three student members, Wyman thought, looked offputtingly 'bohemian.'

Mick would be, as in all things, the final arbiter. But Mick makes a point of remembering almost nothing of his career as Rock and Roll's Lucifer. 'I can't remember things from day to day. Some songs have memories. "Under My Thumb" – that's all pink. We were in LA when we wrote it. I can visualise girls' pink lipstick, pink room interiors, pink cushions. "Angie" has definite memories. "Time Is On My Side" – that's girls of the teenage romance variety. Some funny moments stand out. Otherwise it's just a blur. I can't even remember which prison I was in.'

The Stones are not merely together after 20 years. They are also remarkably cheerful about it. They show none of the amnesiac self-loathing that ultimately overtook the Beatles. The Stones, of course, have managed to hold on to everything

13

the Beatles lost. They kept their unity, their money and – most surprising – their friendship. 'It's good fun,' Mick Jagger says when asked how they can bear to go on tour again. 'We've always had fun on the road. We still do. We have a good time. That's what it's all about.'

It was Keith Richards, in fact, who late last year began the long process of enticing his fellow Stones from plutocratic semi-retirement, back to the life they had apparently left for good after their last tour, in 1978. Jagger, as expected, took longest to persuade. As years pass, it becomes more daunting to reach the peak of fitness required to sing 'Jumping Jack Flash.' 'It means going into training, then on the wagon for three months. I knew when I got back onstage, I'd enjoy it. But performing's like sex. You might like it, but you don't want to do it non-stop.'

What finally emerged was the biggest, most ambitious and arduous tour the Stones have ever made, lasting for 14 weeks, visiting 26 cities, crossing and re-crossing the American continent by way of such unlikely stops as Buffalo, NY, and Boulder, Colorado, playing to a total audience of three million people. Its earnings, from ticket-sales alone, are estimated at $40 million. Then there are corollary earnings from the Stones' new album, *Tattoo You*, already several weeks at number one in the American chart. There are proceeds from souvenir T-shirts, authorised by the Stones, retailing at $12 each. There are proceeds from film, TV and video rights, and from the permission granted to Jovan Inc, a perfumery firm, to print its name across the top of every admission ticket.

The event is one calculated to bring an entire generation out of retirement. Sixties children, in relics of Peace and Karma, are clamouring for this chance to recollect an era, now distant as Edwardian sunshine, before Punk Rock, unemployment, pattern baldness and Mark David Chapman. That is the least part of the Stones' following – of the crowd now thundering its welcome at JFK Stadium. 'Every time we go out onstage,' Bill Wyman says, 'I always think to myself, this time, the *really* young kids won't have bothered to come and see us. But there they are, every time.'

*   *   *

14

Here they are, the front row of 90,000, teenagers, sun-dazed and hose-draggled, stretching up arms to an idol old enough to be their father; swaying in ecstasy to a song recorded almost before they were born. It is 'Under My Thumb' from 1965, the lost world of Kings Road bistros, boutiques and Courrèges boots. The singer has forsaken his peacock robes for athletics kit. But the voice has not aged a day. It is still undecided between pseudo-American and too blatant Cockney, still triumphantly classless, careless, heartless and remorseless.

Whole eras can be summoned up by the outfits in which Mick Jagger has appeared onstage. There was the shock of his matelot shirts in 1964, around the northern Odeon circuit. There was the girl's frilly dress he wore in Hyde Park in 1969, reading Shelley as a requiem for the dead Stone, Brian Jones. There was the semi-drag and warpaint of 'Jumping Jack Flash.' where rock music seemed nearest to a pact with the Devil.

Decades as a figure of quintessential fashion have left Jagger in 1981 strangely muted, vague and contourless. With his scarlet vest, white knee breeches and red stockings, he might belong in almost any century. It is the gradual working up of the vest, to show a torso flaunted like an undeveloped bust, which proclaims this is no medieval troubadour. It is the snagging of the waistband down, and further down, which tells us this is no eighteenth century cabin boy.

Clothes are mere adjuncts – as songs are – to Jagger's real art, the projection of sex across wide open spaces by gargantuan physical effort. That girlish toss of his head is a challenge delivered equally to 90,000, both female and male. That strutting, elbow-pumping walk carries its suggestion over the full expanse of heads and arms and waving banners. They can see the glare on his face, the very pout of his lips, from terraces a quarter of a mile away.

Even Jagger cannot hide the fact that the Stones, after their three-year lay-off, sound nothing like the world's greatest surviving Rock band. The figures of Keith Richards and Ron Wood, mooching with their guitars round the pink dais, serve only to underline the incongruousness of Rock in a stadium on an overcast afternoon. They have opted for safety – a straight

15

run through the Jagger-Richards songbook, varied by simple old favourites like 'Black Cadillac' and 'Just My Imagination.' The effect, despite six weeks' intensive practice, is of a rehearsal no one quite wants to begin. 'Woody,' never the most tuneful lead guitarist, has as little control of his instrument as a man with a pneumatic drill. Richards, bent almost double under Jagger's ballet leaps, often constructs barely half of some essential driving chord.

As mistakes continue, the roar from the stadium becomes subdued. Philadelphia has realised it is being used for a two-day tuning-up session. Jagger by himself cannot win them, though he tries with all his might, teasing, goading, stripping to the waist, prancing down the catwalks, rolling himself, like some child at bathtime, in a cloak made from the British and American flags. 'Can you hear me at the back?' he keeps asking. 'All right! All *right*!' After one fluffed intro, the two guitarists stop and start again. 'It's no good,' Jagger says, burying his face in his hands.

Backstage, with an hour still to spare, the Stones' entourage begin preparing their escape from JFK Stadium. Photographers are invited, by jabbing fingers, to withdraw into the deserted rear grandstand. Below the stage-ramp, three minibuses wait in evident order of seniority. Jagger's girl friend, Jerry Hall, and his nine-year-old daughter, Jade, hold themselves in readiness to rejoin the court as it passes. Jerry is the world's top model, a Texan girl of wideawake beauty, with pale blonde hair, dressed entirely in gold. Jade looks bored, as nine-year-olds usually are at formal grown-up occasions.

The final hour is an unbroken run of classic Stones rabble-rousers – 'Tumbling Dice,' 'Honky-Tonk Woman,' 'Brown Sugar,' 'Street-Fighting Man.' Backstage, the 'paramedics' stand in symbolic readiness with stretchers and oxygen. Outside the stadium, police sirens explode in mad whirligigs. Spectators on the top terrace look outward with sudden interest. Meanwhile, from the under-stage girders, a security man comes high-stepping, beckoning yellow-shirted colleagues from all directions. A posse of 10 or so plunges in

16

after him. They emerge with their quarry, a school-age boy, restraining him by the arms and legs and shoulders and ankles and throat.

The Stones have been onstage for two hours, 20 minutes. The climax – there can be no other – is 'Jumping Jack Flash.' Keith Richards, contorted like a jungle fighter in ambush, beats out the malign tattoo which almost by itself killed off the smiling Sixties. This version, almost 10 minutes long, ends with Jagger scaling the left-hand stage tower and climbing into the open cab of a 'cherry-picker' crane, to be swung out, 30 feet above the audience, gasping 'It's a gas' and flinging down long-stemmed carnations.

A prying radio station has discovered which hotel the Stones are using for their one-night stopover near Buffalo. In exchange for maintaining secrecy, the station is allowed to interview an anonymous hotel employee on its morning rush hour show. One might be eavesdropping on a direct telephone link into some embassy held by terrorists.

'– so the Stones checked in late last night?'
'Yes, sir. They checked in real late.'
'And they're still in their rooms as of now.'
'Yes, sir. All still in their rooms.'
'Not moving round the public areas at all?'
'No, sir.'
'Just staying real quiet in their rooms, huh?'
'Yes, sir. It's been real quiet.'
'Real quiet, huh?'
'Yes, sir.'
'No screaming groupies – nothing like that?'
'No, sir.'
'So the Stones can come back?'
'They sure can!'

The system was perfected long ago when a Rolling Stone ranked as a public enemy. They run from the stage, straight into their vans, to be driven off at high speed among police motorcyclists, under a diversionary blaze of fireworks. They are taken directly to their privately-chartered Boeing 707 and flown to the next city, arriving after midnight in hotel lobbies conveniently deserted. Next day, until early afternoon, no sound comes from their quarters but orders for room-service.

The hotels are unextravagant – mostly Hyatts and Marriotts, block-booked at advantageous rates. Jagger claims not to mind their standardised anonymity. 'I've stayed in most of them before. I know they're okay – for what we need anyway. It doesn't matter to me where I stay. The only thing is, I *do* like to wake up in the countryside.'

He has awoken this morning at the Amherst-Marriott, a glum, grey tower block just beyond the industrial wasteland of Buffalo, N.Y. The rooms are uniformly equipped with brown and orange chintz bedspreads and heavy pseudo-Victorian ceiling lamps. The coffee shop is a lighted labyrinth, so perplexing that your 'hostess' cannot seat you without prolonged consultation of a flashing operations board.

Buffalo's importance is its nearness to Canada. The Stones are still unwelcome there as a result of Keith Richards's conviction for heroin-smuggling during the 1978 tour. Canadian fans are already crossing the border in thousands, skirting the rainy sliproads to Niagara Falls, asking directions to Rich Stadium in low, earnest tones that earn mistrustful stares from the Mountie-hatted highway patrol.

Buffalo's chief autumn feature is a tattered grey sky which, for all its apparent stillness, harbours frequent rain squalls and wind of a malign ferocity. At Rich Stadium, 25 miles away, the wind scuds down the empty stands at a steady 40 mph. A dozen scaffolders cling around the Stones' pink and purple stage set like sailors working an Indiaman around Cape Horn. By midday, the wind has shredded the set to its bare girders. The show will proceed none the less. As American promoters blithely phrase it, 'this is an all-weather ticket.'

The wind is so fierce, it smashes Jagger's hand-mike back against his teeth, loosening the small diamond embedded in his right upper molar. The others play, chins sunk into silver neck collars, gripping their guitars like imperilled umbrellas. For much of the time, they cannot hear themselves. The wind snatches the vast kilowattage from the speaker-mouths, whirling it off over their heads, into the great mass of Canadian fans, whose hair forms a continuous brown mass like good quality manure. The wind gulps the applause even of 65,000 sucking it away with the balloons and hats and errant frisbees that dance on the perpetual updraught.

For all that, the five wind-buffeted figures, panoramically visible through denuded girders, have suddenly begun to play like the Rolling Stones of old. At Philadelphia, there was only Jagger, fronting undisciplined Rock 'n' Roll reprobates. At Buffalo, some freak of whim or weather has summoned up their collective power. It is a power of which Jagger himself, however dominant, represents just one fifth. It requires as well the chords that only Keith Richards can shape, and only he can strike in a way to plant the song in the brain before Mick has sung a word. It needs Woody's bum notes and Bill Wyman's taciturnity; an impetus that only sorrowful-looking Charlie can give to drums. All this happens, all at once, at Rich Stadium. They stand in the teeth of the gale like a band in some basement, jamming for love of it.

That new strength inspires Jagger in turn to still greater exertion. The sprawling pink stage, with its two 30-yard purple catwalks, finally becomes too small to contain him. He dances down to the left, kicking out like a drum majorette, beckoning and taunting all 20,000 faces along that curve. He springs up the right-hand catwalk, leaps to the scaffolding, climbs six feet or so and hangs there, leaning out as far as his fingertips will reach. One whole side of Rich Stadium strains to touch hands with him.

Outside, over a 10-mile radius, the police stand ready in grey, wide-hatted clumps. But their fears prove groundless. Sixty-five thousand people disperse, southward and to Canada, in a satiated hush. The Rolling Stones are back in the bloodstream.

*   *   *

One corner of Bill Wyman's motel room is devoted to his travelling furniture. There is hi-fi, and a video recorder on which all the Stones have kept up with the summer's cricket. There is also the custom-built metal case that houses Wyman's private computer. His first act on returning from each concert is to feed the day's data into its ever-growing banks.

His vocation as Rolling Stones' archivist began with a diary kept even before he joined them in 1962. At home in the South of France, his log of their life as a group now runs into volumes, both journals and photographs. He is aided by a prodigious memory, still able to distinguish between 1964 appearances at the Odeon theatre, Hull, or the ABC, Stockton-on-Tees.

He is the neatest as well as quietest Stone. His room at the Hyatt-Orlando is as tidy at midnight as the maids left it this morning. Next to the TV set stand an array of liquor bottles and an untouched Florida salad. 'If you want a beer, there are three Heineken in the bathroom. I don't drink it myself, but I always order three bottles.'

He is also, by a considerable margin, the eldest Rolling Stone. Estimates of his age vary between 40 and 44. In 1962, when Mick and Keith were still students, Bill already had a wife and a flat. So he married young? He smiles, spotting the trap. 'If you like. . . .' He has a son aged 19, studying economics at Birmingham University.

He sits on one half of the couch, in red and black sweater and bright white flannels: a figure still ageless in close-up, still slender as an ungrown boy. 'That's because I don't eat. See my dinner over there – 'aven't touched it. I have to have a *real* cup of tea. Made with milk, not Half-and-Half. But they never bring you the water boiling. Mick carries round his own little portable heater.'

Bill Wyman's 20 years as least-noticed Stone ended last summer with the release of his first solo single, 'Si Si, Je Suis Un Rock Star'. The song was inspired by a decade in tax exile in the South of France, vanquishing a foreign tongue with pronunciation still firmly rooted in Blenheim Road, Penge.

The song was genuinely witty, and it succeeded. Mick plugs it at every concert; it plays during all the intermissions.

Not that among the Stones he ever felt thwarted. In business, if not performance, they maintain absolute democracy. 'We haven't had a manager since 1969. It's all equal shares. Like this tour . . . we all had to vote to do it. And when Stew (Ian Stewart) plays with us, *he* gets a vote as well. The other day on the plane, we had to decide what backing musicians we wanted to use in the future. All of us were given about 40 names on a list, and we had to tick off the ones we wanted.'

The computer is his pride and obsession. He taught himself to use it during the Stones' six-week rehearsal in rural Massachusetts. 'I've put my whole address book into it now. It gives you games to play as well. In Massachusetts, Mick and I played this one called "Dungeons and Dragons".'

His computer-stored address book naturally has a strong feminine bias. 'I've calculated that in the past 20 years, I must have had contact with about a thousand women – sexual and otherwise. And I'm still friends with all of them. They come and see me here, or get in touch with me in France. If anyone comes over, they've got to bring me things I miss about England that you can't get in France. Bird's Custard. I love custard. Jelly, blancmange, Branston pickle. . . .'

The first of two concerts at Orlando's 60,000-seat Tangerine Bowl happens to coincide with Bill Wyman's forty-something birthday. The other Stones plot vaguely to buy him a Goblin Teasmade, but settle for a party in his honour, cruising in a riverboat up and down the lake at nearby Disney World.

There is also a 'singing telegram,' delivered to him backstage at the Tangerine Bowl by a girl in a tailcoat and black net stockings, wearing a toy monkey that claps two cymbals fitfully in time. The girl, seeing her big chance, stretches her song of greeting to almost a quarter of an hour. After a while, a belly-dancer comes into the garden to join her. The girl steps back, clapping her hands, clashing her monkey's cymbals and honking a motor horn concealed in her bosom.

Jerry Hall has again flown in from New York to see Mick.

21

Bereft of gold clothes and make-up, she has taken Jade and assorted other children for a full day at Disney World. 'A lot of freeloaders, aren't they?' Jagger pants as he jogs round the artificial lawn. 'All they came here for was Disney World.'

'Mick doesn't approve of Disney,' his publicist said.

'It's not that I don't approve of it,' Jagger said. 'I just don't want all the fuss of going there. I do like a good Big Dipper. . . .'

There is delay owing to the late arrival, yet again, of Woody and Keith. Two Lear jets have been chartered to bring them from their separate hotels at Palm Beach. They reel in at last, with the usual entourage. 'What time do you call this then?' several colleagues inquire.

Ian Stewart, the sixth Stone, looks up into the humid, balloon-filled Florida sky.

'I'd give anything for a good pint at my local now,' he says wistfully. 'A nice pint of Directors'. Even Watney's would be all right.'

In the main backstage area, security arrangements have been entrusted to Dr Daniel K. Pai, Grand Master or 'White Dragon' of the Pai Lun system of martial arts. Dr Pai is a squat Chinese gentleman in a baby blue tracksuit, from one sleeve of which dangles a small, metal-edged fan. 'The fan,' one of his disciples explains, 'is the emblem of the White Dragon in our order. It's a handy tool in this heat. And it is – er – a weapon.'

Dr Pai is on guard next afternoon also, with sundry disciples, outside the Stones' sequestered block of the Hyatt-Orlando. He sits in the alley on a folding chair, still in his baby blue tracksuit, still holding his killer fan. Occasionally he rises, assumes a fighting stance and pensively lunges and slices at the unthreatening air.

A black man stripped to the waist, his huge muscles shrouded in the corridor twilight, forms a second line of defence. This is Mick Jagger's personal bodyguard and gym-partner. He taps on his master's door, just once, very lightly, then inclines his great, smoky neck in an attitude of intense listening.

The door opens on a sitting room in twilight and chaos.

Clothes, room service dishcovers, hi-fi, cigarette packs, shoes and papers lie strewn over every surface. Heavy drapes shut out the mid-afternoon Florida sun. Amid the disorder, Jerry Hall stands, Vogue-cover fresh, gazing with amusement at a small portable razor that whirs softly in her hand. 'Can you believe that?' she says. 'None of us can get it to stop.'

Jagger comes from the bedroom, pulling on his trousers. 'Let's go out in the garden,' he says. Behind him, two lines of defence still await all comers. He pushes through the curtains, stepping out unguarded on to the motel's public poolside lawn.

Under the sun umbrella, he looks boyish and, in a strange way, virginal. The years, the parties, the scandals, the scouring camera lenses have left no visible scar, or even blemish. Outside his performing self, he becomes the person one imagines he must have been before it all began. His shirt is still untucked from his trousers. His feet are bare. His voice is quiet, almost deferential. His only ornamentation is a businesslike wristwatch and, sparkling like frost on one upper tooth, that diamond.

He is saying that what he really misses about England after all these years is the cricket. When he comes over, it is usually in the hope of spending a day or two at Lord's with his father. He likes, if he can, to see a match played by his own home county. 'I've always been fond of the Kent county ground, right in the middle of Canterbury. . . .' He pauses, almost wistfully. 'Right next to Boots'.'

Jagger frequently seems to pine for Kent. He chose his chateau in France partly because the country around Amboise, in the Loire Valley, looks a little Kentish. 'There's lots of fruit trees – apples lying round everywhere. The French are into the countryside the way the English used to be. My next-door neighbour at Amboise breeds wild boars.'

There is also New York, where Jagger lives with Jerry Hall, in Jerry's apartment, and leads an off-stage life he likes to characterise as that of 'dilettante Englishman.' '. . . It means being interested in lots of things in a casual way. Doing other things than going round to clubs and making a fool of yourself.'

Jerry's apartment is only a couple of blocks from the Dakota Building, where Jagger's old friend John Lennon once sought similar anonymity. Since Lennon's murder, it has been widely speculated that, of all New York's rock star emigrés, Jagger would be among the first to choose some safer adopted city. He insists it did not cross his mind. 'New York's still the place where I mostly want to be. In fact, I can't wait to get back there for a few days next week.'

Jerry's beneficial impact has been widely noticed. Her attraction for Jagger – even more than her thoroughbred beauty – is her resolute independence. She is the first woman in years whom he has not suspected of being chiefly interested in his money. He speaks admiringly of her separate income, and the horse ranch she runs with it. Before this tour, Jerry told him he need not go on singing if he dreaded it: her modelling could easily support them both.

He stays in close touch with his father, the former physical training instructor he has come to resemble in so many ways. Mr Jagger was recently in America on a lecture tour. ' "Physical Training from the Renaissance to the Present Day",' his son quotes with rather paternal pride.

'It amazes me when I see him with my daughter . . . he lets Jade get away with *anything*. If I'd done the same when I was her age, I'd have got a thump or a task to do. When I tell him so, he says: "Was I *really* as hard as a father as all that?" '

All the Stones, excepting Charlie Watts, have long since left the English country mansions that, in the Sixties, became so attractive a target to the Drug Squad. Jagger's own Gothic pile was sold almost a decade ago. His town house, in Cheyne Walk, Chelsea, remains his, but unavailable for tax reasons. On visits, he stays with his father or with friends. For all his wealth, he is the kind of person friends put up on a sofa.

But also lord of a Loire chateau built in 1710 ('the same year as my Cheyne Walk house') which, Jagger insists, is not *really* large as chateaux go. 'Well it *is* a big 'ouse. Some of those chateaux, that were built for people's mistresses, are

24

minute. Too feminine for me. My house is big but it's airy. It wasn't ever fortified or anything like an English castle. And the interesting thing is, it's got no servants' staircase. So, for some mysterious reason, it had no indoor servants.'

He smiles tolerantly, fingering the heavy wristwatch. He has been asked a question whose banality is designed to pierce this vast unassumingness. What are his greatest pleasures? If you are Mick Jagger, and have been for 20 years, is pleasure still something the body registers?

'Reading's a pleasure. Eating. I ate everyone else's dinner in the restaurant last night.'

He ponders.

'Sex is a pleasure. It gets better and better. Whereas' – he grins, with a pinpoint sparkle from an upper tooth – 'chocolate biscuits do tend to pall.'

He walks barefoot over the synthetic grass, back to his untidy motel room, his recalcitrant electric shaver, his Texan princess and Dr Pai. Only half of America left to go. Only another million people, wanting him.

I Was Never Lovable: I Was Just Lennon

One of the more persistent myths surrounding John Lennon claims that he was brought up in poverty by working-class Liverpool parents. It makes a too-neat antithesis to imagine the musician who jolted, entranced and exasperated his generation starting life as a grimy, Northern street urchin. In fact, he grew up in a respectable suburb, in a mock-Tudor villa near a golf course. His school, Quarry Bank Grammar, had uniforms, a Latin motto (*Ex Hoc Metallo Virtutem*), and masters in gowns who could administer canings.

The Quarry Bank punishment book between 1952 and 1956 records for what diverse crimes J. W. (for Winston) Lennon and his crony, Pete Shotton, were beaten: 'Throwing blackboard duster out of window'; 'Cutting class and going awol'; 'Gambling on school field during House match.'

Mimi Smith, the aunt who educated John and whom he resembled in his not inconsiderable virtues, remembers those lawless school days. 'I used to dread it when the phone went at ten o'clock in the morning. "Hallo, Mrs Smith, it's the secretary, Quarry Bank, here." "Oh, Lord," I'd think, "what's he done *now*?" '

As John himself was to remark 15 years later, when the world's adoration had turned to puzzled resentment: 'People try to put me into their bag. They expect me to be lovable, but I was never that. Even at school I was just Lennon.'

John Lennon was born in October, 1940, during one of the fiercest German air raids on Liverpool docks. His father, Freddy, an itinerant ship's steward, had vanished overseas months earlier. His mother, Julia, a frivolous, pretty girl,

26

entrusted John to her elder sister, Mary – Mimi – whose husband George ran a small dairy farm. To John, Mimi spelled rules and discipline: his mother was more like an elder sister. He loved her easy-going ways and the jokes she played to amuse him and his friends. She would answer the door wearing knickers on her head, or with spectacles that had no glass in the frames.

Though Mimi strove conscientiously with him, John proved to be exactly like Julia. He never cared what he said or did. By the age of eight, he was an incorrigible truant, leader of a gang which terrorised sedate Woolton, shoplifting, breaking windows, even trying to derail trams. At school he stayed resolutely bottom of his class though he loved reading, writing and drawing.

In 1956, 16-year-old John Lennon, together with every British boy his age, was galvanised by a jagged, uproarious American noise. Rock and Roll music, the white man's version of negro 'Rhythm and Blues', sung by a palpitating, silver-torsoed young bruiser named Elvis Presley, gave teenage rebellion its first anthems, its first knee-trembling god. With Presley came the 'skiffle' craze for America hobo songs, strummed and beaten on cheap guitars, tea-chest basses and kitchen washboards. When John heard Elvis's 'Heartbreak Hotel' and saw Lonnie Donegan's skiffle group, only one very Liverpool word could describe him: he was 'lost.'

Aunt Mimi, tight-lipped, bought him a £12 Spanish guitar. He formed a skiffle group, the Quarry Men, from friends at Quarry Bank and at the more illustrious Liverpool Institute Grammar School. They played at sixth form dances, church socials and on the backs of lorries at street parties. John, an embryo Teddy Boy, to his Aunt Mimi's great dismay, was the undisputed leader. Since he could not remember song lyrics, he took to making up his own.

On July 6, 1957, the Quarry Men were playing at Woolton Parish Church's annual fete. Ivan Vaughan, the tea-chest bassist, invited a Liverpool Institute class-mate, Paul McCartney, to cycle over from nearby Allerton and meet John. The songwriting partnership destined to outshine any in history was formed in St Peter's Parish Hall when 16-year-old John, smelling strongly of illicitly consumed beer, looked over Paul's shoulder to copy the guitar chords he was playing.

John and Paul became friends, though their temperaments could have hardly been more dissimilar. John, bitingly curt, forthright and reckless, hated pretension, loathed authority and laughed at anything serious. Paul was virtuous, conventional, socially ambitious, diplomatic to the point of two-facedness.

What drew them close was their passion for music – for Elvis and Buddy Holly, the white American idols, but also for the more raffish black Rhythm and Blues music brought home by stewards on the transatlantic liners. As the skifflers left, a new recruit appeared in George Harrison, a bus driver's son from Speke, also a Liverpool Institute boy. John, two years older, at first reacted angrily to 'this bloody kid, always tagging along.'

He himself was attending Liverpool Art College, in much the same lack-lustre spirit as school. His attitude changed radically after meeting Stuart Sutcliffe, a brilliantly original young painter who looked like James Dean and dressed more stylishly than any Teddy Boy. Stu Sutcliffe stimulated John to draw and paint, and to an awareness of art as a revolutionary medium. John in his turn asked Stu, who was never a musician, to join his group on bass guitar.

That summer, while crossing the road near Mimi's house, John's mother Julia was knocked down by a car and killed. John, though he showed little emotion at the time, carried the scar of Julia's death for the rest of his life.

In 1960, the-still-unnamed John Lennon group made several important acquisitions. The first was a manager Allan Williams, in whose coffee bar John would idle away his student terms. The second, sorely-needed, was a drummer, Tommy Moore. The third was a name. They wanted something with a chirpy sound like Buddy Holly's Crickets. Stu Sutcliffe suggested: 'beetles'. and John, punningly, changed it to 'beat-les'. The revelation was greeted with such scorn by fellow musicians that it became 'Long John and the Silver Beatles', then 'the Silver Beatles'.

Allan Williams, though sometimes erratic, got the group their first work as professional musicians. In May, 1960, they toured Scotland as backing group for a singer named Johnny Gentle. Shortly afterwards, Williams managed a more dazzling coup. The Beatles, as they again defiantly called themselves, were sent to Hamburg to play at a club in the St Pauli red-light district. Lacking a drummer again, they hurriedly recruited Pete Best, a handsome, if taciturn, boy whose mother ran a small coffee club in suburban Liverpool.

Hamburg's Reeperbahn proved anything but glamorous. The five Beatles, John, Paul, George, Stu and Pete, lived in squalor behind the screen of a small cinema. For five or six hours each night, with only minimal breaks, they blasted out their music before the indifferent eyes of whores and clients at a downstairs club called the Indra. It was in an effort to enthuse this audience that John would launch into writhing parodies of Rock and Roll idols like Elvis and Gene Vincent. To keep awake the boys took Preludin, a German slimming tablet which arouses the metabolism to goggling hyper-activity. John, ever the leader and experimenter, swilled beer and gobbled 'Prellys' until he literally foamed at the mouth.

By day, he was hardly less outrageous. He would loll around the Grosse Freiheit in his underwear, or build effigies of Christ to shock the Sunday morning churchgoers. At length even the Reeperbahn demurred. The group broke up after a fire at their lodgings and the deportation of George Harrison, Paul McCartney and Pete Best.

They reassembled in Liverpool to play at their most celebrated venue, the Cavern Club. This was nothing grander than a brick cellar under warehouses in Mathew Street, with walls streaming with condensation and dead rats under the stage. The Beatles performed at lunch-time, in the evening, sometimes all night, employing the vast repertoire and almost subconscious unity they had acquired in Hamburg. It was at the Cavern one lunch-time, by one of the vast coincidences that were to occur throughout their career, that Brian Epstein stumbled on them.

There seemed no logical reason why Epstein, the son of a

Liverpool Jewish family well established in the retail trade, should suddenly decide to manage a group of down-at-heel Liverpool rockers. As director of his family's NEMS record shop in Whitechapel, he already ran a large, profitable business; his taste in music, like his appearance, was deeply conservative. Though himself only 27, he was worlds apart from the fans who queued daily among the fruit boxes in Mathew Street.

But Brian, unknown to his employees, his close friends, even his family, was also a homosexual with a barely-subdued passion for drama, even danger, in his clandestine affairs. His interest in the Beatles centred, not on their musical talent – though he recognised that – but on the boy in front whose toughness and crudeness were relentlessly affected. That first day at the Cavern, Brian Epstein fell hopelessly in love with John Lennon.

On the strength of his inadmissible adoration, Brian became a manager unprecedented in the pop music business for flair and taste, and also decency and square-dealing. He transformed the Beatles in a few months from scuffling stage-arabs to smart little bandsmen in high-button suits. John, though he railed bitterly against this 'selling out,' went along with the common vote, just as he was to do again and again in the future. At this point, he came perilously near to quitting the Beatles and joining his friend, Stu Sutcliffe, who had left to study art in Hamburg under Eduardo Paolozzi. Stu's death from a brain haemorrhage, on the eve of the Beatles' breakthrough, opened a second, secret void in John Lennon's life.

Brian, meanwhile, after a discouraging round of the London record companies, managed to audition the Beatles with Parlophone, an obscure label in the EMI group, whose solitary 'A & R' man, George Martin, was best known for making comedy records. Martin signed the Beatles at a royalty of a penny per record, and, after some misgivings, allowed them to make their debut with a Lennon-McCartney composition, 'Love Me Do.' On the eve of the session, their drummer Pete Best found himself ousted in favour of a frail, melancholy boy named Ringo Starr, whom the others enticed from a rival Mersey group.

'Love Me Do' rose no higher than 17th in the British Top 20. It was the Beatles' follow-up, 'Please Please Me,' number one in March, 1963, which stamped their outlandish new sound and look over a heavily snowbound Britain. From the very beginning their sound and their appearance seemed to focus on the chirpy, anarchic figure, unidentified yet as John Lennon; an anti-star, even when stardom came, who told reporters that his heroes were Chuck Berry and Ingmar Bergman, his favourite film star was Juliette Greco and his 'type of car' was 'bus.'

Beatlemania, the *Daily Mirror*'s coinage for that madness which gripped Britain first, then the whole western hemisphere, owed its genesis to a Fleet Street trick. The papers sensed their readership to be sated with the dingy adventures of John Profumo, Christine Keeler and the tottering Macmillan government. But the mania, once noticed, proved bigger than any front page. A whole generation, left intact by 20 years' peace, unstiffened by National Service, with fortunes to fritter on its youthful pleasure, established the unsteady decade in one great, shivering scream for John, Paul, George and Ringo.

As simple freaks of fame, however vast, the Beatles would have quickly expired. They remained because they were like no teenage idols before them; clear headed, sharp witted, above all endowed with the flash-quick repartee of their native Liverpool. Though the repartee was communal, somehow it was John who grunted out the devastating one-liners that are still quoted today. To George Martin, he was like a precocious child, scarcely conscious of the joltingly funny things he said.

America succumbed to Beatlemania in February, 1964, thanks to a still larger, and eerie, coincidence. The previous November, on the very day the Beatles' second LP was released, President Kennedy was assassinated in Dallas. The deep-seated American jingoism, which had always barred immigrant popular music, now dissolved in a tremor of self-disgust, an outward searching that alighted on the four British mop tops with almost therapeutic relief.

The Beatles' song 'I Want to Hold Your Hand' bounded into

the US Top 10 with sales of 1.5 million copies. The Beatles landed in New York, to a carefully-staged welcome that grew to dementia far exceeding Europe's. When the Beatles appeared, for a pittance, on the Ed Sullivan TV show, they were watched by 70 million people. Billions of dollars were generated by the sale of Beatle merchandise – toys, wigs, clothes and bubble gum. They themselves, thanks to unwise agreements signed by Brian, never saw a cent of profits literally beyond computation.

In Britain, they were a teenage fad no longer; they were a national treasure. Harold Wilson, that artful Socialist newly in power, saw the advantage of reflecting their vast popularity upon his administration and himself. The Beatles were given Variety Club lunches, modelled for Madame Tussaud's; they appeared in the Royal Command Variety Performance, whose audience was charmed by John Lennon's suggestion that it could either clap or rattle its jewellery. In 1965, Harold Wilson's first Honours List awarded each Beatle an M.B.E. John wanted to refuse the honour. He submitted, with only an undone shirt button to signify his distaste, and a marijuana joint puffed surreptitiously in a Buckingham Palace washroom.

By 1965, apart from the awesome sales statistics they represented, John Lennon and Paul McCartney were acknowledged as a song-writing partnership unique in popular music. Few of their 150-odd songs, in fact, were total collaborations. They wrote together only while touring, rattling off a dozen numbers at once as sound-track albums for their films *Help!* and *A Hard Day's Night*. More often, one would write three-quarters of a song, then come to the other for help with the chorus or 'middle eight.'

The songs they wrote, like the harmonies they sang, derived freshness from a perpetual contest, even clash, of two wholly unalike minds. John, with his sarcasm, ruthlessly cut back the cloying sweetness to which Paul was often prone. Paul in turn rounded off and honed the lyrics John could not be bothered to finish.

32

John's was the renegade, the adventurous talent. The emergence of Bob Dylan in the mid-Sixties inspired him to break out of simple formula 'yeah, yeah' lyrics; to bend his songs around the same punning and surreal word-play that made best sellers of his two books of nonsense verse. His words ceased to be teenage *cris de coeur*: they became, instead, fragments of current autobiography. 'Norwegian Wood,' on the *Rubber Soul* album, was a tale of edgy infidelity to his first wife, Cynthia. 'Nowhere Man' was a self-scourging for his cosseted life in a mock-Tudor mansion now, in Surrey's stockbroker belt.

He began to loathe the repressions of his Beatle life – the diplomacy and politeness on which Brian, abetted by Paul, always insisted: the bowing and scraping to mayors and officials. It caused him particular revulsion, as a remorseless mimic of human frailty, when crippled children would be wheeled into the Beatles dressing room to touch them in the hope of healing.

Drugs had been a part of his life since the 'Prellys' he would gulp down in St Pauli. Drugs became increasingly a means to allay the boredom of limitless self-indulgence – marijuana first, then purple hearts, French blues, cocaine, and finally LSD, the 'mind drug' with which a dentist friend laced his after-dinner coffee. From the sterility of his outward life, he turned avidly to the grotesque visions which 'acid' provided; he later admitted that he 'ate the stuff,' taking in all perhaps 1,000 'trips.'

He was now visibly splitting away from the Beatles' cosy well-mannered quadrille. In 1966, on the eve of what would be their last concert tour, he said in an interview: 'Christianity will go. It will vanish and shrink. We're more popular than Jesus now. . . .' The assertion – which, typically, John did not deny – provoked anti-Beatle rallies and LP burnings all through the American South. Brian Epstein offered to pay $1 million out of his own pocket rather than expose the Beatles to danger below the Mason-Dixon Line. Brian, in his maternal concern for John, always dreaded what did indeed ultimately happen: that one night, a fan would walk up, smiling, then pull out a gun.

It was John's bothered spirit, his vagrant and soon fatigued brilliance, which raised the Beatles as dictators over an era which lasted one year but lingers still as a nostalgic after-glow. In 1967, the lisping insurrection of hippies – Love, Peace and Flower Power – was personified in the Beatles LP, *Sergeant Pepper's Lonely Hearts Club Band*. The concept, of a psychedelic panto, was Paul's. The stunning visions were John's: 'Lucy In The Sky With Diamonds', drenched in acid sparkle; 'Being For the Benefit of Mr Kite', with its acrobats turning 'somersets'; lastly, 'A Day in The Life', that strange, tingling elegy leading to a crescendo of symphony orchestras played backwards which John had told the Beatles' producer, George Martin, must be 'a sound like the end of the world.'

Even the acclaim for *Sergeant Pepper*, and for 'A Day in The Life,' as comparable to Eliot's *Waste Land*, did not satisfy John. He grew impatient with the hippy disciples, encouraged by Dr Timothy Leary who studied and debated his lyrics like Holy Writ. 'I just shoved some words together, then shoved some sounds on,' he insisted. 'I'm conning people because they give me the freedom to con them.'

Nineteen sixty seven was also the year of death, dissolution and false dawn. In August, Brian Epstein, a wealthy and sad victim of drugs, conscience and cruel boys, was found dead at his Belgravia house. The Beatles, led by George Harrison were, that same weekend, undergoing initiation as disciples of Transcendental Meditation under the Maharishi Mahesh Yogi. The holy man giggled, but seemed to give comfort. All four Beatles later went with their women to the Maharishi's Indian ashram, leaving Neil Aspinall, their faithful road manager, to organise the business corporation which Brian had planned to offset their gargantuan income tax liabilities.

In 1966, at a London gallery, John had met the mildly notorious Japanese 'performance artist' Yoko Ono. She was not beautiful like a Beatle groupie. Her small, unsmiling face floated between clouds of hair, black as her clothes. She talked, and John, to his great surprise, listened raptly. Her views on the nature of art startled and fascinated him. Her fierce independence jolted him out of his Northern chauvinism; he fell in love with her via an unused organ, his mind. For the next two years, nervously and guiltily, he kept in touch with her.

In 1968, while his wife Cynthia and son Julian were away, he plucked up courage to invite Yoko to the house. They spent all night taping avant garde music; it was only when dawn broke that they got around to making love. Later that day, John said to his old friend, Pete Shotton: 'Will you find us a house to live in with Yoko? This is it.'

The Beatles, recording their *Yellow Submarine* film soundtrack album, suddenly found Yoko's black shape in their midst, clinging close to John, as he did to her, breaking a ten-year bond and brotherhood. Though months remained to run, that was the overture to the end: when John discovered a partner he needed more than he needed Paul McCartney.

Meanwhile, the Beatles' Apple enterprise had begun, intending to fritter away only £2 million as a tax loss on clothes, boutiques, a record label, a film company, publishing and, Paul's brainchild, the Apple Foundation for the Arts. By late 1968, the fresh green empire was water-logged with hangers-on, gorging drink and meals, lounging on white leather sofas and stealing anything portable. The Beatles could not be bothered to be bosses, nor to delegate executive power: they themselves had been locked in the record studio for eight months, trying to finish the new album that was to eclipse even *Sergeant Pepper*.

The result was the two-volume *White Album*, an audible conflict between Paul's commercial instincts and John's determination to create electronic 'sound poems.' Though hailed as a masterpiece, it was, with some exceptions, an undisciplined mess, its chief virtue the creation of a vacuum in which George Harrison could emerge at last as a credible song-writer and instrumentalist.

In Yoko, a super-charged hustler and implacable showwoman, John found inspiration to do things he had never dreamed of daring. Together they embarked on a programme of consciously ludicrous 'happenings,' each drenched in a Beatles publicity glare – 'sculptures,' that were acorns, 'exhibitions' of balloons and rusty bicycles, 'concerts' given from inside paper bags, 'films' of John's penis in close-up. His wedding to Yoko in 1969 was followed by the notorious Bed-In, a week's honeymoon spent in bed at the Amsterdam Hilton to promote world peace.

His arrest for possessing cannabis in 1968 indicated how thin he and his Japanese consort had worn the Establishment's patience. A year earlier, Paul and George had been able to admit with impunity to using LSD. The day John and Yoko appeared in court, Apple released their *Two Virgins* album, the cover of which showed them both with arms entwined, naked. EMI refused to market the record; dealers would sell it only in plain brown wrappers. Another album sleeve showed Yoko in hospital, pale and ravaged after the loss of their first baby together, with John camped beside her in a sleeping bag. Though his persecution was self-induced and self-aggravated, there began to be something chivalrous in the way his slight body shielded Yoko's still slighter one.

He announced he was leaving the Beatles after their disastrous *Magical Mystery Tour* film, their chaotic sessions for the *Let It Be* album and their brilliant stop-gap album, *Abbey Road*. As John put it to the others; 'I want a divorce.' He was persuaded to keep silent to enable the Beatles' new manager, Allen Klein, to negotiate a massive royalty increase with their American record company, Capitol.

John kept his word to hush up his resignation. In a strange way, his and Yoko's continuing notoriety served as camouflage. Late in 1969, he returned his MBE to Buckingham Palace as a protest against the war in Vietnam and Biafran genocide. He espoused the cause of Black Muslims, student activists, anti-apartheid demonstrators and James Hanratty. With a hybrid group, the Plastic Ono Band, he produced songs that showed his gift for creating instant crowd chants. 'Give Peace A Chance', recorded at his Montreal bed-in, became the anthem of disaffected college campuses throughout the world.

Early in 1970, sickened by the mutilation of his music on the *Let It Be* album, Paul McCartney announced his own secession from the Beatles. He did so, not pleasantly, in a self-interview packaged with his solo album, *McCartney*, hinting at his fury against Allen Klein and also at John's escapades

36

with Yoko. John replied to Paul in a song called 'How Do You Sleep?' and a vicious parody of the sleeve of Paul's *Ram* album. In 1971, Paul started legal proceedings to dissolve the partnership, which, in John's mind, had ended three years before.

The Beatles together had given the Sixties their shout of youthful optimism. Separately, they seemed to represent what the Seventies became; a jumpy, neurotic decade, nail-biting with nostalgia for last year's past, whose music was only plagiarism or parody. In the Sixties, things happened. In the Seventies, they unhappened.

John, now living with Yoko in New York, made the strongest beginning as a solo musician. His individual albums returned joyfully to his Hamburg and Liverpool Rock 'n' Roll roots: after Primal Scream therapy with Arthur Janov, he produced songs of blunt agony, culled from the threshold of childhood. The multi-layered Sergeant Pepper sound was stripped to a style as plain and confined as a confessional. In October, 1971, the drifting flakes of a lone electric keyboard ushered in the song he will be best remembered for, 'Imagine'.

In 1975, he stopped making records. He settled with Yoko, after a brief infidelity, in the Dakota building in New York, devoting himself to buying up the adjacent apartments, looking after his new baby, Sean, and trying to obtain the 'green card' without which, as a convicted drug user, he would be barred from re-entering America.

Massive income still accrued via Apple from his song copyrights. He spent it on impulse buys of estates in Florida and Long Island and a herd of Holstein cattle worth thousands of dollars each. He gave up tobacco, even sugar. He looked on himself as a New Yorker. To John, the city's racy, cosmopolitan feel was an all-night version of his lost Liverpool. He always remembered the excitement of standing at Liverpool's Pier Head, looking up the Mersey and knowing that 'the next place was America.'

Throughout the Seventies, as Rock music grew duller, the Beatles were a lingering, then a growing force; billion dollar offers were made to them to reunite. Of all their rumoured second comings, the biggest occurred early in 1980 when Paul McCartney organised a concert in aid of Kampuchean refugees. George and Ringo seemed willing to play but John would not be drawn. At one point, the UN Secretary-General, Kurt Waldheim, was said to have telephoned him on a coded number; but in vain.

Then, late in 1980, came his first album for five years, *Double Fantasy*. A letter he and Yoko had written to the American press babbling of angels and prayer, aroused deep foreboding. But here, miraculously, was the original John Lennon; older, evidently wiser yet still as he used to be when amazing years could not amaze him; his emotion bright, his intelligence unimpaired, his honesty, whether crass or heroic, fierce and incorruptible. His song 'Starting Over' might have been sung in the Abbey Road studios in 1963 with George Martin, chin on hand, listening critically.

Lately, John had been asking his Aunt Mimi to send him mementoes from childhood – a Royal Worcester dinner service, his Uncle George's photograph, even his Quarry Bank school tie. Once when he telephoned Mimi, they had a row over the repainting of the bungalow in Bournemouth which he bought for her. 'Damn you, Lennon,' Mimi cried, slamming down the 'phone. Later it rang again, 'You're not still cross with me, Mimi, are you?' John's voice said anxiously.

Early on December 9, another trans-Atlantic call came through to Bournemouth. Mimi picked up the 'phone, thinking the same thought she had since John was nine years old: 'Oh, Lord, what's he done *now*?'

Yoko: Life Without John

It is five months since the shots were fired. The Dakota
Building shares in that relief which Spring fleetingly gives to
New York. Beside the gloomy Gothic archway, red geraniums
spill out of the big iron vases. There are tourists now, as well
as grief-stricken fans, lingering on West 72nd Street. Dis-
passionate eyes and cameras search for a glimpse of the
guard, still shut futilely in his copper box ten feet from the
place where Mark David Chapman stepped forward and John
Lennon fell.

Under the arch, it becomes strangely like some shipping or
insurance office from the Liverpool of John's early childhood.
Narrow steps lead through old-fashioned double doors into a
wood-panelled vestibule with a polished counter. Behind the
counter, another guard watches over his console of TV monitors. An automatic lock gives access to further stairs, a
passage twisting to the door marked 'Studio One.'

Inside, two young men loll over desks in a cluttered, high-
ceilinged room. One of them withdraws for a moment, then
returns. 'Go right in,' he says. 'Yoko's ready.'

Yoko works alone behind a gold-inlaid desk in an office
filled with small trees, white sofas and pastel-coloured art
deco lamps. Her clothes are black, as they always have been:
sleek trousers, high-heeled boots, an undone shirt and tie. Her
hair, drawn back to a single tied mass, reveals a smile that
few outside these walls have seen.

The broad, taut cheekbones, the fierce, dark eyebrows,
have so rarely seemed capable of smiling. Yet she does so
often, even when talking about the day after John's murder.

'I couldn't eat anything. Then all I wanted to eat was chocolate. I kept remembering how much John loved chocolate. When I would go out, I'd bring him a little chocolate something home, and he enjoyed it so much. Now it was all I wanted to eat. Elton [John] was so sweet – he sent me a big chocolate cake. My diet went crazy for about a month afterwards – nothing but chocolate and mushrooms.

'A few days before it happened, I remember looking at John. And he looked so good, so beautiful. I said to him, "Hey, you're even better looking than when you were a Beatle!"

'He always wanted so much to be thin, but he never really was. Even when he was a Beatle, there was this little pot belly under the Beatle jacket. When we split up and then got back together in '74, he said he *really* wanted to lose weight. I said, "Okay how much do you want to lose – twenty pounds?" And he did it. His body had gotten to be just the way he always wanted.

'And he was so happy. Both of us were. A few days before it happened, I remember thinking, "This is so good, I wonder if things can go on being as good as this." '

It was a feeling almost as strange as bereavement, for Yoko to realise that people do not hate her any more. For the hatred had seemed as durable as the Beatles' own legend. It followed her even after John and she escaped from London to New York; even after their artistic partnership had ceased to puzzle and exasperate the world. No forgiveness appeared possible for the Japanese woman who sundered the Beatles' magic entity, luring John away from lovableness into avant-garde aggression, from pop music into mystifying 'performance art' escapades – 'bed-ins' and 'bagism.' The rumours are multiplying even now about Yoko's alleged pursuit of John: how she intruded on the Beatles in their secret recording sessions, how she once even followed John into the men's lavatory.

'People said that I ran after him, pursued him. What really happened is, neither of us went after the other. We were both too scared. Each of us was married at the time. John was terrified to make any move because of the Beatle thing. After

40

we first met at that gallery [The Indica, where Yoko had an exhibition in 1966], we were circling around one another for about two years. I wouldn't make a move. I never did. I had left London for Paris and John was in India. At that point, I thought we would probably never get started.

'The one time he did try to make a move, it was so sudden, so clumsy, I just rejected it. John had invited me to the record studios. He suddenly said, "You look tired. Would you like to rest?" I thought he was taking me to another room, but instead we went off to this flat – I think it belonged to Neil, the road manager. When we got there Neil started to fold this sofa down into a bed. Maybe John thought we were two adults: we didn't have to pretend. But it seemed so crude, I rejected it. I slept on the divan, I think, and John went into another room.

'I *never* pursued him. If I had, I would have got nowhere. After we started living together, it was John who wanted me there all the time. *He* made me go into the men's room with him. He was scared that if I stayed out in the studio with a lot of other men, I might run off with one of them.

'Jealous! My God! He wrote a song, "Jealous Guy", that should have told people how jealous he was. After we were together, he made me write out a list of all the men I'd slept with before we met. I started to do it quite casually – then I realised how serious it was to John. He didn't even like me knowing the Japanese language because that was a part of my mind that didn't belong to him. After a while, I couldn't even read any books or papers in Japanese.

'I used to say to him, "I think you're a closet fag, you know." Because, when we started to live together, John would say to me, "Do you know why I like you? Because you look like a bloke in drag. You're like a mate." '

'He was a genius, but he had this huge inferiority complex. He was brilliant as an artist, but he didn't think he was capable of it. Like when he was asked to do his lithographs – he was just too scared to get started on the drawings. We both took mescalin and then he tried. I told him, "That's brilliant, it's

41

beautiful." John said, "But it's only a circle, like a child would do." I said, "Maybe it's childish, but it is still beautiful."

'It was the same when he was asked to write a sketch in the *Oh! Calcutta!* show. "What am I going to write?" he kept saying. I said, "Write that thing you told me about when you were a boy and you used to masturbate." He and his friends all used to masturbate together, shouting out the names of film actresses – and then suddenly John or one of them would shout "Frank Sinatra." So he made that the sketch, and it was marvellous.'

The decision to separate, in 1973, was Yoko's. She had given John his escape route from Beatledom, but in the process, had sacrificed all her own ambitions and identity as an artist. She had two husbands before John: she was used to marriages that ended. So John left New York for California and the confused, drunken year which he later described as his 'lost weekend.'

'He came to New York a few times and asked me to go back to him. I wouldn't. I was going out with other people – several others. One of these young guys persuaded me to go to that big concert of Elton's – and suddenly John walked out on to the stage. I didn't know he was going to be there. The audience gave him a terrific reception. But when he bowed, it was too quickly and too many times. And suddenly I thought, "He looks so lonely up there."

'The young guy I was with wanted to go backstage afterwards. I didn't want to, but I said "Okay." And John, of course, was there with a young chick. He said, "Oh, I'm so *happy* to see you." We sat there, talking, holding hands. His young chick and my young guy were still standing there, getting more and more uptight.

'After that, John asked me out. We went to an art show together. We started dating all over again.'

They settled down for good, so it seemed, in the strange, old Manhattan apartment building, decorated with dark turrets and cast iron sea serpents, where John had been gradually buying up leases. Yoko got his weight down: he even stopped smoking his eternal Gauloises for the sake of the baby they both wanted. New York, unlike London, left them alone. They bought houses in Florida and Long Island, and prize Holstein cattle for their Dream Street farms. 'All of it was for our old age,' Yoko says, with a wry smile. 'And eating the right foods to keep ourselves healthy. It's so ironic. Since December I've been telling Sean [their son], "Eat anything you want. It doesn't matter".'

On the seventh floor, a guard sits, nursing a raincoat, outside the apartment where John and Yoko spent their five years of role reversal. Opposite is a second apartment, equally large, which they used only for storage. Two smaller ones, lower in the building, were bought by John for specialised uses, like storing and cataloguing their videotape collection.

We enter the principal apartment. A tiny hall, with a single lamp burning in it, leads to the vista of a dozen white rooms and skyscrapers beyond, set down at random among the Central Park treetops. Far beneath, near the place now renamed Strawberry Fields, a glint comes up from mirrors heliographing messages of sympathy.

It was in a small side room that John spent his long retreat, 'watching the trees change colour.' The room is empty now, but for cardboard cartons and the huge TV set he had specially shipped from Japan. In the passage is a painting he did, aged 11, at Dovedale Primary School. There are pictures of Julian, his elder son, of Sean, and Yoko's daughter, Kyoko. His clothes still hang in the corner dressing room: revolving boutique-racks crowded with epochs of brief fashion and their attendant cloaks, caps, hats and shoes. Yoko does not use the dressing room any more.

There is a room devoted to Egyptian art, including a full-size mummy in a case. It averts its golden eyes from the mantel of schoolcaps and straw boaters and the tubular steel sculpture spread on the carpet. Nearby, a thin Perspex column supports four silver spoons. The inscription says: 'Three spoons, YO 1967.' What attracted John to Yoko in the first place was the humour in her work – perhaps it was there

43

all along. The room where Yoko now sleeps is modest, quiet and formal. Along the hall, a seamstress sits bent over her work. Sean, the second baby to be born with that uncanny Lennon face, is away at the Long Island house. Three pedigree cats roam at will down the immense but comfortable kitchen. Next door in the playroom, John and Yoko are painted on the wall as Superman and Superwoman, carrying Sean with them up into the sky.

For three months after John's death, apart from dignified messages to his fans, Yoko remained silent. She then decided to release her song 'Walking On Thin Ice', which John had been helping her to record on the day of his death. Her voice, once so outlandish, sounds normal by today's standards. With the record came a video sequence of scenes from John's last month – his 40th birthday party, his view from the Dakota, his face and Yoko's in the closeness of making love. The same unclothed frankness that disgusted the world on their *Two Virgins* years ago, now seems perfectly natural.

Helped by Phil Spector, the American record producer whom John idolised, Yoko is at work on a full solo album, driving herself and those around her to finish it in a fraction of the usual time. Meanwhile, adulation continues for *Double Fantasy*, the shared album they had just released last December. Ironically, John's most commercially successful music since the Beatles will probably be 'Starting Over,' 'Woman,' and other calm, simple elegies to his life with Yoko.

Contact with the ex-Beatles is rare. They once called her contemptuously 'Flavour of the Month'. Yoko refers to them drily as 'the in-laws'. After John's death, only Ringo Starr flew to New York to see her. Paul McCartney, John's partner into songwriting history, provokes a bleak and bitter look. 'John said that no one ever hurt him the way Paul hurt him. But it's in the past. It's gone.'

She is talking again in the long, dim salon with its trees and soft lamps and huge, solitary inlaid desk. For Yoko Ono Lennon, as for all who suffer loss, small, silly details give passing comfort. 'He would never swear, you know. At least, not in front of Sean. And if I let out a word, he'd clear his

44

throat and say "Oh oh – Mother's getting agitated".

'He would never have gone back to England. But he still loved England – that's not a paradox. On Sunday nights we would always watch the TV dramas from England, like *Rebecca*.

'John used to say he'd had two great partnerships – one with Paul McCartney, the other with Yoko Ono. "And I discovered both of them," he used to say. "That isn't bad going, is it?" '

The Beach Boys: Not All Fun, Fun, Fun

Wherever Brian Wilson goes, his cousin Steve is never far away. Cousin Steve sits in the hotel room as Brian wanders fitfully back and forth, a tall, helpless-looking figure with shorn hair, white cotton trousers and eyes that can suddenly fill up with terror or tears. Sometimes the eyes close; the bristle-bearded face is uplifted in silent, pleading anguish. Then Cousin Steve appears beside him, talking in a murmur and kneading the muscles of his neck. It is done with evident tenderness and concern.

For Brian Wilson to be even visible is a historic event in popular music. He is the founder of the Beach Boys, undisputedly the greatest American Rock and Roll band, still intact after a career spanning 18 years. As a songwriter he ranks with the select few, in any idiom, who have created a potent and self-contained dream world. To Wilson we owe the California idyll of surfing, sun and hotrod cars apotheosised in songs such as 'Little Deuce Coupe', 'Help Me Rhonda' and 'Fun, Fun, Fun' which brought happiness, ironically, to everyone but their composer. Throughout the past decade Wilson has been ill and disturbed, a recluse unable to perform with his band or even finish the writing of a song.

The Beach Boys' story forms a chapter of modern American mythology. In 1960, then a 19 year-old high school student, Brian Wilson formed a band with his younger brothers Dennis and Carl, their cousin Mike Love and Brian's schoolfriend Al Jardine. Their early records celebrated the cleanly outdoor pursuits and inamorata of Californian youth, with fresh white vocal choruses superimposed on urgent black

Rhythm and Blues. From this they developed intricate harmonies and studio techniques, culminating in the album *Pet Sounds*, in 1966. *Pet Sounds* contained Brian Wilson's masterpiece, a song called 'Good Vibrations', a multi-track oratorio that made the Beatles' *Sergeant Pepper* seem unambitious by comparison.

The years have been kinder to the other Wilson brothers. Dennis, age 35, and Carl, age 33, are respectively lean and plump, bearded and long-haired West Coast conservatives. Each is king to a private retinue; each acknowledges Brian, in his solitary torment, to be the source of all melodic inspiration. His brothers grow alert when Brian stumbles, as by instinct, to the piano. His touch there is firm. 'Nice change, Brian,' Carl says interrogatively. He waits, as all do, to hear what Brian will play next.

So it always was, Carl remembers, when they were growing up in Hawthorne, Los Angeles. Their father, Murray Wilson, had a small import business. Brian was always the dominant boy, gifted in languages, sport and mimicry. Carl remembers lying in bed at night in the room the three brothers shared, helpless with laughter at the stories Brian told him. Grown-up Brian remembers this, too, pauses in his wandering and suddenly smiles. As a boy he had a pure soprano voice. His brother Dennis remembers him running home from school in tears because the other boys had teased him about it.

His musical imagination developed in early adolescence. For inspiration he turned, not to the anodyne pop music of the day, but to the early 1950s' close-harmony singing of groups like the Four Freshmen. He schooled his two brothers in drums and guitar and part-singing, reaching for chord-sequences beyond the comprehension of other teenage musicians. His harmonic skills are the more remarkable because all his life he has been totally and incurably deaf in his right ear.

The first instruments were bought with lunch-money left for them when their parents went on holiday to Mexico. Their name, inspired by a brand of beach-shirt, was to be the

47

Pendlestones until a friend casually rechristened them the Beach Boys. Their first concert appearance, in 1960, was for $5 apiece in Long Beach, at a memorial concert for a dead singer called Ritchie Valens. Despite a largely black audience, their appearance was as successful as any they have since made. No one in the band can remember playing to people who did not enjoy their music.

It was after a European tour in 1965 that Brian ceased to appear with them in concert. While they continued travelling, he laboured in the studio, staying in touch by telephone. Carl remembers being rung up in North Dakota and hearing the outline of 'Good Vibrations' played by Brian down the telephone. The whole *Pet Sounds* album was planned and largely recorded before Brian summoned the others to fill in their vocal parts. The album established a precedent in studio wizardry as well as in length of preparation. Somewhere in California, Carl Wilson says, there is an entire shelf of tape canisters housing unused material from 'Good Vibrations' alone.

Brian's mental turmoil and gradual isolation stemmed from fear that he would be unable to surpass the *Pet Sounds* music: his mind buckled under the necessity of going one better. He had dabbled in drugs and was haunted by a fear that his deafness might spread. From this exile came a single album called *Smile*, rumoured to be masterly but unlikely now ever to be released.

Brian inspires affection and forbearance in an industry not noted for its humane qualities. There is his cousin Steve, always there to massage his neck when the horrors come. He has been happily married for 14 years to a kind and understanding wife. Another factotum called Rocky describes how Brian's weight has been brought down from 16 stone and his consumption of cigarettes reduced from 60 a day to three or four. He hasn't touched drugs for a year and a half, Rocky says with pride, and he runs miles each week on a treadmill rigged up for him at home.

The band has now broken from rehearsal on a sound stage at Pinewood Studios, just outside London. 'Rocky, can't I have

48

a smoke in the break?' Brian pleads. 'Can't I, Rocky, *please*? I'm working hard, Rocky, honest. I've got no high notes.' He sits at a piano to demonstrate that his voice, still pure and high like a teenager's, is unsullied by cigarettes. 'Okay, now, change key,' Rocky orders. Brian obeys. 'Again,' Rocky orders him. 'Again.'

The remaining two Beach Boys defer to their leader while remaining calmly individualistic. Al Jardine, the bass-player, is wry and school-masterly. Mike Love, the vocalist, studies advanced Transcendental Meditation in Switzerland and has a sharp way with clumsy radio interviewers. Neither has known contentment as great as that to be found by singing and playing in the Beach Boys. 'What we've evolved from our being,' Mike Love says, 'is that harmony feels good.' Al Jardine remembers their last Wembley Stadium concert when he was tortured by earache, but still went on with the performance. 'It's like being a doctor. You can be sick, but you still prescribe the drugs.'

In recent years, both the younger Wilson brothers have produced solo albums. Each drew on the confidence of superstardom, and a coterie of superstar session-men. Each wondered, with some trepidation, what Brian would say. 'When my record was finished, Brian was the first to hear it,' Dennis Wilson says. 'In the middle of some tracks he'd say "I can't stand this" and walk out of the room. Sometimes he'd laugh. Sometimes he'd cry. I guess he was thinking that he'd seen me grow up as a musician.'

Elvis: The King is Dead

(The Times obituary, 1977)

Elvis Presley will be remembered as the first and the greatest exponent of Rock and Roll music, whose recordings of 'Blue Suede Shoes', 'Hound Dog' and 'Heartbreak Hotel' establish the music's otherwise fitful claim to be a 20th century art form. Presley was not the first to play Rock and Roll, nor can he be numbered among its faithful adherents, but such details have long become irrelevant in the immensity of his legend. To his own generation and to others born after his career began, to the uninformed as well as the aficionado, Elvis Presley remained 'The King'.

A new art form, a youth revolution were not among the objectives of Presley or his promoters. He was launched in the middle Fifties as a moneymaking confection with a life, possibly, of six months. It was inconceivable that the catchpenny excesses of the moment – the slicked hair and shaking torso; the guitar, flashed and flourished and spun – would create a style to fascinate millions of young people for 20 years afterwards. As a symbol, Presley dominates Rock music, pop art and unnumbered private ways of life; as a person he was largely untroubled by mortality. That he himself never did or said anything remotely outrageous, significant or even interesting has only added to the purity of his myth.

Elvis Aron Presley was born in January 1935 in the small town of Tupelo, East Mississippi. His parents were poor, eking out a precarious sharecropper living as factory workers or farm hands. Elvis was one of identical twin boys; his brother Aron died at birth. Throughout his childhood, a doting affection was lavished on him especially by his mother

Gladys. Elvis, in return, became devoted to his mother, and was deeply affected by her death in 1958.

It was propitious that he should have grown up in that region of the American South. The lands around the Mississippi River, for all their outward dreariness, have fostered two distinct and vital musical cultures. From the Negro came slave and work songs, later formalised into the Blues. The white man, too, evolved music to express his superior caste, with fine clothes and sentimentality and rapid banjo and guitar-picking. The two styles met, but did not coalesce, at the city of Memphis with its rich merchants and its depressed hinterland, nurturing the Blues tradition of the famous, and infamous, Beale Street.

The Presley family moved to Memphis when Elvis was 10, living first in one room, then in an apartment-house for poor whites. Elvis had received a musical education no greater than any Southern boy, picking up the rudiments of guitar-playing singing in church or at county fairs. When he left school, it was to work for the Precision Tool Company of Memphis as a truck driver. At the age of 19, he was signed to the local Sun record label by its proprietor Sam Phillips, who had heard him singing in a record-your-voice machine. Phillips was the first to see the possibilities in a white boy who could sing black music: it was Phillips who encouraged Presley to develop a style unlike anything ever heard in Country and Western music. The result was 'That's All Right, Mama', released on the Sun label in 1954.

Presley might nonetheless have enjoyed a merely regional popularity but for the intervention of 'Colonel' Tom Parker. A man in his 40s, of doubtful fairground antecedents, Parker had already gauged what convulsions were threatening American popular music. In a market hitherto dominated by crooners and ballad singers, new and violent noises could be heard, compounded partly from Boogie and Bebop, partly of Rhythm and Blues and other Negro styles traditionally stigmatised as 'race' music. Already, the appearances of an ex-dance band called Bill Haley and the Comets were providing scenes of impulsive hysteria among young people. With

51

masterly timing, Parker wrested Presley away from Sun and signed him to the wealthy RCA label; under Parker's personal and exclusive management, the young man from Tupelo was launched upon the world.

From 1956 to 1958 Presley's music and his appearance became the scandal of America. He was universally denounced as an immoral influence on the mobs of girls who shrieked for him at his concerts, who tore at his clothes and covered his cars with lipstick. A new species, the 'teen-ager', became the preoccupation of the American establishment, and Elvis was condemned as the embodiment of its rebellion and uncleanliness. Nor was business slow to perceive the commercial advantages in this new species. Every record that Presley made generated fortunes: 'Heartbreak Hotel' alone stayed two months at number one in the American hit-parade. Merchandising empires were built up around his name. Films followed: *Love Me Tender, Jailhouse Rock, King Creole*. The sale of guitars rose to unprecedented figures. And all proceeded under the skilful tutelage of Colonel Parker, orchestrating 'Elvis the Pelvis', his gold suits, his pink suits and gold Cadillac cars, together with intriguing glimpses of a quiet, religious and respectful Southern boy. His fame grew subsequently in England but Parker, cautious of the fate of other teen-idols, saw to it that he played no concerts here. Rumours of his coming were to recur, however, throughout his career.

It was Parker's most adroit piece of management which brought about the end of the Presley golden age. In 1958, Elvis entered the Army for two years' service. This potential disaster was converted, with the aid of the military authorities, into a commercial transfiguration. The film *GI Blues* signified the birth of a new Elvis: rebel and outcast no longer, but an all-American hero, clean-cut and close-cropped and dutiful.

The years which followed his discharge were devoted to the playing of this anodyne part. Throughout the early and middle Sixties, Presley was cast in a series of second-rate musical films. His recording output – with such notable exceptions as 'Return to Sender' or 'His Latest Flame' –

entered the same decline. His public grew accustomed to his remoteness. Inordinately rich, he lived as a recluse in the mansions he had built for himself, maintaining a squad of his ex-Army friends to be his aides and to allay the boredom of his wealth. In 1967, he married Patricia Beaulieu, an Army officer's daughter who he had met in Germany. They had one child, Lisa Marie. The marriage was dissolved in 1972.

Although the influence of Rock and Roll appeared to wane during the Sixties, it was to provide the stimulus for most of the next generation of young musicians, including the Beatles. Inevitably the commercial 'Rock revival' brought Presley out of retirement, first on a television show, then by personal appearances in the Las Vegas clubs. Overweight, self-conscious, self-mocking, he seemed astonished by the ovations which he received. The standard of his records improved, though inclining to middle-of-the-road Pop. As he passed the age of 40, surrounded by countless youthful imitators, his command of the hit parade had been restored.

His private life remained largely a matter of speculation. There were rumours concerning his erratic temper, his indifference to beautiful women, his diffidence, his preoccupation with his mother and religion and his addiction to drugs. That he never visited England was felt by many to be a betrayal of his most faithful audience; to others it was part of his incalculable fascination. His total record sales are estimated at 150 million copies. He leaves behind clubs and associations dedicated to impersonating his voice and his appearance, and unable to believe him guilty of even the smallest aberration. What lay behind the music was never clear – if indeed, there was anything at all. But, merely by innuendo, he is assured of his place in history.

The Everly Brothers: Growing Apart

Phil is the fastidious one. Don was happy to stay at another motel with a northern draught sweeping its gallery and cows grazing round the back. Phil preferred the formality of a private hotel 10 miles off, hung with barometers and gongs; and so separate cars were necessary each night to secure the union of their voices. Phil said, not altogether playfully, 'You're witnessing the end of one of the greatest sibling rivalries of the 20th century.'

They do not pretend to be boys any more. It is, after all, 16 years since 'Bye Bye Love' sold a million copies. Their big-eyed good looks are haunted slightly by a lifetime of travelling and night; their chins thrust into mufflers against the wind of the road. they will no longer do 'Ebony Eyes', the song about an air crash, though it is always requested. In all else, for the hinterland of Leeds as for anywhere, they are miraculously the same – the skip of a drum, a ruff of steel chords, a high and a higher voice. There is no mark on their harmony's perfect face.

'I was thinking the other day,' Don said. 'We've been the Everly Brothers for 20 years. I was thinking, we're the best duet there is.'

'We may never see the gold of another hit record,' said Phil, 'but I know what we're doing is valid. After all this time I know that it isn't just something I'm feeding to myself.'

As individuals, too, they are the same – that is to say, still as dissimilar in temperament as in the colour of their hair. Don the elder brother is homely and tractable, the softer of the two for all that his share of trouble has been greatest. Phil,

54

two years younger, is more intense and volatile; he hates flies and grasps at the air if he suspects one to be in the vicinity. Yet they have been vexed, all their lives, by being treated as identical twins. As they advance into their thirties, to continue as one voice, one guitar, suitors for the hand of one girl, is the most fatiguing part of keeping faith with their music.

They agree that they have not noticed the passage of years. Perhaps no-one has; it is possible that Time is accelerating. Their songs remain indestructibly young – never more than when considered with the senile pretensions of newer music. One can only judge the distance they have come when they speak of their contemporaries; of other youths raised up by Rock and Roll into bigger gods than the world had seen, but afterwards thrown back, dead. One of their great friends, especially Phil's, was Buddy Holly, the brilliant 22 year-old, killed in an air crash in 1959 before he could elaborate on the charm of his first four chords. 'He wrote "Not Fade Away" for us,' Don says. 'It burns me up when I read "reportedly written by Buddy Holly for the Everly Brothers".'

Of the years when they were worshipped, their recollections are mixed. Walled in by screams that were being released for the very first time, they were understandably bemused. 'We liked it,' Don says. 'Anybody would. You didn't have to do anything.' But Phil's abiding memory is of disparagement, even as they were idolised, even as the disparagers themselves were making a fortune. 'They were always saying, "What are you going to do when the bubble breaks?" Our line was "Yes Sir, No Sir." ' Phil's face clouds at the slights of a decade ago. 'Fear and guilt, that's what we were disciplined by.'

And also by a harmonious upbringing. They were born in Kentucky, where children pick guitars instead of their noses. In a family of coalminers their maternal grandfather was named Blueatrice Embry and they had uncles Zerkel, Shirley and Prock, christened after the first word he ever spoke. Their father, Isaac Everey – Don's first name is Isaac – wanted to form a singing family, a proposition dear to the heart of Country and Western music. To this end his child

55

bride, Evie Embry, took up the double-bass and their little boys were put to singing early. 'It was good practice,' Phil says. 'We had to be always watching Mother in case she drifted over into our part of the harmony.'

That was the start of treating them as twins. No eternity is greater than a difference of two years between boys, but they were dressed alike and made to share a birthday party. To compensate, Don was held back and Phil brought on; Don had to wait for his first sports jacket until Phil was old enough for one. The family lived in Iowa before settling in Nashville, and there, at the age of eight, Don was given a little radio programme of his own, singing and reading the commercials for Deacon's Rat Poison. Then the six-year-old Phil was brought in, telling jokes. 'That was downfall for me,' Don says. 'I was a has-been at eight.'

The Everly Family sang for 90 dollars a week in the early morning for the farm workers of Knoxville, Tennessee. Afterwards they would go across the street for hot chocolate and Krystalburgers, a small but pungent rissole. This was scarcely preparation for what befell them when Country music laid the surprising egg called Rock and Roll. Don says, 'When Phil and I first hit New York, we were still wearing baggy pants. It was the first time we ever saw shoes without laces or socks that came up your leg. We met Buddy and the Crickets up in Montreal, they saw what we were wearing and said, "Gee whizz!" The only publicity picture they had then was of them all down in Lubbock, Texas, in T-shirts, settling tiles on the roof.'

In the pains and rages of adolescence, how one longed to change places, to inhabit the pleasant teenage world they sang of – motorcycles and Claudette and dreams unharried by skin blemishes. No-one could conceive of stardom as anything but dwelling in the songs. 'Buddy Holly,' Phil says, 'put me to bed with a girl. And he *laughed*. But I can remember him another night playing me all of his songs and asking me why he couldn't get a hit record, he was so low. Then he said, "Will you put me to bed?" '

Don almost joined the others whom stardom rapidly killed.

56

Scarcely out of his teens, he had one broken marriage behind him. His wits were clouded by amphetamines, so long before they grew to be fashionable. A British tour had to be cancelled through what was then described as a nervous breakdown. He tried to kill himself twice, while staying at the Savoy. 'I was so high, it didn't matter whether I went on living or not.'

Out of the tunnel of the years, however, they appear as very normal men. Their slightly feminine Southern charm has a strong effect on the Yorkshire manner, which as a rule is dour and defiantly familiar. At the motel, the chef himself emerged from the kitchen with a pot of tea for Don; one of the chauffeurs involved in the nightly rendezvous with Phil vouchsafed them to be 'a decent set altogether'. They were engaged on a long provincial tour, into Europe and out again, accompanied only by a manager and three musicians. No special trumpets were played for their presence. But everywhere there was someone whose adolescence they assuaged once, who still wears his hair in a brush like they did or wishes that he could strike the E Major chord at the beginning of 'Dream'.

Though the road still endlessly unwinds, both seemed to have attained emotional stability. Phil seems much the younger because his movements have the vividness of first love – his second wife, Patricia, is as fragile and pretty as the china displayed in the Yorkshire private hotel. As for Don, he has divorced a second wife. He says his children did not notice; he was always away in any case. Now his companion is Karen, a severe-looking but tender-natured girl, of both Cherokee and Apache descent, who keeps his engagements noted in a book; Don himself seems content to inhabit the present. 'I like beer,' he says, 'champagne. Vichy water, I would drinks quarts of that. Anything with bubbles.'

They are pursued at a distance by Pat Eadey, their most constant admirer. In Canada, in Yorkshire, in Southend, in Australia, Pat Eadey will appear and tape their night's performance and so studiously avoid imposing on them that now they look for her and ask how they played tonight. Glasgow-born, she emigrated to America and began to follow them:

over the past eight years her fan worship has matured into a warm but logical regard. Which is Pat Eadey's favourite song? ' "Dream" . . . I've seen them laugh too many times during that one and Don sneezed once in it, too, in Canada. "Devoted to You" I like. "Let It Be Me" I could listen to them sing every night – and I do.'

Musically their problem was knowing how to progress from early material which was, of its kind, perfect. In the 1960s they suffered a decline, as did most Rock originals who were overtaken by their English imitators. Yet their partnership, that most vulnerable thing of all, remained always intact in the binding of their voices. Their strength over all the refugees created by Pop music is in knowing their destiny to be joined however their personalities may dispute it. And in not being proud. So they advance by reaching back – far back to the Country music of their Knoxville days in the beautiful album *Roots*; voices flying together above orchestras and banjos and flowerings of steel guitars.

Lately, their career has described a circle. They have signed with RCA Records, whose famous Sam Sholes secured Presley but once turned the Everlys down. This places them under the supervision of Chet Atkins, doyen of Country guitarists, who heads RCA's Nashville repertoire from an office full of jars of peanuts, of butterscotch and all his shining-faced guitars. When the Everly Family sang on Radio KROL in Knoxville, Atkins was appearing on KNOX. He has helped them unselfishly ever since. It was he who played the E on 'Dream', and other chords throughout their hits whose quavering entered the disorder of so many a young boy's glands.

They have already completed an album with him; the Everly Brothers produced by Chet Atkins being a formula likely to impress many as close to perfection. It is, however, part of their survival to experience the bureaucracy which music has become. While they were in Yorkshire they heard that a minor RCA executive, who according to Don had lent a marginal hand with the album, was rewarding himself by amending the credits to: 'The Everly Brothers co-produced by Chet Atkins and David Kirstenbaum'.

'Can you imagine,' Phil said, 'some young guy telling Chet Atkins what to do?'

He continued, his voice rising, 'It wouldn't mean a thing if it said, "co-produced by Freddy Fudpucker and David Kirstenbaum". That's more presumptuous than I would be, Donald, and when people are presumptuous, I don't even give them the courtesy.'

His fingers played notes of annoyance up and down the keyboard of his guitar.

'Maybe they thought they'd like to do something for the boy . . .'

'Do nothing for the boy!' Phil answered passionately. 'Nobody ever did anything for us.'

Tonight they were appearing in Batley, Yorkshire – was their audience in Batley ever young? The formality of working men dressed up denies it; under the floor of blue smoke, all are as stiffly ageless as the women's pointed wigs. Applause here is given strictly in proportion to labour; yet at first beat of their guitars applause begins of the gentle sort which flutters out of memory.

' "Ebony Eyes",' several voices shouted.

'Er . . . we have to travel by plane occasionally,' Don said in apologetic refusal.

Backstage they were imperially treated. A waiter arrived with champagne glasses like honeycomb through his fingers. Phil cuddled Patricia as if he had only just met her, and Karen cuddled Don. The ghost of the irritating David Kirstenbaum came sometimes into the air. Pat Eadey arrived; they asked her how they had played tonight and she replied better than last night. Finally they were driven out by the smell of ammonia with which the club was being fumigated. In the freezing car park, a lady in a flame-coloured chiffon evening dress was waiting for an autograph.

Phil came back to Don's motel; a journey which took longer than it need have owing to the inordinate pride of the driver in carrying them. Even a minicab driver felt the pulses of teenage once, before his hair melted downward into his moustachios. The night-porter, no less admiring, opened up the bar.

Phil is the raconteur, although Don sings lead. That night Phil became almost incoherent with laughter as he summoned up their beginnings, when they wore Chartreuse-green shirts and had a girl named Scooter Bill for a manager. They only got the chance to record by surprising a record-company executive with a lady friend in the Sam Davis Hotel, Nashville.

'She was his mistress,' Phil said. 'A few years ago I couldn't have said that but now I can. She was his mistress.'

Their wanderings, and the California law of community property after divorce, have deprived them of copies of much of their best early work.

'I don't have all of it,' Phil said. 'I thought maybe I'd advertise for it through the fan-club. In a few years we're going to be really collectable, Donald.'

'We can take it steady,' said Don, 'for the next five years. Maybe they could do a film special on us, you know? Like they do on species that are disappearing.'

'– You mean all in long camera shots? Like the screaming eagle.' Phil laughed, then was abruptly serious. 'But we aren't disappearing. Donald. You'd have to say where we're disappearing to'.

Marianne Faithfull: My Credit is Good

When Marianne Faithfull goes out nowadays, it is usually to the Chelsea Arts Club. The whitewashed house in Old Church Street, a cross between country pub and seaside repertory theatre, has become her main refuge from the prying eyes that still pursue her, even into her own home. I met her just back from the Chelsea Arts Club, where she had been telling a fellow member about a photo-session she was shortly to do in West Berlin. 'How appropriate,' the friend remarked. 'You and Berlin have so much in common. Armies have passed through you both.'

Marianne herself tells the story, accompanied by a husky, foreign-sounding laugh. 'It *was* a bit strong, don't you think? Armies have passed through us both! I made him modify it in my case to just a platoon.'

Sitting on a rug, holding her knees before a slumbrous log fire, she seems almost eerily unchanged and untouched. Blue eyes through a parted gold fringe look upward, still trustingly. The face is the same in which that first brash young Pop promoter spotted the bewitching conflict of convent girl innocence with helpless sensuality. Only when she pats her cheeks, bewailing the effect of heroin-dependence on the complexion, does one remember that life did not keep its promise to handle Marianne Faithfull like precious china.

Most who remember her do so in the vague, still-reeking colours of the era she so unwillingly personified. For Marianne *was* the Sixties: in London, in Pop music, in the money and in trouble. She was the shy-voiced girl who made the Top Twenty safe for young ladies, but who fell from grace

61

by her liaison with Society's arch-enemy, the Rolling Stones. She was the scarlet woman who became Mick Jagger's mistress; the 'girl in the fur rug' at the decade's most notorious party; the quintessential Ophelia who first played the role onstage and afterwards, in Sydney, Australia, swallowed 150 Tuinol tablets and lay down to await death. It was already 1969. The Seventies, though less notorious, would prove even more nearly fatal.

Tonight in Chelsea, you would think the Sixties long dead and buried. The Kings Road, roaring close by, is just another rainy thoroughfare. On Cheyne Walk, a few streets away, the Georgian house where Mick and Marianne lived, turns darkened windows to the chill illumination of Albert Bridge.

Yet the past still harasses her, in small-time, almost self-parodying ways. There was the night recently, in a previous flat, when she woke up in bed with her husband Ben to find a man photographing her through the half-open window. As late as November last, police arrived suddenly at her present address to search and afterwards take away 'substances' for analysis. The game, she found, had changed none of its rules. 'There's nowhere they can't look. There's nothing they can't say to you. Then they read your statement back to you. "Er . . . for the record, officer . . . sorry, no pun, intended . . .!" I'm supposed to have *said* that.'

Since recovering from her heroin-addiction, Marianne has struggled to win recognition, not as a Rock star's consort nor the victim of an era, but as the dedicated musician she originally hoped to be. The voice, which used to sound so diffident, is now rich, raw and nicotine-stained. Two record albums, *Broken English* and *Dangerous Acquaintances*, distil the lessons of her 35 years with bitter world-wisdom but a still-game insouciance. She has become a cult figure in America and in European markets like West Germany. Once or twice a month, she has to get up early to take some or other short-haul flight, alone.

Her manner frequently evokes the absent-minded grandeur of some emigrée Austrian countess. She does not carry money – a habit unconnected with sometimes not having any.

The jargon of Pop, which she must speak to survive, is varied by recourse to fluent French and serviceable Latin. She had just heard that a newly-famous young record-producer was willing to supervise her next album, so long as he received his £75,000 fee in advance. 'He's just a young *arriviste*,' Marianne said. 'He doesn't realise how it would *benefit* him to work with someone like me.'

It puzzles and annoys her that, with two highly-regarded albums to her credit, she still does not rate as high in promotional terms as her manager's other main female client, the shock-headed Toyah. 'I know this country still bears me a grudge. People think I betrayed them in some way. I know they think of me as a rich, spoilt kid who doesn't really have to work. In fact, Ben [her husband] and I are nearly skint at the moment.

'I do want to make it again, and I know I deserve to. There's a foreign part of me that still rather likes to be thought of as a gifted amateur. But what I am is a highly-trained professional, brought up by another highly-trained professional.'

Her mother, Eva Sacher-Masoch, Baroness Erisso, was the daughter of an Austrian count who fought the Great War from a string of seven cavalry chargers. On the baroness's side, Marianne can trace her lineage back to the man who gave his name to masochism. Eva herself became a dancer in Vienna with the Max Reinhardt company and, but for the outbreak of war in 1939, would have gone to Hollywood and become a film star.

Eva met Marianne's father, Glyn Faithfull, through her brother Alexander, who fought beside him in Yugoslavia with Tito's partisans. Glyn was a philologist and – Marianne believes – a British secret agent. The war over, he brought his Austrian baroness back to Ormskirk, Lancashire, and became a lecturer at Liverpool University. They parted when Marianne was six years old.

Marianne spent most of her childhood with Eva in a small house, packed with grand Viennese ornaments, in Millman Road, Reading. 'My mother had to adapt her whole posture to that house. She couldn't *sweep* across rooms any more. But when we went to the shops, she was still the grande dame. She told me I'd got to smile at everyone. And the poorer they were, the nicer I had to be to them. Millman Road wasn't the worst part of Reading, but it was close to quite a bad part, which I had to walk through to buy my mother's Woodbines. "Darleeng", she'd say, "You go out and get me some Voodbines . . ." '

A local Catholic convent, St Joseph's, accepted the baroness's daughter as a weekly boarder on semi-charitable terms. The girls had to put on shifts directly after bathing, to avoid the sin of looking at their own bodies. By the time she left, Marianne had read her way through the entire 'Index' of literature forbidden to Catholics.

At 16, she was singing folk songs in a Reading coffee bar. 'I lived in a Renoir painting . . . long, blonde hair, sunny days, straw hat with ribbons . . . There was no doubt in my mind or my mother's that I'd go on the stage. The only question was, how? My mother had taught me that being beautiful was a thing one should recognise and put to use. I always knew that my looks and my voice were a devastating combination.'

She was 17 when her Cambridge undergraduate boy friend John Dunbar introduced her to a friend of his named Andrew Loeg Oldham. An inspired young hustler, Oldham was already far advanced in his plan to launch the Rolling Stones as a shaggy, threatening antidote to the so-lovable Beatles. Mick Jagger, then spotty and studentish, was at the same party but made little impression on Marianne. Oldham there and then offered to manage her also. Within weeks, her version of the Mick Jagger-Keith Richard ballad 'As Tears Go By' was in the British Top Ten. 'Greensleeves Goes Pop', one newspaper headline said.

The idyll seemed perfect when she married John Dunbar and had a son, Nicholas. Dunbar ran the Indica Gallery, focal-point for London's swinging young aesthetes, the place where John Lennon fell under Yoko Ono's irresistible spell. It was art dealers as much as Pop musicians who encouraged Marianne's first essay into drugs. 'This gallery-owner friend of John's called me into another room, showed me a pile of white powder on the mantelpiece and said "Take a sniff." I was so innocent, I snorted up the lot. He was very offended.'

In 1966, she left John Dunbar and began living with Mick Jagger. 'It was really very simple. I needed a friend. Mick was a good friend, who also happened to be a millionaire.'

She was with Jagger throughout the Rolling Stones' transition from snarling delinquents to peacock-robed leaders of a new London elite. Mick Jagger, above all, relished his ascent to the salons of families like the Guinnesses and Ormsby-Gores, and the friendship of Society legends like Tom Driberg and Lady Diana Cooper. 'Those were the people who were never shocked by us – the Dribergs, the Diana Coopers,' Marianne says. 'They'd seen it all before in the Twenties. "Cocaine!" they'd say. "My dear, I was at dinner parties before the War when every silver salt-cellar was *full* of cocaine!" '

The relationship with Jagger was never easy. Sixties Pop stars, after all, were chauvinists unrivalled since the Victorian paterfamilias. 'I was always trying to run away. I'd rush out of the front door clutching a £5 note and a lump of hash. Mick would come chasing after me and bring me back.'

Their four years together, though rife with bizarre and ugly incident, also brought both of them genuine domestic happiness. Jagger was fond and fatherly with Nicholas, Marianne's son, who lived with them at the Cheyne Walk house. 'I remember Mick telling me in horror that John Lennon wouldn't let his wife Cynthia have a nanny to look after their son, Julian. The Stones always thought the Beatles were so provincial. When Mick hired a nanny for Nicholas, he did it as if he'd had servants all his life.'

In January, 1967, 24 police officers raided the country home of the Stones' rhythm guitarist, Keith Richard*, during a weekend party at which Jagger and Marianne were present. Jagger, Richard and the art-dealer Robert Fraser were charged with drug-possession. Marianne, though not named

---

*Richards dropped the 's' during the Sixties and restored it in the late Seventies.

in the case, became notorious as 'the girl in the fur rug', centrepiece of a drug and sex orgy which the 'bust', allegedly, had interrupted.

The raid followed a deeply suspect tip-off to Scotland Yard by a Sunday newspaper which had accused Jagger, quite inaccurately, of heavy drug-taking, and which Jagger was now suing with every prospect of success. The 'drugs' found in his jacket pocket amounted to four pep pills of a type prescribed quite legally outside Britain. Nor were they even Jagger's – they were Marianne's. 'I'd got them in the South of France and just left four of them in that jacket. Mick played the English gentleman and took the blame.'

There followed the heat-hazed, unreal summer in which Jagger and Keith Richard were convicted, imprisoned, then released, chiefly at the intercession of a *Times* leading article headed 'Who Breaks A Butterfly On A Wheel?' Jagger was afterwards flown from his prison cell by helicopter to a televised summit conference with MP's and bishops in the garden of the Lord Lieutenant of Sussex. 'Mick was pretty vague – he'd been given Valium, I think,' Marianne says. 'As we sat in the garden in front of those cameras, I couldn't help feeling he'd only have to say one word out of place and the same helicopter would have flown him straight back to Wormwood Scrubs.'

By 1969, her life as Chief Stone's consort was driving her to despair. 'I found Mick's other affairs hard to take, but that wasn't the main reason. I felt I was pinned against the wall by the whole Sixties superstar thing of non-communication. Because in those days, you couldn't show any emotion. You had to be *cool*. One of the troubles was, there was never much drink around. If Mick and I had been able to get drunk together a few times, we might have had a chance. But it all got bottled and bottled up inside me. I remember, on one of those trips to Morocco, being with all of them in the middle of the Atlas Mountains, and just bursting into tears.'

Her suicide attempt late in 1969 was the culmination of a year in which the whole multicoloured era could be felt expiring. It was the time of her miscarriage of Jagger's child;

of new drug charges against them both; of the death of Brian Jones, most musically-gifted Stone, at a country cottage once owned by A. A. Milne; of the Stones' free concert in Hyde Park before half a million people; of Mick Jagger in a frilly frock, reading Shelley for his dead colleague, then flying with Marianne to Sydney to make a film as the Australian outlaw, Ned Kelly.

'While all that was going on, I'd been playing Ophelia in *Hamlet*. To do the part, I'd willed myself into a suicidal frame of mind. I'd also cut off all my hair. I can remember waking up in this hotel in Sydney with Mick, looking into the mirror – and suddenly seeing Brian Jones looking back at me. I remember very deliberately ordering hot chocolate from room-service to wash down the 150 Tuinols. It was Mick who saved me – not just from dying but from the major brain damage I could have had. He got me rushed to hospital in minutes.'

She lay in a coma for six days. 'I remember that feeling – as if I was in a place with no weather. No sun, no cold: nothing. And Brian Jones was there. He was terribly pleased to see me. He said he'd woken up, frightened and confused, not knowing where he was. Then he'd realised he was dead. He was actually quite funny about it. "Hey man . . . strange thing . . . opened my eyes, reached for the pill-bottle, then found out I was dead . . ."

'I remember walking – or rather jogging – along with Brian for a long time in this place where there was no weather, until we suddenly came to the edge of a gigantic drop. Then Brian said, "I've got to go on from here alone." And I could hear voices behind me, calling me back. One was my mother's. One was my son Nicholas's. And one was Mick's.'

Her decision to leave Jagger a year later was, she says, the inevitable consequence of her growing addiction to heroin and the threat it posed to Jagger's career. 'I truly didn't want to damage Mick any more than I had. People always assume I became a junkie while I was still with him, but I didn't. It was still an experiment I was making with my eyes wide open. I started on heroin knowing *exactly* what I was doing.

'I *did* love Mick very much, and he loved me. But I felt that an era was over and nothing could ever be the same again. Besides, various influential people with the Stones were letting me know I'd become superfluous. The Stones were getting chic, and I wasn't chic enough.'

Her heroin-addiction, at its deepest point, effectively obliterated 18 months of her life. All she can remember is that she spent each day standing by the same wall in Great Windmill Street, Soho, waiting for the next fix.

The memory is not all horrific. 'In a way, I found it *fascinating*. All my life, you see, I'd been looked at. Now I was looking at life as it passed me by, not even recognising me. And I was never harmed. I wasn't mugged. I wasn't raped. The whole of that underworld, for some reason, treated me with incredible gentleness.'

Even at her personal nadir in the mid-Seventies, she continued to turn down the large sums offered by various Sunday papers for the story of her life with Jagger. 'Well – I did do one. I worked out exactly how little I could get away with telling them for the money they paid me. I still don't want to do anything to hurt or upset Mick. He was good to me and he was very good to my mother as well. It was Mick who bought her the cottage she lives in in Berkshire.

'I'm still fascinated when people bring out books that claim to be the real inside story of the Stones. Like that Tony Sanchez book, which couldn't be published in England. Do you know who Tony Sanchez was? He was their drug-pusher. *Vere Dignum Justum Est*. Truly it is right and just.'

Her second husband is Ben Brierley, a gifted songwriter-guitarist whom she met in the punk rock era when he performed under the stage name 'Ben E. Ficial'. In their sitting room, remnants of Marianne's baronial past mingle with Ben's guitars – a Martin, a historic Les Paul Special. Ben himself, a witty, pale Mancunian, sits framed against the antique bureau, tinkering on a fretless Fender bass.

Ben, though not a member of Marianne's backing-group, is her main encouragement. 'Let's play something together,' Marianne pleads. 'Let's do "She's Got A Problem".' The lyric, written by a novelist friend, Caroline Blackwood, was considered too personal and explicit for her last album.

'Oh, please let's, Ben.'

'No, I don't feel like it.'

'Oh – *please*, Ben!'

'Go on then.' He plugs the Les Paul into his practice amplifier.

Her son Nicholas, now a teenager, lives with his father, John Dunbar, but comes over often for guitar-lessons with Ben. Nicholas can remember just flashes of his life in Cheyne Walk with Marianne and Mick.

'I remember being in the little music-room that smelt of cat-shit while Mick and Keith were writing a song. It was "Street-Fighting Man", I think.'

'And you remember when the three of us went off to South America,' Marianne said. 'Mick used to take you off along the beach for hours.'

'I remember Mick telling me. "Put on your sandals". And I remember when you both got stoned.'

'We were often stoned, darling.'

'No . . .' Nicholas said. 'I mean, when these people started throwing stones at you.'

Her future, in the past few days, had become even brighter. Her record company, Island, wanted to release a third album this summer – including the previously censored 'She's Got A Problem'. More important, she felt she was at last beginning to defeat the malice that the Rock business whispers about her to crucial figures like the Island Records boss, Chris Blackwell. 'It's so easy. If anything goes wrong, whoever's to blame, people have only got to raise one eyebrow and say "Oh well . . . you know . . . Marianne . . ." ' Chris Blackwell, after a long talk in Nassau, had offered to be her new album's executive producer.

Meanwhile, 'nearly skint', Marianne and Ben are looking round their flat for things they can sell. 'I'm always skint,' Marianne says. '– always was and always will be. If I've got anything, I spend it. But one thing I can say . . . one thing I've always been able to say. My credit is good.'

Eric Clapton: God is a Guitarist

George Harrison sat with a painfully thin fellow in a motorway restaurant, a graveyard of the digestion outside London. As the Beatle picked at the grisly fringes of a piece of toffee-coloured fish his companion ate through the largest blend of fats the place was capable of – egg, chips, bacon, sausage, beans, and trifle computerised into a frilly cup – while behind them a group of rubbish-trolley ladies grew more and more unsettled. The boldest of these finally crept up on Harrison, darted back to her friends, then returned to lean over his shoulder and stare into his face, breathing excitedly through a fine grey moustache.

As he autographed a paper napkin – 'for Sharon and June and little Willis?' – Harrison nodded to the other person at the table, Eric Clapton. 'Why don't you ask Engelbert for his?' he suggested drily. The fat lady bridled at this, scanned Clapton's features and demanded: 'Are you Engelbert?' 'No actually,' Harrison went on in his expressionless way, 'that's the world's greatest white guitarist – Bert Weedon.' But the woman continued to stare challengingly at Clapton who, outside of a millionaire's fur coat, seems ill-nourished and weedy and lacks the alabaster complexion of total indulgence that all the Beatles have. 'Are you a group?' She looked as though she wanted to shake him. Clapton said: 'No, just a hanger-on.'

He really likes going on tour – even the ulcer-making things: service areas instead of proper bathrooms; the musicians' changing-rooms filled with orange-peel, beer bottles and choc-ice wrappers; the Northern hotels that smell of old cinema carpets. He has fond memories of a particular stop off the M1 near Birmingham: 'The Blue Boar. You could get away with anything in there. Throwing plates of fried tomatoes around, anything.' It was genuine pleasure in this kind of life that led to one of last year's better tours. Clapton, largely at his own expense, brought over Delaney and Bonnie, a kind of rocking Ma and Pa Kettle, who appeared on the same programme when he was in America with Blind Faith; now Clapton appeared as one of their musicians, and his close friend Harrison had joined the party to play supporting guitar to him.

Harrison's admiration for Clapton's music is that of every other soloist who will gladly play chords as Clapton leads. Whereas the others picked up their skills largely in front of paying audiences, Clapton's brilliance seems always to have been complete; he is the most gifted of a society in which every other private citizen apparently owns a guitar; and his friend and caretaker Ben Palmer can recall this opinion forming locally almost as soon as he began to learn. It was in 1966 – when he was with John Mayall's Bluesbreakers, before the endlessly-applauded Cream – that a slogan appeared first on London walls, at the dawn of slogans. 'Clapton,' it said, 'is God.'

He has a following like no other in Pop music, a neat and tidy adulation from men and youths who simply wish they could change places with him. It is based entirely on the sound he can conjure from electric equipment, every trick and note of which seems played for the first time: he transforms the solid guitar from fingernails on metal bars to a species of rare wind instrument blown by bellows, heated by voltage. When the Delaney and Bonnie tour opened at the Albert Hall, Clapton had the most tremendous reception; yet on stage he is so thin he seems to melt into spotlights; you see only his sleeves. Afterwards, the tunnel to the stage babbled with beautiful parasites – staring teeth, unoccupied eyes and white skin coats. Clapton was indistinguishable among them, except to a bearded man his size who called: 'You're great, Eric.'

He is so self-effacing as to appear to disguise himself in the company of the moment. On this tour he was plainly influenced by the unquiet manners of Delaney, who embraces or clouts his wife and roisters generally like Attila the Hun dressed for motorbicycling. Clapton's malleability could be explained by his troubled childhood. Or else his character failed to come to a final dimension because of the lengths of time he has spent practising in rooms by himself – he lived for two years in a photographic darkroom in John Mayall's house, getting out of bed only to eat and play his guitar; the eyes of his mind shut tight. 'He *becomes* different people,' says his publicist Robin Turner. 'When he was with George Harrison a lot he bought a big house like George's and a big Mercedes – George gave him his Indian-painted Mini. When he was with Stevie Winwood and Blind Faith, he went back to jeans and wanting to live in the country. When he met Delaney and Bonnie he gave up travelling first-class and just climbed into their bus.'

Clapton seems equally uncertain about what he really looks like. During rehearsals he was wearing an expansive beard, a curly Saxon monarch affair that had disappeared by the night of the Albert Hall concert, but was beginning a mask of stubble again by the time the bus approached Sheffield. He has a pointed and pinched face, with a fleeting look of Gene Vincent, and dull teeth. Famous women like this: Clapton was once reported to be engaged to Alice Ormsby-Gore, Lord Harlech's daughter, and Christine Kaufmann, Tony Curtis's ex-wife, is also a friend of his. The only word, in fact, that Ben Palmer's wife will say against Clapton is that he isn't good at being with women and treating them as adults; he seems to benefit most from the company of the girls who follow the bands about.

He is also courteous and quiet and puts up with earnest fools. His mind has unexpected resources – mostly the result of gigantic reading sessions at Palmer's house in Oxford – and quite the best practical result is his vocabulary. Pop musicians as a rule have to use one or other of an inflexible set of phrases to describe any emotion that strikes them. In one of the tour dressing rooms the guitarist Dave Mason laboured to put into words the effect on him when Stevie Winwood left their group Traffic to form Blind Faith with Clapton: somehow the endless expression 'trying to get it together' seemed hardly enough to describe being thrown out of employment so cruelly. And later, at the buffet-supper after the concert, a girl vocalist refused to be assisted on the grounds that she was getting her own salad together.

As Clapton never says 'get it together', it is possible to ask him for the explanation many people believe he owes – why, in 1968, did he allow Cream to disband? Commemorated on five albums, including the record of their final appearance at the Albert Hall, they could have aroused little more emotional response from audiences if Clapton and the other members, Ginger Baker and Jack Bruce, had all been killed and their music released posthumously.

Clapton himself was never content with what Cream did or what he did for them; he says he saw himself differently; not as a soloist on whose every note the world hung but as a complete Blues player and singer. 'I've got confidence in my voice until it actually comes to getting in front of the microphone. I wasn't really proud of anything Cream did, but there are things on the Blind Faith album that I'm proud of.' In that case, why didn't he make an effort to keep Blind Faith on a permanent footing after their 1969 Hyde Park concert as the world's first supergroup? 'I like playing with Stevie and I expect I will again. If I've got a responsibility now, it's to other people.' Robin Turner remarked: 'In Germany he was practically in tears because the audience started shouting they didn't want Delaney and Bonnie, they wanted Eric to play on his own.'

His wealth is gigantic, though, in common with Royalty, he does not carry ready cash. To pay for the fry-up in the café he had to borrow a pound. When Delaney and Bonnie's musicians arrived in London, Clapton gave them four amplifiers costing £500 each; these failed to provide sufficient power so Clapton had another five air-freighted from Los Angeles. His own guitars are not opulent, and anybody is free to borrow one. Clapton's favourite is a black Gibson that was made

15 years ago, congested with electrical pickups, piped in white that has become nicotine yellow – he got it in exchange with the lead guitarist of the Free. And recently he also paid £50 for a relic of the 1930s, a self-amplifying metal guitar half-way between a viola and a biscuit-barrel that he afterwards gave to Delaney. The one instrument he does set store by as a possession is a 12-string Country and Western guitar that was specially built for him, inlaid with purple West African wood, picked out with silver like a hussar's jacket.

Before Clapton was rich he wasn't particularly happy. His grandparents, Mr and Mrs Clapp, brought him up in Ripley, Surrey, and he went to Surbiton Secondary Modern school. 'I call my grandparents my parents; I was born illegitimately I think. I looked at my birth certificate the other day and where it said "Father" there was just a dash.' The only thing he was ever really good at was art. 'I've heard I was top of the class and really doing well – then my real Mum came back to stay with us. From that moment they say I was moody and nasty and wouldn't try. We had to go through this whole thing of pretending she was my sister. At school I used to hang around with all the weeds. I was always getting hit – on the hand with a ruler, or the side of the head.

'My parents bought me my first guitar on the HP – a Kay. It wasn't cheap and flash; it was expensive and flash. I was pretty terrible at the start – kept doing the same three licks. I'd learned a whole Chuck Berry album off by heart and I played it one night at the Marquee, with *terrible* feedback; I got a mike and stuck it on a box and did it sitting down. I really started to play when I was thrown out of art college because it was the only thing I was interested in that nobody else was.'

He joined a group called Rhode Island Red and the Roosters, which met to practise in the Wooden Bridge Hotel, Guildford, and once also included the late Brian Jones. They more or less dissolved after one engagement in Brighton, during which a lot of French students indicated displeasure by holding up handkerchiefs tied in hangman's nooses. After that Clapton was with the Yardbirds, but left when attempts

74

were made to discipline their behaviour. John Mayall's Bluesbreakers, with whom he played next, for 18 months, have in fact been an unusual academy for good musicians in Pop and Jazz: Mick Taylor of the Rolling Stones, Jack Bruce and Mick Fleetwood of Fleetwood Mac.

It is difficult to explain the avalanche that Cream started, and the legends that still surround them; such as the night they assembled 115 amplifiers at once. As a psychedelic group their average power was 1000 watts (as opposed to the Roosters' 30); yet their songs, notably 'I Feel Free' 'Badge' and 'Strange Brew', were genuinely lyrical. Some of the romance about Cream in England stems of course from the time they were in America, and some from tales that its members were always fighting. Clapton says this is true: blows were at one point exchanged between Jack Bruce and Ginger Baker, a drummer of satanic brilliance, who, if he saw ushers mishandling audiences, used to fire off drumsticks to hit them in the neck, and never miss a note.

It isn't true, however, that America was at once at their feet when they arrived. On the first visit they had to play for two weeks on a non-stop Murray the K Rock and Roll show at the end of which Clapton wanted to have a flour and egg fight backstage. Murray the K heard about it and threatened not to pay them, so Clapton and his friends contented themselves with using the materials to create a huge moving pudding in the showers, and throwing Pete Townshend of the Who into it.

If Clapton adores anything as well as the guitar it is making a mess. His face lit up as he described a food fight that took place after one Delaney and Bonnie concert in Scandinavia. When the coach with George Harrison aboard reached Sheffield, Clapton at once disappeared to try to buy water-pistols but instead brought back a number of horrid-faced little clockwork toys, oranges and lemons that dragged their feet when they walked.

During the first half of the concert he took a clockwork orange and released it on the stage, along the rim of the electric organ belonging to a trio named Ashton, Gardner and Dyke; after they had finished laughing they played with rather more spirit than before. Clapton, meanwhile, stood in front of the dressing-room mirror, combing his hair back and up into a cowlick style popular among Elvis-worshippers almost a generation ago: possibly he remembered the Lyceum, the gilded Muscovite ballroom where Delaney and Bonnie rehearsed, and where entire galleries are devoted to mirrors for greasy heads. Delaney and George Harrison copied him, for a laugh; but, at that moment and in the concert, Clapton seemed a different person.

Almost everyone else from the coach was on the stage as he and Delaney and Bonnie played. It is a dizzy experience to stand close to powerful equipment, listening to the buzz of the loudspeaker fabric, looking into a darkness bejewelled by green Exit signs. They did a medley of Little Richard songs, demented old classics like 'Long Tall Sally', and Clapton, for the first time that anyone could remember, leapt about and angled his guitar like Gene Vincent on a good night. He is 24. Earlier, in a room already ruined by waste paper and clock-work fruit lying in puddles of wine, he had been asked what he'd be doing when he was 30. 'What I'm doing now, I suppose,' he said.

Bill Haley: A Piece of Gold in my Pocket

Close to his 50th birthday, Bill Haley seems to be in excellent repair. His hair is at low water, but then it always was, stranding the kiss curl on his brow like a small, wet scythe. His jowls have descended, but the baby face remains, with cheeks as plump as if pressed between invisible hands. Dignified, judicious, given to use of the Royal we, he embodies an age when popular music was still played by our elders and betters.

His visits to London with the Comets are still accompanied by minor, commemorative violence. His last concert, at the New Victoria cinema, had to be curtailed after a crowd of Teddy Boys in cylindrical coats began fighting among themselves for possession of the stage, and kicking at one another with blunt and wedgy shoes. One spectator was observable being dragged by his mate towards the exit, unconscious, blood-boltered, and almost with a sense of vocation. It reads like 1956, save that some of the Teddy Boys were parents, with grown-up sons standing by.

Haley's career as king and founder of Rock and Roll music has always been a source of amazement to him. He was no wild Country boy. He was raised in the Philadelphia suburbs. His mother came from Liverpool. His father was a horticulturalist. As a teenager, he left home and travelled to the American South, riding the boxcars, wary of the railroad detectives who patrolled the roof. The 'race' music he heard in the South he strummed in his own way while working at the radio station in Chester, Pennsylvania. His earliest Rock and Roll hit, 'Rock the Joint', in 1951, was released without publicity, to create the impression that he was black.

He remembers the mad days of 'Rock Around the Clock' with a mild, almost professorial detachment. The famous visit to England in 1956 was small stuff compared to Berlin, where rival East and West German gangs broke up the Sports Palace, and Haley and the Comets had to seek shelter up in the rafters. In Argentina, he was carried bodily into one theatre by a column of police, breaking heads on all sides with their clubs. A fan grabbed his tie, and almost garrotted him. He had to live in that theatre for a week. He ran risks in America, playing concerts in the South at segregated theatres. He once finished a concert having been informed that there was a bomb set to go off beneath the stage. It was, he says, the quickest version of 'Rock Around the Clock' he ever played.

He has been trying to retire for years, to go back to his young family and his fishing business in Mexico. But he still enjoys singing 'Rock Around the Clock – which, with frequent re-releases, has by now sold some 26 million copies. 'It's always the same good feeling when I start those words. "One two three o'clock four o'clock rock." It's like a piece o' gold in my back pocket.'

Ringo: A Starr is Bored

Ringo Starr was to be viewed ceremonially last week, in
Paris. He and his courtiers were accommodated at the
George V hotel, where *Salade Belle Nuit* can be obtained
nowadays for as little as £9 per portion. Obediently, a contin-
gent of the European press gathered downstairs, checking
earnest-looking tape recorders into cloakrooms and nervously out again, leaving nothing on the saucer for the
concierge. Our self-appointed leader was Tony Prince, a
Radio Luxembourg disc-jockey with vertical black hair, the
physique of an ageing stripper, and a manner intended to be
keenly observant of his surroundings. 'Lots of posters to Mao
about,' he remarked. 'Mao Tse-tung. He's the guy who's just
died, right?'

Ringo dealt with his inquisitors upstairs, at half-hourly
intervals. He is in Europe to promote his new record album,
Rotogravure. The name, as is customary, arises only from
personal caprice. He was sitting in bed once, watching *Easter
Parade* on television, and Judy Garland sang a song that mentioned 'the rotogravure.' He believes it has something to do
with newspapers. You notice his little feet, and little hands
covered with gold that now looks somewhat tarnished. His
hair, formerly shaven, has grown back into a tonsured,
curious shape, like a grey pocket handkerchief. His dark
glasses provide double reflection of the half-drawn blinds.
His voice, glum but not gloomy, has withstood the
depredations of time. Between his feet, a half bottle of Mumm
Cordon Rouge champagne gives open-mouthed aid in his
ordeal.

The George V has special Beatle memories. That was where they stayed in 1963 – some in the group downstairs remembered it – when *Salade Belle Nuit* was, possibly, just £5 the portion, and 'I Want to Hold Your Hand' first broke through the American charts. Coincidentally that day, a full page in the *International Herald Tribune* had been taken by a Mr Bernstein, a New York agent, pleading with the four former Beatles to perform together again, for the hope of Mankind, as Mr Bernstein emotionally expressed it, and a purse cautiously estimated at some 200 million dollars. The advertisement had been shown to Ringo at lunch time, when he awoke. He found too many words in it, he said, for his taste.

Besides, his fame as a solo musician has flourished in America: even his. In England, he was always the neglected Beatle, the fourth, the funny one, but America gave him equal billing with John, George and Paul. They appreciate drummers there. He cites the case of Charlie Watts of the Rolling Stones, another of history's great bit-part players. His albums go high in American charts. He has remained on amicable terms with the other Beatles, even McCartney: they have all gone down to Los Angeles to play on his records. So have Nilsson, Peter Frampton and other celebrities tickled by the new affectation of anonymity. Ringo, least of any Beatle, seems troubled by former glories. The cover of *Rotogravure* depicts the door of the Beatles' Apple building in Savile Row, covered with years of desperate graffiti messages, pleading with the Beatles to be reborn. But how amusing, Ringo's courtiers murmur, to put that on the cover. He accepts the tribute modestly. Rock musicians are noted for their keen and sensitive wit.

He regards himself as still primarily an instrumentalist. Who, on hearing his voice, could dissent from that view? He admits that he finds the singing difficult. 'Singing with the boys used to be easy, because John used to take me through the lyric. I'd stand there, thinking I was Stevie Wonder: then I'd go in the control box and find out I was Bing Crosby. I've got a lot more confident, but I can still feel it shaking' – he pulled at his Adam's apple – 'in here. I've got the range of the common housewife.'

He has long since joined the pitiable brotherhood of tax exiles. He resents this. Good old fashioned, unshapely resentment surfaces through the mock artistic gestures of superstardom. He worked in a factory once, didn't he? He worked on the railways and in the Navy. Why shouldn't 'e 'ave what's 'is? Materially, he is not deprived: he has a rented house in Los Angeles, a house and furniture business (for sale) in England, and a flat in Monte Carlo. But there are subtler forms of poverty. His 10-year-old marriage is over, with three children in the custody of their mother. His life is on short-term rent. A few keepsakes from the old days are in a tea chest somewhere, awaiting a permanent home.

He admits that he has never really saved money. He could never restrain himself from buying new toys. A couple of years ago, he discovered credit cards. Previous to that, one gathers, like Royalty, he paid for nothing. 'But I've been good lately,' he said, to the wider audience in the room. At this point, one of his retainers looked round the edge of a green plush armchair. The retainer wore a velvet coat, like a cloak, and a single earring. Curly grey hair stood wildly around a bald pate: the yellow fanged smile was both predatory and protective. 'Yes,' this apparition agreed. 'You've been *very* good lately.'

Fleetwood Mac: Carrying the Albatross

Fleetwood Mac have returned to Britain, a decade after their song 'Albatross' set a new mood and mellow tone for the rock guitar. But that original psychedelic Fleetwood Mac are to the present group like cousins many times removed. The band since its first success has undergone almost a dozen changes of personnel, and a chapter of accidents and ill luck which might have disheartened many a more robust community. Now based in America, they view their current British revival as small recompense for the years of real pain and genuinely broken hearts.

Mick Fleetwood, the band's drummer and co-founder, is the antithesis of a rock freak. Hugely tall and stilt-legged, healthily white, precise of thought and speech, he is betrayed in his vocation only by institutionally long hair.

The son of an RAF officer, he spent his early childhood in Egypt, during the Suez invasion, and then Norway, where his father served with NATO. He attended King's School, Sherbourne, distinguishing himself in acting and fencing, and privately dreaming over the catalogues issued by drum manufacturers. He remembers standing in the school grounds, vowing to become a drummer, with tears in his eyes.

His first engagement was in a London night club, playing for £7 per week and a nightly plate of spaghetti. From this, in the middle Sixties, he graduated to John Mayall's Bluesbreakers, a band famous for the diverse talents whom Mayall, an insecure man, hired and fired. It was in the Bluesbreakers that Fleetwood met two inaugural members of Fleetwood Mac: John McVie, the bass guitarist, and Peter

Green, a guitarist of unusual talent who had joined Mayall as replacement for the demigod Eric Clapton.

Their initial phase as Fleetwood Mac was deservedly acclaimed. It produced 'Albatross', an experiment with harmonising guitars, and one of the earliest intimations that Rock was capable of melody. There was also 'Oh Well', a song containing the first, perhaps the only lyric in which Rock musicians made fun of themselves. 'I can't help about the shape I'm in,' the lyric ran, 'I can't sing, I ain't pretty and my legs are thin.'

In private they remained individualists, shunning offers from management companies who might have tried to influence their output. As a result, they stayed poor and grew accustomed to hardship. Mick Fleetwood remembers the scabies caught from dirty bedclothes; the terrible all-night drives; the agony of coiling his long legs inside a cramped van with condensation grey on the windows. When Christine McVie first met them, they had begun to do a little better. She recalls her envy of their Transit van, fitted with aircraft seats.

Christine McVie, composer, singer and pianist, came to Fleetwood Mac in 1970 with exceptional abilities and fractured self-confidence. She grew up in Birmingham, the daughter of a music professor, and drifted into rock while studying sculpture at art school. In the late Sixties, she joined a band called Chicken Shack playing piano, largely unaware of her soft, low, flawless singing voice. She left Chicken Shack and, some months afterwards, was astonished to find herself named as Top British Female Vocalist in the *Melody Maker*'s annual polls.

There followed a short, catastrophic career as a solo singer on tour. She got as far as Nottingham, was overcome by her own imagined defects and ran off the stage in tears. She married John McVie, Fleetwood Mac's bass guitarist, after a courtship of two weeks, and prepared herself for the hectic, uneasy existence of a Rock and Roll wife.

By 1970, the original Fleetwood Mac had all but disintegrated. Peter Green, the 'Albatross' guitarist, resigned, and with his departure, the band's obituaries were as good as written. To add to their demoralisation, an ersatz Fleetwood Mac began touring, until persuaded by legal means to desist. The real Fleetwood Mac, working now mainly in America, were bedevilled by arrivals and desertions. One member went out to buy a newspaper and never returned. They discovered that he had joined a religious sect. Almost by default, Christine became keyboards player in the band. This, as she recalls, did little for her self-confidence.

It was by sheer coincidence, in California, that the present personnel coalesced. Mick Fleetwood happened to hear an album recorded by the American boy-girl songwriting partnership of Lindsey Buckingham and Stevie Nicks. This, as it happened, was Buckingham-Nicks' only album. Disgusted with their manager, they had virtually given up music. Buckingham rose early in the morning to canvass advertisements by telephone in the different time-zone of New York. Stevie Nicks, the daughter of a wealthy businessman, worked as a waitress to support Buckingham and the sound engineer who lived with them.

In 1975, after a single meeting, Buckingham and Nicks were invited to join Fleetwood Mac. 'They didn't even want us to audition,' says Lindsey Buckingham, a thin youth with the composure of a young Moses. 'The only time they ever auditioned anyone, it was absolute disaster.'

Fortunately, Buckingham and Nicks brought with them a quantity of unrecorded material. After only 12 days' rehearsal, the first album of the new Fleetwood Mac was produced – the one they now call 'the white album'. It contained 'Rhiannon', sung by Stevie Nicks, and 'Over My Head' and 'Warm Ways', both sung by Christine McVie as if she had never felt a qualm. The album was destined to sell better than any other in the history of Warner Brothers Records. Four million copies have now been sold, a tiny proportion of them in England.

Their alliance proved to be the salvation of more than a musical approach. At that time, Christine had left John McVie to live with a lighting technician. Buckingham and Stevie

Nicks had ceased to be lovers. Even Mick Fleetwood had parted from his wife. All were casualties of a life perpetually on tour, lacking any respite from each other, even after the different love affairs had terminated. John McVie, in particular, had to pull himself back from the edge of suicide.

All made a conscious decision to subdue emotions for the sake of the band. In return. McVie thinks, hard work soothed the agony and affront of seeing his wife with another man. He and Buckingham now have new girl friends, happily accepted by Christine and Stevie. And Fleetwood is reunited with his wife.

Their life on tour is civilised, even domestic, with limits. There are two nannies in train, and a quantity of little daughters, peeping through Mick Fleetwood's long legs, Fleetwood maintains that he dislikes stability – his attitude to money remains the same as when he would use his National Assistance money to fill up his Jaguar XK 120. Yet the prevailing atmosphere on the road seems to be 'not in front of the children.' If the men wish to misbehave, they go to a Chinese restaurant in Beverly Hills which never objects when they plaster their food on the walls.

They were in two minds whether to undertake this present tour. To begin with, they stood to make little money from it. And even Mick Fleetwood felt apprehensive about returning to England after so many years of indifference. Buckingham and Stevie Nicks were terrified by what the others told them – how small British audiences were, and how implacably strange.

The first of their concerts was in Birmingham. Christine's home town, where she and John McVie had spent their honeymoon. They walked onstage, upset by this painful coincidence. The concert, however, proved to be the best one of the week.

'We were very surprised,' Christine said.

'Very relieved,' Mick Fleetwood put in.

'Very exalted,' Christine said.

Debbie Harry: Rhapsody in Blonde

In a tall, draughty brownstone house, off New York's Second Avenue, preparations are afoot to videotape a sequence for Blondie's new single record, 'Rapture'. The two-minute film involves some 20 costume characters, among them a Martian, a Red Indian, a Rastafarian, a policeman, a troupe of voodoo dancers and a presently docile, though deeply pessimistic-looking goat.

Upstairs, Debbie Harry, Blondie's lead singer, is applying her own makeup like the professional cosmetician she used to be. The face reflected at her has the same flawless, pouting, impersonal gloss that has improved the circulation of magazines as far apart as *Cosmopolitan* and *Penthouse*. Unpinning her platinum-bright hair, she combs it carefully into its formal appearance of having been rumpled playfully by a force nine gale. She wears a vestigal black bodice, a pair of evening trousers cut to thigh-length and a black crocheted shawl.

The word for Debbie Harry and Blondie, in Pop jargon, is 'hot'. Their songs – 'Atomic'; 'Heart of Glass'; 'Call Me' – are modern Pop at its ultimate: brief, shallow, disco-distant, as blandly evocative as the magazine covers on which Debbie so often features. She is Pop music's first pin-up and, as such, ministers to needs more complex than mere listening and dancing. They call her, with good reason, 'the Monroe of the Eighties.'

I was to meet her and her boyfriend Chris Stein, not at the record studios, as is usual, but in my own New York hotel room. This slightly cloak-and-dagger air was increased by their arrival half an hour early. In the corridor, only one person was visible; an ordinary-looking bespectacled man of 30, with grey flecks in his hair. Down the hall lurked a second figure swaddled in scarves and knee-warmers and a balaclava topped off by large black spectacles. 'Hi, I'm Chris,' the young man said. 'This,' he added with some admiration, 'is Debbie.'

Such caution, necessary for all Manhattan public faces, has intensified since John Lennon's murder, not far from Chris and Debbie's own apartment. 'We never go out of any building without looking both ways,' Debbie said. Living on the East Side as she does, she has been threatened innumerable times, both by guns and knives.

The woman who epitomises New York, in all its seedy and chic allure, was born, 36-odd years ago, in Florida. Her mother, a concert pianist, had her adopted as a baby by a couple named Harry, living in suburban New Jersey. Her upbringing was quietly provincial until, with a like-minded teenage girl friend, she began creeping off from New Jersey, over the river into Manhattan. The two would hang around Greenwich Village in the afternoons, gaping at a new species, the 'beatniks', with their berets, dark glasses and bongo drums.

Her first job was as a secretary in the BBC's New York office. She learned to work a Telex machine and edit radio tapes. Her hair was darker then, coiled into an elaborate beehive full of air and pins. Alert, quick witted, rather bookish, she has always felt bored by the sheer hard labour involved in being beautiful. 'What is hair, anyway?' She twisted a white-gold lock downward and reproved it. 'External protein!'

Her music career began in the late Sixties, with an unsuccessful band called Wind in the Willows. In between, she worked as a waitress and, once, as a Playboy Club bunny, learning to smile even as customers' wives malignly stubbed out their cigarettes on her stockinged thigh.

One of her waitress jobs was at Max's Kansas City, the New York restaurant which, around 1971, nurtured Punk

Rock in its original up-market form in which music was united with avant garde art. Debbie Harry, crop-headed and dye-streaked before her time, formed a three-girl group called the Stilettos.

Stein, Brooklyn-born, grew up in the era after Debbie's. Like every post-Beatlemania American boy and girl, he had a guitar, grew long hair and camped out at Rock festivals. He hitch-hiked to Poland, lived with London's hippies, studied photography at the New York School of Visual Arts, took LSD and, as a result, spent a year in what he refers to cheerfully as 'the nuthouse'.

When they first formed Blondie in 1975, Debbie still worked as a waitress and Chris was on the dole. Strange as it may now seem, the idea of a female 'fronting' a Rock group used to be thought highly eccentric. Debbie's persona, innocent yet sluttish, arrogant yet waif-like, was consciously rooted in America's most mystical of all sex objects. 'I *did* identify with Marilyn. But it was more the blonde thing in general. Blonde hair we equate with glamour, success, desire. It was just a great hook.'

Their style was mid-Sixties: the era of sighing girl groups and Phil Spector's 'wall of sound' technique, traditionally revered more in Britain than in America. Early Blondie singles, like 'Denis' and 'Sunday Girl', were British hits that made little impact on their home market. It was American interest in British Punk and New Wave, ironically, which took them in the US Top Twenty. 'Heart of Glass', then 'Call Me' each sold a million copies. Debbie Harry's face, meanwhile, became a means of advertising any commodity from 'contact' magazines to cine equipment. Rock as an industry finally awoke to the possibilities in simple female sex appeal.

Six years of success and two Platinum Discs have left Debbie and Chris only a little wealthier than in Debbie's waitress days. Disputes with their original management and record company led them to spend several million dollars on buying out the contracts of both. More millions have vanished through the use of Debbie's face on unauthorised merchandise. 'We never saw the money, so we don't miss it,' Stein says.

Stein, even now, remains an underground figure, mistrustful and contemptuous of the commercial Pop world. He and Debbie argue constantly over the value of Blondie as culture. 'I say that to entertain people is enough,' Debbie says. 'Chris thinks we should be doing something more.'

As well as its 20 costume characters, the videotape sequence featured a graffiti action painting by two young men, one black, one white, who make a career of decorating New York subway trains in their marshalling yards after dark. The trains, bearing elaborate landscapes or rainbows, cause spontaneous applause as they enter subway stations. 'That boy,' Stein said, pointing at the black graffitist 'is a true artist of our time.' The artist, concurring, pointed to himself and added: 'This coat used to belong to Thelonius Monk.'

The two-minute sequence took 12 hours to film. The goat grew gradually less acquiescent, its sphincter tensing ominously. At length, it bolted through the TV equipment, carrying its handler with it.

Much later, Debbie Harry, in crocheted shawl and cut-down evening trousers, sat with her stockinged feet on a ledge, gnawing an apple. The composition, once again, could hardly have been bettered by *Vogue* or *Cosmopolitan*. Downstairs, one of the extras had smuggled in a copy of *Forum*, the sex magazine, its cover proclaiming that Debbie Harry had 'told all.' All she has told was that she prefers Chris Stein to other men; that she goes 'half-crazy' if he so much as looks at another woman.

Stein thinks their fan-mail gives the finest indication of Debbie's effect. 'We get letters from parents saying: "Our son never showed interest in girls before, but now he's hung a picture of Debbie over his bed." It's not a complaint. "We want to tell you," they say, "we're really *glad* it's only Debbie".'

89

Johnny Cash: Jailhouse, Jesus and H.G. Wells

The heavy carved front door into House of Cash, Johnny
Cash's state mansion, in Madison, Tennessee, swung inward
to reveal blinding sunshine and the awe-struck face of a
tourist. His eyes grew wider still as he surveyed the sump-
tuous foyer, its heavy brocades, its gilded Tennessean Louis
XIV furniture, its massively-framed photographs of Johnny
Cash, his wife June Carter, his new baby son and his celebrated folk-singing mother-in-law. Not until this point did the
tourist descry Cash himself, on an unexpected visit, lounging
in a high-backed armchair.

'Well – good gosh. I'm all excited!' the tourist said with a
gasp.

Cash seldom laughs. His life beats in an unease of his large
muscles, in shifting feet, a collar turned up against the
draught; nerves more conspicuous since he keeps no flat-
terers and sycophants to shield him. But laughing, suddenly
he relaxes. The serious battlements of his face dissolve. His
teeth glow brightly and small. Like now – he chuckled,
grasped the corners of the chair above him and repeated:

' "Good gosh, I'm all excited". That's a great line.'

Thus encouraged, the tourist returned with 60 others, followed by 60 more. They were the contents of two excursion
buses from Nashville here only to worship, as they had
thought, the gravel of the drive. Sandals muffled in the
carpet, with their strange, merciless reticence they all
swooped at Cash. He rose from the chair, his face anxious,
shoulders in a fidget, and walked straight towards them.

'Hi folks, glad to see you,' he said, 'You all havin' fun?'

'Hell-o,' a woman gasped, 'How are you?'

'I'm fine, thanks,' Cash said, 'Hi folks—'

They passed him endlessly and shook hands: old men and matrons, young men, boys with sandpaper heads. Speechless with love, and the fear of being charged a supplement for it, nevertheless few of them could look up into his face. 'And I'll put my arm around some of 'em to say "Glad to see you" . . .they'll be tremblin' all over,' Cash says, 'Like they had St Vitus' Dance there.'

For he is all that they desire for themselves; all strong, outdoor things. Country music is the palliative of imprisoned city whites and Cash is king of Country, embodying the most of its supposed virtues. In the monolithic simplicity of his singing, freedom seems conjoined with absolute dignity – they see him moving over trackless land into the sky, but always in tailored black, well-shod. Few such heroes remain to them now that the Wild West has been turned by their enemies into pornography.

His estate is 15 miles from Nashville, and far from the spirit of it. There is a house on Old Hickory Lake; an office across the highway like nothing so much as an English rectory made of some washable substance. Since it is part of their dream of him that Cash should often be absent – air travel being, after all, only a modified form of riding the boxcars – the biggest shock his worshippers normally receive is in the decoration. Cash and June Carter his wife are fond of oyster shades and carved German dressers, not the plated horrors and wild beast horns to be seen in other Country stars' homes. On the mind of the Nashville tourist, the effect of this sudden taste has yet to be measured.

June's office is displayed across a red cord like the drawing-room of a queen. She is in fact Country and Western royalty; a daughter of the Carter Family. With the tubercular Jimmie Rodgers, the Carters all but founded the music 40 years ago, when Cash's father was still trying to scratch a life from the hard lands of Arkansas.

She met Cash in the 1950s, just as Country music was turning into Rock and Roll. He had been signed to the famous

Sun record label and was on tour with the other Sun acquisition Elvis Presley. 'Elvis had been raving about what a great singer Johnny Cash was,' June says. She and Cash were both married previously. 'My little daughter used to love "Folsom Prison Blues" and I'd rock her to sleep, dancing to it with her in my arms. But the first time I saw him I thought: "Why, maybe some of the other guitarists would go out on the stage and help him." There was just John all alone, and Luther Perkins's guitar going "boom chuggachugga boom".'

She joins him at the microphone now; against his towering black, an innocence of Southern lace. It is marriage to her which. Cash says and intimates with every movement in their duet, has been the proper adjusting of his soul. 'I was evil,' he says solemnly, 'I really was.' Certainly he was wayward; sometimes compromising his early career. June is quick to point out, however, that he was never a monster; that she did not, by a womanly miracle, reclaim him; he simply, at a certain point, pulled himself together. But the white races love nothing better in their heroes than penitence. Even as he sings Gospel, they love to think of him, as well, when he was bad.

Yet his life has really been no more lurid than any self-made American millionaire's. As a boy he picked cotton until too tired to speak, let alone sing 'Cottonfields'. He spent, as in the song, horrible nights in Detroit city where he worked as a punch-press operator in an automobile plant. He has been in jail, but not for the long sentence to which his prison shows have been attributed; it was more like one night. The scar on his face was made by a cyst. Some years ago one of his many imitators offered money to be hit with a signet ring in hopes of reproducing the disfigurement.

And also he was once a door-to-door salesman; a difficult notion for those of us who think of him moving only with the four winds. 'I used to worry about people puttin' themselves into debt. I'd say, "You don't want any of this, do you?" They'd say, "Hold on there, what are you selling?" ' As for his Service career, it left no mark on him more serious than the ability, to this day, to read Morse code at the rate of 60 words per minute.

His face will also relax while imparting or receiving knowledge. He has discovered that he lives on land once occupied by an Indian tribe called the Stone Box, who happened to hit on the secret of internal plumbing. He seems – almost biologically – incapable of guile; but it is the way of the world for the plainest liberal statement to be received with contempt by all liberals. Together with the odium conferred on anyone with a successful television show, Cash has been attacked for most of his interests – his concern for prisoners, for Indians, and now his singing of religious music, despite the fact that no one ever thought to question the sincerity of Jazz Gospellers.

His passion is gardening. To indulge it when at home he has to get up at six if he wants to escape the eyes of tourist boats scouting the lake. 'I raise beans, peas, okra, cabbage, squash. I got an orchard with Jonathan and Bartlett pears, Winesip apples, and I'll have Chinese chestnuts and paper-shell pecans.' Part of the garden is the site of Roy Orbison's house which burned down and killed his two little boys. Cash promised him, when he took over the property, that something good would at least come out of the ground. One can somehow see him promising that to Orbison, who always looked desperate and pale even when happy.

'We own a mansion,' Cash admits, 'but that's home; we're dug into it. I got some woods over there, maybe 80 acres of woods. In the middle there's just a two-room shack. I'll go over there and sit around – read a lot. I read novels but I also read the Bible. And study it, you know? And the more I learn, the more excited I get. Some of those stories are as wild as any H.G. Wells could drum up. And that Jesus! He really cuts me up! I worship him, but he tickles me to death.'

Even in his troubled years, the time of records such as 'Big River', when Cash was by his own admission alternately flying and falling on pep pills, he went through the works of Joyce and Dylan Thomas. 'We got books all through the house

93

but most of 'em I got rat-holed in my study. I been reading the writings of Josephus, the histories of the Jewish peoples. Other night I was reading the works of Ecclesiasticus. I got my books all ready to take to England – Winston S. Churchill's *History of the English-Speaking Peoples* volumes one through four. I'm really looking forward to going to England so's I can get back to Foyle's.'

When those busloads crept speechlessly into his presence from Nashville, an English tour had just been announced and sold out in 24 hours. So it is everywhere. The following day the Cash company flew to Toronto to appear at the Canadian National Exhibition; their route lying roughly parallel with the hurricane then brushing with angry skirts at the edges of the Americas. As the long official Cadillacs moved towards the visor of the grandstand, the skies were already dark as a madman's painting, pricked by the turning lights of the Ferris wheels.

June Carter is beautiful in a wide-lipped way with hair like a girl's and a voice full of honey and nuts. It is part of the South's domestic art that she can make almost homely their constant passage through the rich hotels and draughty Blue Rooms of the world. Her mother, Maybelle, of the original Carter Family, appears with her, and the two daughters who make up the present Family, and Carl Perkins, doyen of Rock and Roll guitarists, who smells pleasantly of antiseptic lozenges. The retinue has also been increased in the person of a baby son John Carter; an exceeding gratification to his father's respect for learning of any sort.

'He sure knows some difficult words. "Chandelier"—'

'And "platypus",' said June.

'– and "Daddy come here *right now*".'

Cash's friends are younger than himself. There is Bob Dylan with whom he appeared on *Nashville Skyline*; a figure often overlooked when the Conservatism of Cash's following is being reckoned. And there is also Kris Kristofferson, who flew in to see him in Toronto. A former Rhodes Scholar, with daemonic eyes and a suit like suede pipes, Kristofferson has written the first songs worthy to be called White Soul music, like 'Me and Bobby McGhee'. with rhymes as good as glasses softly touched. Charley Pride came in, too. He is an even more revolutionary figure: a *black* Country and Western singer.

Both of them owe a lot to Cash. Kristofferson used to receive unnumbered mentions on his television show, many of them without the younger man's knowledge. That debt is now being repaid in the Kristofferson songs Cash sings. As for Charley Pride, Cash virtually talked him into the unusual position he now occupies. 'I ran into him one night,' Cash says, 'when I was roamin' around Chicago. I told him, if that was what he really wanted – if he really felt it . . . that's all there is to Country music. If people know it comes from the heart, no matter how prejudiced they are, they'll invite you home to a chicken dinner.'

He himself does not sing without effort, as his limbering moosebellows demonstrate in the wings beforehand. The very production of his voice is heroic. Arising from walls and bands of muscle, it passes nowhere near the cells of artifice; it cannot change – that is why they love it – and cannot lie. He performs in an empty stage, with only the guitar-bass beating as metronome, because the voice is deeper than any darkness which encircles it. But, as with all feats of strength, it is a precious part of every performance that the voice might suddenly fail.

By the time he ran out into the spaces of the Toronto stadium, the air was already tropical with menace, struck by flash cameras high and low. His guitar was over his back, as if he had sprinted, to reach them, over rocks. In a moment the rain started. His voice, all around him, said: 'I'll stay out here with you if you'll stay out here with me.' The stadium did not move, and the rain passed through the spotlights like coloured silk and coloured rope; the wind lashed the curtains of the stage overhead to bursting and twisting white flags. His head was flattened by rain, his sleeves weighted by it. His voice continued the same, all around him.

Afterwards he and June raced madly for their car along a tarpaulin path like Flanders mud. As the black door sealed them dry, still there were people with little cameras, break-able in the rain, pleading, 'One more Johnny, one more Johnny – please Johnny . . .'

His head coddled by a towel, suddenly Cash grinned, stretched his arms and said, 'I almost lost 'em back there. For the minute I couldn't remember any song I'd recorded. Then I grabbed 'em again. I wouldn't let Kristofferson see me flop.'

June had wanted to join him out on the promontory of the stage but was restrained because of the electrical danger.

'I been laid out,' Cash remarked. 'Flat on my back in Balti-more.'

'I was knocked out too, Baby,' June told him. 'When the Carter Family played concession stands at State fairs. I been knocked flatter'n a fittercake. And heat. We played 110 degrees in Kentucky. That heat bakes your brain.'

'Oh, Mother!' her daughter Rosie protested.

Cash looked impish.

'Ain't you ever had baked brains to eat, Rosie?'

They sat at dinner now, in dry black against the scarlet ban-quette, holding hands. They looked like a pair of benevolent, resting Borgias.

'Oh but I love that rain,' Cash said solemnly. 'You know: back in that shack. It came on to rain. I stripped down to my shorts and just lay on the rock and let it come down on me like bricks.'

'Better'n flying through the woods,' June remarked.

He gave a shrug and a giggle.

'I used to get high and think I was an Indian flyin' through the woods. Till I woke up beside the lake with no shoes on and my foot in a stumphole there.

'I had a book when I was a boy: it was called *Long Bull's Mistake*. It was about an Indian brave, Long Bull, who stam-peded the buffalo herd, and the whole tribe starved that winter and they hung Long Bull up by the thumbs. I read that book through so many times; I'd think "only 12 more pages till he stampedes the Buffalo".

'The other braves in the tribe, they told him, "If you see the

96

buffalo herd, don't do anything, just come right back here and tell us.'' But he made all the mistakes he could have, crawling out there single-handed, wounding one buffalo, scaring the others off.'

He chuckled as he occasionally does.

'Guess I might once have dreamed I was Long Bull.'

Sting and Police: The Rhetoric of Stardom

It is not Sting but his alter ego Gordon Sumner who opens the door of the smart Hampstead house, one hand restraining a large, black, comfortingly ugly dog. His band, the Police, have taken a break between world-conquering concert tours. For Sting, this evidently also means a rest from being the apotheosis of fashion.

The most adored Rock musician since Paul McCartney turns out to be a smallish 30-year-old with features less heart-stoppingly beautiful than crinkly and good-tempered. His hair, after its punk uprising, has almost learned to lie flat again. His waistcoat, tie and tan-coloured cowboy boots seem oddly conservative. Across the hall, a scrubbed table-top is covered with papers strewn round a portable typewriter. He could easily be Gordon Sumner, correcting the homework of his class of Durham nine-year-olds.

Instead, under his waspish nickname, he personifies a Rock group acclaimed for high talent and, hardly less, for refreshing iconoclasm and good sense. As musicians, the Police now enjoy recognition unsurpassed since the mid-season Beatles. They have, at the same time, managed to be more successfully subversive than Punk Rock at its most furious. The current album, *Ghost in the Machine*, stands comparison, in end-to-end quality, with the Beatles' *Revolver*. One would hardly notice the insurrection woven into its spry Latin rhythms, its elegant guitar-twists and the high, strange, anxious lead voice that, in a recent Top Ten hit, defined politics as 'the rhetoric of failure'.

The voice, with its near-operatic range, is a source of

constant, well-publicised anxiety. 'Taxi-drivers are always turning round and saying "Ere, Sting, I'll tell you what you wanna do for your throat . . .' I'll try anything. Ginseng. Pineapples. At the moment, I practise the Alexander method. Before a concert, I lie flat on the dressing-room floor for 20 minutes and try to get my back exactly level with the ground. If the body relaxes, so will the larynx. I also breathe steam through a facial sauna.'

It is not a scene generally associated with Rock stars' dressing-rooms. What has made the Police different – and ultimately made them rich – is their determined rejection of all Rock's mythical excess and megalomania. They are the antithesis of bands who demand that the backstage quarters be provided with 1804 Napoleon brandy. And if it is 1805 Napoleon brandy, no one will play a note.

'Most of the bands never realised they were being *charged* for things like that,' Sting says. 'American promoters are the worst. They charge you for everything in the dressing-room – even the couch you sit on. A really good tour accountant, like we've got, can protect you from most of it. When we go on tour, we take our own food. We take our own furniture. The couch we sit on is ours.'

The life is one that Gordon Sumner never imagined, growing up in Wallsend-on-Tyne, attending St Cuthbert's Catholic grammar school, helping his dairyman father with the 4 a.m. milk-round, even on Christmas Day. 'I don't make a big thing out of being a Geordie. I've lost my accent, deliberately. We weren't a particularly happy family. It was the sort of family you inevitably go away from. No one in it had ever done anything extraordinary, excepting my Uncle Joe. He was decorated for keeping up the morale of his fellow soldiers on Crete during the invasion, which he did by playing his accordion. I always liked the idea that he got a medal for not killing people.'

At St Cuthbert's, his reports said 'Has ability but doesn't try.' He compensated by becoming Northumberland's junior 100-metre sprint champion. His friends called him Sting because of his buzzing energy and a black and yellow striped football shirt he wore.

He read English for a desultory year at Warwick University, then drifted into teacher-training college. His first job was in Cramlington, a Durham pit village, teaching nine-year-olds everything from football to handwriting. 'I might think I've come a long way to get here, but if I'd been born 20 years earlier, I'd never even have become a teacher. All along, I've had the maximum advantage of social mobility.'

He was still teaching in 1976, married with a baby and playing in a Tyneside Jazz-Rock group called Last Exit, when he fell under Police drummer Stewart Copeland's prescient eye. It was Copeland's ambition to fight the pretensions of mid-Seventies Rock with a three-man group, simple but brilliant, like Cream or the Jimi Hendrix Experience. Stewart Copeland persuaded Sting to pack his wife, baby, bass guitar and dog into a battered Citroen and head for London and rehearsals. The subsequent group chose its name as an ironic reference to Stewart's father, Miles Copeland, formerly Middle East director of the Central Intelligence Agency.

Punk Rock, for its brief, ghastly season, served the Police, in Sting's phrase, as 'a flag of convenience.' Under their energy and aggression lay the finesse of Andy Summers, a lead guitarist whose inventiveness encouraged Sting to write songs like 'Roxanne', a cult success in 1977, then the first Police chart-topper, 'Message In A Bottle'. Stewart Copeland's brother, Miles Junior, became their manager and founded their own record label, Illegal. The world's cleverest tour accountant was now not far behind.

Their other great virtue as performers was a willingness to recognise an audience outside the well-worn Europe-America tour circuit. The Police made a point of giving concerts in Egypt, Venezuela, Hong Kong, even in India under the auspices of the Bombay Time and Talents Club. That, Sting says, was probably the best of all their performances. 'We had every caste watching us, from Parsees to untouchables. I'd said into the microphone, "This is basically dance music". So everyone danced. Old ladies in saris with umbrellas danced on chairs. It was like being back in the Fifties when Rock and Roll first came to England.'

Just such a gesture at the end of their last American tour, when they gave an additional concert in Chile, has brought the Police their first serious dose of bad publicity. How could Sting especially, a paid-up member of Amnesty International, do business with a regime under which, as Amnesty frequently reminds us, so many thousands have been murdered, tortured or made invisible?

'I don't believe we condoned the regime by playing in Chile any more than by playing in England we'd be condoning the regime of Margaret Thatcher. It's different in South Africa, where there's a white elite that craves acceptance and the performers who go there provide that acceptance. I'd never go to South Africa. In Chile, we played to 30,000 kids. I didn't see any political torturers among them.

'Amnesty had given me a message in Spanish to read out – "This next song is for The Disappeared." But, looking at all the machine-guns that were surrounding the place, I decided not to read it. I've been in those countries before. I know how instant the violence can be. What we took to Chile was the message of the music, which is, anyway, pretty rebellious. It's like giving out pamphlets, but cleverer.'

He is married to an actress, Frances Tomelty, whom he met in Newcastle while still a humble backing bass-player. He has himself begun to act, notably in the film version of Dennis Potter's banned play *Brimstone and Treacle*, for which he also composed the theme music. It excited him to rehearse with a full orchestra at EMI Records' Abbey Road studios, on the very spot where the Beatles made their albums. The Beatles, Sting says simply, were 'gods'.

His new house in Hampstead once belonged to a dancer with the Ballet Russe. E. V Knox, the essayist, used to live next door. 'And Kathleen Ferrier across the road . . . this is real blue plaque country,' he says, with minimal apology. 'I don't feel I belong here any more than I used to belong in Wallsend. On the bedroom ceiling, there's the design of a Cross, which I like. Probably my Catholic upbringing coming out.'

On tour, he plays the oboe and reads the works of Jung. As a result, he is apt to define Rock as 'a tonal range which evokes a collective response.' But the performer in him knows he simply shuts his eyes and lets it happen. 'My favourite moments onstage are of silence, when the Police stop playing. There's just this great blank for the audience to fill in. I often find myself looking out at them and wondering how I got here. I still don't think I really belong. Sometimes it's a depressing feeling, but often it's exhilarating.'

Suzi Quatro: The Girl in the Gang

A separate dressing-room had been provided upstairs, but
Suzi Quatro preferred to use the same one as her band. It was
large, clean, grey and brightly-lit; and there were some hours
to wait. The band settled to cards around an upturned guitar-
case, with a carrier-bag of pennies and halfpence. Suzi
inserted two grips in her hair and opened a small makeup
bag. Above and all around them hummed the unique vitality
of the BBC Television Centre.

'What's that you're playing?' she asked the band.

'Brag.'

'Stupid game,' Suzi observed without rancour.

She returned to her face in the mirror. With the grips
pinning her hair back, it is the face of a large-eyed little girl or
boy. On one cheek there is a violet mark like a bump which
children sustain. She could be a little girl using her mother's
mascara, but for the expression in her eyes. 'I despise doing
this,' she murmured,'I really do.'

To discover her sharing a dressing-room with her band is
no less than one might expect. Of all female rock singers, she
appears the most emancipated: a small girl leading an all-
man group in which she herself plays bass guitar. The image
is of a tomboy, lank-haired, tight-bottomed and (twice) tattooed; a rocker, a brooder, a loner, a knife-carrier; a hell-cat,
a wild cat, a storm child, refugee from the frightened city of
Detroit.

On meeting her it is surprising how the image achieves
reality in a quite inoffensive form. Her life is absorbed into
the band's; she wears its monochromatic jeans and jerseys,

103

and seems unscandalised by its periodic flatulence. On their recent tour through Japan and Australia she spent most of her free time in the band's poker school. She has not worn a dress for years, and remembers, with amused disgust, the worst dress she ever had to wear. 'It was a little silvery mini.'

'Was that the one you puked over, Suse?' asked one of the band.

'No, that was a blue velvet formal.'

The card-game dissolved as the band started to make itself ready. The coins were scooped into their carrier-bag. White jerkins and trousers were unfolded, somewhat in need of laundering; small vests dangled like black string in their fingers. Len Tuckey the guitarist crossed the room in his shirt-tails. 'Where's me trousers gone? These must be Alistair's. They got rust on'em.'

At this point Suzi withdrew to the Ladies' to change.

Studio 8, where the weekly recording of *Top of the Pops* takes place, presents an animated and colourful appearance. All the momentary pop-toppers are there, together with those who can expect to top the pops in a moment or two. Over there stand the Glitter Band with their spangled leotards and honest Co-op assistant faces. There is Steve Harley in a furry windcheater, Alvin Stardust in black gloves, Freddy Mercury in white satin drawers: legends of the week mingling in democratic propinquity with stout-thighed dancers from Pan's People, elderly uniformed porters and many other less purposeful individuals. The cameras rush back and forth on their tracks, dramatically shifting the crowd, with operators suspended high in the air, wearing suits and pullovers and ties.

After several rehearsals, the 'live' audience is permitted to enter. It consists largely of very young girls dressed, in the prevailing fashion, like little old ladies, who are shooed around the studio, with the filming of each act, from one podium to the next. The disc jockey presenting *Top of the Pops* this week is Tony Blackburn. His hair is combed into a fringe and his features are contorted into a smile. He moves with the simian litheness of a man who knows his job and does it

104

supremely well. From camera-angles everywhere one can hear intimations of Tony Blackburn saying, 'Er . . .'

Suzi Quatro's turn comes to mime her newest record. She wears a brown leather blazer piped with white, and cream leather trousers: the faintly cricketing effect is obscured by a great white bass guitar with four silver tuning pegs. The song, like so many songs, is by the team of Mike Chapman and Nick Chinn. She bothers to mime: not everybody does on *Top of the Pops*. At her feet the little old ladies clustered with folded arms, staring upward listlessly.

A *Top of the Pops* executive jumps up on the stage in front of the Suzi Quatro band. His hair is grey and his expression, rather displeased.

'Look!' he shouts at the audience. 'All of you wrote in and asked for tickets, so can you look as if you're enjoying it, or I'll make sure that nobody who wrote in will *ever* get tickets again. Just remember you're not here to get *autographs*. You're here to enjoy a *show*!'

In private she is even smaller than she looks on stage – her feet, in particular, with their stiff little raised heels, endlessly shifting and drumming. She is 24, and says that her body ceased developing when she was 12; by smiling a quick, cute smile – which she demonstrates – she can still get into cinemas for half-price. She is full of such demonstrations, her leather-piped arms flying back now like a Go-go dancer to satirise her former way of life. The staccato speech expected from a rocker is frequently overlaid by the pleasant self-deprecation of a nice provincial American girl.

'I'm not a great singer – but I do know how to put a song over. I'm a pretty good bass-player. A single – that's just a three-minute burst of energy. The lyric's important to me: I can really get into it if I feel the audience getting into it. Whatever happens, I've got to have this' – she clapped her hands decorously together. 'I'm just a ham. But I'm not a nauseating ham.'

Suzi Quatro is her real name. She is one of the four daughters of a General Motors executive, himself a semi-

105

professional musician. Her father is Italian and her mother Hungarian; her mother, in addition, looked after several pairs of foster children. In this gregarious household Suzi grew up to be extrovert but solitary, a worry to her mother, a puzzle to her schoolteachers, pining to see her father during his rare sojourns at home. Only in the separation of the past three years has she discovered a deep attachment to her mother. Her face, if she speaks of her mother, relaxes from its pistol-point of worldly cynicism. 'When you kiss her cheek, it's like kissing cotton.'

From the age of 14 she played in a band with her three sisters called Suzi Soul and the Pleasure Seekers. They remained together for seven years on the same midnight dreary cabaret circuit in short dresses and heavy wigs, not listened to but ogled. Her tattoos, on wrist and shoulder, express her frustration in the captivity of this epoch, which only ended when Mickie Most saw her singing with the Pleasure Seekers in Detroit.

Mickie Most has done well since he appeared on Shanklin Pier as one half of the Most Brothers, 'England's Answer to the Everly Brothers'. From producing the Animals and Hermans' Hermits he has risen to his own label Rak Records, with prodigious success both in recording and music publishing.

Most, a curly-haired, heavy-shouldered, open-shirted man with an astonishing mental appetite for grosses and percentages, is devoutly aware of the alchemy which has allowed him to ride for a decade perfectly alongside the taste of the mass record-buying public. 'When I first went to New York in the early Sixties, I was taken to this restaurant, and Paul Anka walked in. All the waiters were running round after him. I couldn't figure it out. Paul Anka – he hadn't had a hit in six years. Then I realised. He'd been a millionaire at 16; he wrote 'Diana'. He was always the boy millionaire. That was what had stuck in all those waiters' minds.'

Most, like every other producer, knew that there was a vacuum for a girl rock singer which had not been filled since the death of Janis Joplin. He admits, however, that, once he had brought Suzi Quatro to London, he was uncertain of the best way to present her. Pop music in 1972 was embarking on its sequinned phase. Moreover, there were some harsh edges to be rubbed off his new acquisition. He maintained her for a year in an hotel while she mellowed and practised and wrote songs. The way in which she was finally launched – the leathers, the shaking hair and bass – were merely, suggests Most, the realisation of her true personality.

Towards Suzi Quatro now he is understandably proprietorial. 'People in this business are inclined to daydream. What they're usually thinking is, "When I make it, it's going to be great." But it isn't. It's just the same as before. I make things difficult for them. That way, when they do make it, they really appreciate it. I give them lectures. They've got to respect you and they've got to be afraid of you. On their second tour, after "Can the Can", some hotel room up in Blackpool got damaged. It was nothing to do with her – some other people were involved. I sent 'em a telegram saying "Report to this office at two o'clock tomorrow. And if it's five past, don't bother." '

At a mews studio just off Baker Street, a new Suzi Quatro album is being recorded. Several expensive cars stand all day outside the studio's yellow shopfront: a large, thin Mercedes, a smaller thin Mercedes, a fierce silver Porsche and, once, the blue Rolls Royce of Mickie Most. The lady in the adjoining cottage with the doorscraper lets herself out or in, unconscious of these portentous arrivals.

The album is produced by Mike Chapman, co-writer of all the hits for Suzi Quatro, as well as for male groups like the Sweet, and Mud: a gigantic yearly accumulation of chart-success which Mike Chapman with his partner Nicky Chinn dashes off with the casualness of so many greetings-cards. This golden touch is somehow evident in Chapman's person as he reigns over the studio-controls: gold in his spectacles and cigarette-holder, in his crewcut shining under the lights, and in the down on his long, bare arms. He rises from his chair and dances. Glimpses of his goldness rotate in the control-room's perspex wall.

At the moment the band is simply 'laying down' an instrumental base, to be ornamented later by overdubbing and afterthoughts. Suzi sits outside in the studio, wearing bulky headphones, her fingers pecking slowly at the buff-coloured bass, her other fingers over its keyboard, stretching and contracting. Her voice speaks, disembodied, to Chapman at the control-desk. On a nearby table lies a mass of roses wrapped in pink satin, presented to her that day by a German fan magazine. She is not wearing leather. Her jeans are curiously straight and unwrinkled like clothes newly-bought for a toddler.

'Make some coffee will you Suse?' Len Tuckey says.

She does so.

The band is a good one. After the comparative failure of a solo debut-record she went out, with Mickie Most's approval, and auditioned for it herself, at a rehearsal-room in King's Cross where the proprietor wore women's clothing. For a keyboard-player she found Alistair McKenzie, a nervous half-Scottish Irishman with eyebrows whitened by cigarette-burns. For a drummer she found Dave Neal, who is good-natured and quiet even when drunk – he just goes round shaking everybody's hand.

Out of the band's democracy, a private relationship has evolved between her and the lead guitarist Len Tuckey. Two years her junior, but many sizes bigger, Tuckey is an ex-Stock Exchange clerk with a roughness of demeanour that is, at least partly, assumed. In the early days of their association she bit him, quite hard, on one fat arm before they were able to achieve a better understanding. Recently, his younger brother Bill has left a job as checker in a plastics factory to act as tour-manager for the band. Suzi goes to the Tuckey parents at Romford for Sunday lunch. She seems content to shelter in Len's relentless normality. He will grasp her by the scruff of the neck or else push her face away with a large, not unaffectionate hand.

Mike Chapman, this afternoon, was feeling annoyed. It happened to be Wednesday, the day on which the music trade papers are published. The *New Musical Express* carried a review of the new-available third Suzi Quatro album. Chapman, together with a few others, has taught himself to understand the unique prose employed by the *New Musical Express*, and he perceived the review to be, not only critical but abusive towards himself. The article was signed by someone called Charles Shaar Murray.

'I know what I'll do!' Chapman exclaimed. 'I'll send him a wreath.'

He opened the portmanteau on his knee and began to search through it.

'What you want to do,' Len Tuckey said, 'is get a big shoebox and fill it up with pigs' brains and chickens' heads. . . .'

They continued rehearsing into the early evening. They played through the rhythm track many times, and every time Chapman's ear detected something which displeased him. He joined the four of them out in the studio, conducting them with a long gold arm; they tried playing after the style of the Staple Singers, and of the Average White Band; they expanded Alistair's lavicord part; they raised some switches which had formerly been depressed. They returned and stood along the sofa, their elbows along the rim of the desk, as the latest attempt was played back.

'That's 'orrible,' Len Tuckey said.

Suddenly Chapman stiffened in his chair.

'Why don't we do it straight? Just rock it.'

As they watched, his legs and shoulderblades began to move in different time, his gold crewcut to turn back and forth, circling the cigarette-holder before his face. It was as if, deep within him in whispered major chords, an oracle was speaking.

'You've sold me on it,' Len Tuckey said.

They did not, as it turned out, put this new idea into practice. While they were on the telephone, trying to hire a Hammond organ, Tuckey ran around the control-desk and fastened his hands around Mike Chapman's neck. The studio assistant, who had hitherto said little, jumped up, grabbed the producer's feet and attempted to collapse him like an accordion. Chapman escaped, vanished through the Emergency Exit and returned holding in one hand a heavy black fire-extinguisher with a separate nozzle which in his other hand he pointed at Tuckey. 'Woof', went the fire-extinguisher, imparting a chilly haze of carbon dioxide. Tuckey ran through the massive two-deck door into the outer studio and, for a weapon, seized the conical maraca from a drum-kit. 'Woof', went the fire-extinguisher, 'Woof, woof', as Tuckey and Chapman wrestled for it on the carpet. Chapman's sleeve became white. The side of Tuckey's leg became white. The maraca rolled, crushed, into a corner.

Outside, a thin mist covered the cars along the mews. The lady next door had set out her milk bottles. Inside the studio, 12 hours after they had begun, they were playing over the tracks which they had recorded. Chapman and Alistair, Dave Neal and the assistant leapt to and fro behind the control-desk, waving their arms loosely in the air. Suzi Quatro, in her stockinged feet, bounced up and down on the couch.

Mike Chapman subsided, panting, into his chair.

'We make twice as many hits as anyone else,' he said. 'And we seem to have twice as much fun.'

Some days later, the music journalist Charles Shaar Murray was surprised to find in his morning's post, among the free records and invitations to free parties, a parcel containing a portion of pig's brain. Surprised and, so it appeared, a little shaken, for in the next issue of the *New Musical Express*, no reference was made to the gift.

At the studio near Baker Street, the recording was finished. Mike Chapman and his assistant – now restored to taciturnity – were deeply engrossed in the final alchemies of 'mixing'. Dave Neal the drummer had gone to Battersea to look at a Ford Consul, taking Alistair with him. Len and Bill Tuckey were also absent, fetching a new car battery. Suzi Quatro was still there, sitting by herself.

She sat on the couch below the control-desk with the trampled *New Musical Express*, the dented maraca, the carpet which bore perhaps the most eloquent traces of their week's recording.

110

'I can't ever be still – look at me now. At Catholic school I was thrown out of First Grade because the sister said I drove her mad. Sister Inez, her name was. When I was little my mother would hear me floor walking overhead. The only thing that relaxes me is wine. *Côtes du Rhone, Blanc de Blancs* – I've got cases of it standing round. I wake a lot in the night. I can't bear to be in darkness. I always have to have a light in the room.'

She lives in a flat in Crouch End. She does not know its telephone number. 'I'm not *attached*,' she said, with a touch of contempt, 'to anything.'

Her grocer knows who she is, and converses with her in whispers to preserve her incognito.

'He said to me— " 'Ere, if you aren't doing anything Saturday night, why don't you come down our Vicarage for a game of snooker?" '

Her face melted into its charming, fugitive smile.

' " 'Ere", he said, "We don't 'arf have a good time." '

Bryan Ferry: Mask behind a Mask

Bryan Ferry's jeans are as outmoded in style as high fashion can contrive. He wears a blue shirt and black official tie, framed by a grey sweater such as an aunt might choose. The whole effect, reminiscent of nothing so much as an off-duty policeman, is instantly identifiable as superstar regalia, designed both to attract notice and discourage it. His hair is his faithful ally, collapsing into an appropriate shape with each distracted flourish of his hand. His eyes are bright blue and narrowly set. At times they cloud with preoccupation, like a cat watching pigeons above one's head.

Rock music idols nowadays do not fade: they hibernate periodically, living off the fat of their million-sellers. Bryan Ferry is at the point of emerging from just such a retreat. Last week he was completing a new record album, his fourth as a solo performer. In February he begins what is inaccurately known as a 'world tour'. Not with his former band Roxy Music, it is emphasised, but with notable free enterprise musicians like the guitarist Chris Spedding. So you see: he has substance as well as style. This is the current theme insisted upon by Ferry's promoters.

In private, he is deferential, soft-mannered, modest to the point of inaudibility. His origins are unpretentious. A miner's son, the second of three children, he grew up in Gainsborough Avenue, Washington, Co. Durham. At grammar school he was erratic but good at sport; at basketball and high hurdles. He sang with his first group, the Banshees, thanks to a friend he had met at a cycling club. At school, after playing Malvolio in *Twelfth Night*, he was encouraged to take up acting. His father urged him towards the police force, because of the free house.

He always knew that he would go far in music. At Durham University, studying fine art, he sacrificed the chance to turn professional with a band called Gas Board because he still felt unready. It was with Roxy Music, the band he founded after coming to London, that he could carry out his musical ideas. He wanted to combine the fastidiousness of art with the sweat and sex of Rock and Roll music. He explains this in a set speech, then apologises for having delivered it. His eyes are fixed in a stare now, as if the pigeons are roosting on one's head.

His role in cafe society – what survives of it – is irksome to him. Well, is it? Yes and no. The hostility of many critics towards his wheezing voice, and profligate borrowing of decent old songs, should by rights have made him into a recluse. Actually, he says, he rather enjoys going out. He goes to restaurants for company rather than food. His alliance with Jerry Hall, a famous model, is evidently piquant to him. 'There goes Jerry!' he suddenly exclaimed. It was only her eyes, hugely magnified, along the side of a Piccadilly-bound bus.

In the recording studio, he has complete control of his own work. For each album, he says, is like a collection of short stories, to be anthologised in the hit parade. To his credit, he immediately repents of this comparison. 'I like the rhythms of Rock. I like going crazy.'

Rod Stewart: The Familiar Face

Through the colonnades they come, along freezing passage-
ways. Girls look like ventriloquist-dolls, in black plush and
rouge, puffing as dolls do on big cigarettes: boys and girls
alike wear coats, mufflers with which they lassoo each other,
waistcoats, sashes, bow-ties, everything in Hunting Stewart
tartan, though this is Kilburn, North London. Far away the
balconies fill up, and far away the stalls, beneath the
strangely-lit heavens of the old State cinema.

'It's cold out there, Rod.'

Rod Stewart continues to kick a football against the wall of
his dressing-room.

'Rod – can we do the gig?'

'Hang on,' Stewart says in the voice that is very nearly as
hoarse as his singing. 'I've only got one shoe. Anybody seen a
silver shoe?'

'Then can you put on one bronze?'

The other Faces, Woody, Kenny and Mac, hobble on their
high shoes to the door through which, with the draught, comes
the seething of many hearts – but still Rod lingers. He turns
the football on his toe. He holds it against his instep, trickling
it a short way up his turquoise sateen leg.

To be at one with an audience is the affectation of most
performers of Rock music. But the music is essentially contemptuous and hostile, walled-in by its own voltage: that
which its so-called legends believe to be intimacy is more
often self-indulgence and narcissism.

The stage appearance of Rod Stewart with the Faces
therefore has few precedents. They receive, before touching

114

a note, an ovation. Noise is cheap; what distinguishes this is lack of noise, as if each atom in the tumult strives to win his attention by not screaming. It is a noise of embraces; of arms extended, scarves outstretched, a thousand thumbs raised up in some secret signal to him across the roaring darkness.

'Look, I'm sorry we're late,' he says. 'We're going to play our asses off to make up for it.'

This was the first substantial British tour by the Faces since, with 'Maggie May', 'You Wear It Well' and the rest, they joined the rulers of the Rock sub-continent; and also since they acquired a bass-guitarist named Tetsu from Japan. They did not find that their supporters had grown bashful in the meantime.

'You're t'greatest guitarist in t'world, Woody,' screamed a boy in Leeds. 'I voted for you in t'*Sounds* poll.'

'Hey, and where's that Oriental chap?'

'Rod, quick! Have you got anything small on you? A ring – anything small? Kenny! Anything small I can have? Yer hat! Can I have yer hat?'

'Rod!' The girls try to follow him through an hotel's revolving-doors. They are revolved by the night-porter out into the street again, wailing, 'Rod!'

He presents anything but a narcissistic figure. The turquoise leotard he wore last night in Liverpool and will wear tomorrow in Manchester. The stringy biceps, concave torso, the buttocks small as a pigeon's forehead; all are eloquent rather of some long-distance runner rather than the fantasy of today's 14-year-olds. His hair, wound at the neck by his scarf, is a crumpled, greyish sheaf, a high and huge cockade which he scratches, as he sings, with his fingers. He looks as Bob Cratchitt might after playing strip-poker in a heatwave.

And the voice! From the over-sized larynx in his narrow chest the voice rises, already on its knees: there are broken bottles in it, cigarettes and many last gasps, though his songs are of blue skies, hot days, innocent things. Sometimes in the changing lights he will appear next to the guitarist Ronnie Wood, both of them jumping up and down like little girls with a skipping-rope; or he will lie prostrate, kick his football, even wander off the stage altogether.

Then he holds out his arms.

'Come on . . . public house.'

The music stops. The quarry of his voice stops. High and low, with scarves held taut, the audience sings; word-perfect and in tune, swaying like some quiet machinery through the night.

The result of Stewart's individual stardom has paradoxically been to draw him even closer to the four other members of the band. It was the Faces who made him: he scuffed around for years, before their formation, employing his voice neither with care nor attention. They have it all in common – the half-sleeps; the bad dressing-rooms from which, each night, they struggle to the refuge of some hard-hearted British Transport hotel; and the clowning, raucous, incessant, sometimes brutish, by which these things can be made bearable.

They are in Leeds now, playing below the girders of an old tram depot to an audience teeming in light like red ants. On each side of the stage there is a curious dead area in which elongated figures composed of girls sitting on boys' shoulders stagger about, calling 'Rod!' Others attempt to scale the amplifier equipment, crying as piteously as if they are being lowered in doomed lifeboats.

The obvious analogy is with the football crowd. He trained once as a professional footballer; one may debate, even now, whether music has a greater power than football to ignite the spindly dynamo of his limbs. He worships famous footballers as the little girls worship him. He enfolds in his bare arms, his scarf, his hair, a famous footballer's sober suiting and correctly-tied tie.

'We're doing what football ought to do – but it doesn't any more. It's not the same. You'll see the players pushing the fans away. And cricketers do it as well; they push the fans away. We never push 'em away: we always say "How you feeling?" '

'I can't stand being late. If I'm 10 minutes late, I start getting upset. But none of that *discipline*. Not like some of these bands

– like Deep Purple. You go into their dressing-room before a show and there's dead silence. They're all sitting round having a glass of milk and reading the *Evening News*.'

In the struggle of the Faces' dressing-room stands a girl who appears neither to be coming nor going. Her name is Sandy; she is their most devoted admirer and follows them everywhere; even when they go to Germany Sandy is somehow awaiting them with her Napoleonic head and her carrier-bag, speechless in their presence, curt in her dealings with anybody outside her particular hallucination.

'I call you Persephone,' she tells little Ian McLagen, the pianist and organ-player.

'I'm still none the wiser.' He buries his face in a towel.

John Barnes is already moving them on. The proprietor of a car-hire company it is Barnes, somehow, who has become the Faces' most confidential aide, bodyguard and gentleman's gentleman. He waits in the wings during each performance to hand a drink to Stewart or bounce a football in his direction. A little of the drink spills: John Barnes kneels in his lounge suit to wipe it clean. One of his eyes wears a patch, for he had been unexpectedly beaten up after the Birmingham concert.

Desperately Sandy twines her arms around Stewart's leopard-skin coat. 'I'm sorry, Rod.' She is apologising for the helplessness of her fixation.

'That's all right. I didn't want to say that to you, you know. He told me to do it.'

She regards with hatred the efficient John Barnes now carrying from the dressing-room the bottle of port, the bottle of brandy and the bottle of Pimms No. 1.

Stewart balances the football on his yellow boot; he flicks it upon one leopard-skin knee. 'How was the gig?' he inquires kindly.

'It was all right. Only, people kept pushing me around.'

The period between concerts is composed of different, inhospitable twilights. Dinner at dawn; breakfast for lunch; the day beginning in an hotel foyer at tea-time. Girls are still revolving hopelessly in the doors crying, 'Rod! Rod!'

They had been, as they invariably go, to a late-night club:

117

ultra-violet light and sweltering scampi. There they had received evidence that the Faces are approved of as much by males as by females. 'Did you hear what the guy said?' Ian McLagen marvelled. 'He says to his girl, "Go on, show 'em yer bristols – she's got a fantastic pair o' bristols – go on, show 'em." I said to him "Do you want a drink?" He says "Aye, I'll have a Broken Leg." '

'I'm bored,' remarked Kenny Jones the drummer, who is quiet and home-loving, from the corner of the limousine. 'Can we be there, please?'

'Who was that little piece of delight by the lift last night then?' McLagen said. 'I thought she must have had a room in the hotel. I thought "Hello, Stewart's being crafty!" '

Stewart turned round from the car's front seat, an umpire's white hat perched on his cockade in an attempt to hide the long, anteater face.

'Shirley, is that her? No, I just went to bed.

'– up here's my time-off,' he murmured.

The Sunday newspapers carried an account of the latest hotel to suffer depredations from a sojourn by the Who. Not that most of today's hotels do not invite such activity on the part of their guests.

'We've done it as well,' Stewart said. 'Gone down to Reception and said, "Er, we've had this mistake, how much is it going to cost us?" It's terrible really, like people breaking up football trains.' A grin slowly appeared on his face. 'It's great, though. Smashing up the bed . . . the dressing-table.'

The voice was implanted mysteriously through a Cockney mother and a Glasgow Scot. He still, on a reflex, lapses into Glaswegian; that spluttering dialect which seems to take the listener by the coat-front. 'We had a piano at home that nobody played. I used to go to sleep underneath it, watching 'em having their wild parties, getting me Uncle John to pick up sixpence to see if he'd got any underpants underneath his kilt. I had my first bunk-up underneath that piano,' he added thoughtfully. 'This girl and me were going on the march to Aldermaston, banning The Bomb, and I whopped one up her underneath the piano.'

118

His family's gift was equilibrium. It sustained him in the years of his obscurity – the years of 'Rod the Mod', sleeping and singing rough in Blues bands – it protects him now against the grosser surfeits of his fame. Both vagrancy and stardom appear to have been his own decisions. 'People tried to help me, to record me, but I wouldn't turn up for the session or something.' He reflected, then said, 'It's easy living with failure. It's not so easy to live with success.'

Immediately after the concert that night he had himself driven 250 miles in his limousine, gushing purposefully through the night to loiter in London a few hours. The remaining Faces sat about the hotel lounge. Among them sat several little girls of the city, with long overcoats and long, clean hair, whispering incredulously over this piece of impossible luck.

'He's Ian McLagen. Hm, I always did fancy him – remember in the Fourth Year?'

'Ian McLagen. It's funny; I never used to like him.'

'I'll tell him.'

'Ye can.'

'He's Tetsu'. The Japanese bass-guitarist is peacefully sipping whisky and smiling. 'Eh, I read in an interview that Tetsu can only say two things, "whisky-and-soda" and . . . a rude word.'

'He took my bangle and wore it on his head.'

'It could have been mine.'

Ronnie Wood, the most pleasant-natured of guitarists, shows the little girls snapshots of his new car.

'Do you like Gary Glitter?' he asked them.

'Ugh! Him and his big, fat stomach!'

'Paul Raven,' said Woody, employing the pearly phenomenon's previous pseudonym. 'I once shared a flat with him. He used to say to all the girls "Have you ever seen a one-eared elephant?" ' Woody jumped up to demonstrate what Gary Glitter would do if the girls had not ever seen a one-eared elephant. He pulled the lining out of his trousers-pocket and made as if to unfasten his fly.

'– our Pamela will be sitting up.'

119

'Let her. Ee, I've had a talk with him and I've had a kiss off him . . .'

'This mustn't be real, must it? Sitting up late and talking to the Faces!'

Unremarked by the little girls, and properly sardonic because of it, sits a blond, tall, close-bearded man. It was John Baldry who gave Stewart a start, in his band the Steam Packet: Baldry is now opening act on the Faces tour. He still leads an excellent band. Cruel is the fate of an excellent band preceding a charismatic one; to play in the void of anticipation, to be always packing up just as the darkness comes to life.

Baldry's testy humour has inured him to his fate – almost. 'Ah, you're the bitches who were sitting in front, are you?'

'Bitches! Er, we're not bitches!'

The efficient John Barnes hurried past. 'Where's the driver of your coach?' he asked. 'It's been stripped.'

Baldry flushed dark red. 'No! My guitars!' He drank his vodka in agony.

Nearby sat his manager, and Stewart's, Billy Gaff; a dainty man who, even at stable moments, communicates an air of imminent catastrophe. Glumly he pressed the side of his watch. On its plain black face a row of scarlet figures shone. He pressed the other side. Half a row of scarlet figures were illuminated.

Baldry returned from the scene of the theft, smiling with desperation. 'I can't even do a Folk gig now,' he said.

'Haven't you got any more guitars?'

'One. At home.'

'– they got John's guitars and suede suits, and they got Sammy's dobro . . .'

'– No, man, it must have been to sell them. No musician, however broke he is, will ever steal a guitar.'

A star can be immune. Invisible. Carried by an immense length of shadowy motor, in whose heated depths cigar-lighters mysteriously become erect, the star goes first to his mansion, Cranbourne Court, Ascot, then forth again to begin the day after midnight. 'I read somewhere,' he said, 'that

120

when a man is tired of London he's tired of life.'

He goes to Tramp, a club just like any club except that stars go there. The darkness is worth thousands of pounds a yard. He watches from this darkness with amusement as the long-bodied, tight-bellied, expensively-tousled girls combat ferociously among themselves for his attention.

'Why can't a woman be more like a man? You know, there's a lot of truth in that saying. With a man you can have lots of mates. Look at 'em!' he pointed derisively into the shadows. 'I gave *her* that red lion T shirt and *she* hasn't twigged it yet. *She's* got the needle 'cos I was talking to that spade bird so she's dancing with her hairdresser – and they're both wearing scarves, trying to look like me. At the Kilburn concert I had four of 'em. I put all their seats together so they could kick the shit out of each other.

'My Dad's a real straight Scot. He doesn't believe the things he reads about me. After that thing in *The Sun*, about me taking dirty pictures with me Polaroid, I couldn't face up to him for five days. He would have hit me.'

The audience in Liverpool was better than ever before. A wild plantation of heads, scarves, entreating arms, barely held in check by the curving front row, whose white blouses and little bow-ties gave the effect of a Viennese choir, ferociously buckling. He danced; his lips against the wound scarf as if playing trains. He threw the long microphone up into the lights.

At another perimeter, one of the stealthy efficient and inoffensive road-managers was challenged by a group of 'stewards'. The recruitment of these officials is arbitrary and their qualification sometimes dubious. They knocked the road-manager down, trampled on the ribs beneath his T shirt and kicked his face; he was dragged clear with his jaw fractured in three places, leaving a pool of blood under the illuminations, silver changing to mauve.

The concert-promoter asked to see the manager of the theatre. Beside him, earnestly joining in the debate, stood a species of 'steward'. Middle-aged, he wore a flat cap, a red jerkin embroidered with the name 'Rocky.'

121

A woman assistant to the manager said, 'Look, don't tell me what you want!'

'I want to see Mr—. The stewards in this theatre are responsible for what's happened, and I want to press charges.'

The audience, beyond, were singing. Her face crumpled into hate. 'Yes, we all know whose fault that is don't we? Just clear off will you! Just clear off!'

In the wings the note of the bass-amplifier enters one's own chest and beats, two-and-four, in one's heart. It is like eaves-dropping on an earthquake. At the end of the front row, the very tip of the raging continent, sat a girl. She wore a grey sweater. Her body inclined forward, as only new bodies can, with arms mixed up in her long hair, she clapped her hands.

Stewart himself, bouncing suddenly offstage, appeared in the wings and peeped out.

'I've always wanted to get Rock and Roll concerts . . . like public houses,' he said, panting. 'What we've got tonight we must never lose.'

Part Two
Blues and Soul

Soul on Fire

Stevie Wonder crosses the hotel lobby, resting on the elbows of two other people. That he is blind, has been blind from birth, is nonetheless difficult to comprehend; for Stevie smiles constantly, his face turns as if into fresh breezes, his glasses mirroring two worlds not dark but sunlit. He is long, thin, gentle and tormentedly restless. He wears a fur coat, yellow shoes, a denim jacket with the sleeves turned modishly back. He smiles, though he is ill, as his brother Milton leads him through the hotel, out to a waiting limousine.

'Milton,' he said. 'Could we stop the car and get some orange juice or something? Only if it's no problem.'

'We're almost into the Tunnel,' Milton told him.

'Okay.'

A hotel is all the home he needs. After a concert he will ask one of his musicians to bring an instrument from the band to his room, and play on it until morning. In his arms he carries a large recording-machine; his fingers, normally so languid, so obedient, dance over its buttons to release his voice, blissful in a dozen different ways. He does not eat, only sucks lemons. His music is his house. His voice dwells there, up on the top-most floors.

'This one's called "Shine in the Night".' His fingers pressed for it rapturously. 'All the people rise up to put an end to the bad things in the world, and they shine in the night. The words of this one go "I took a worthless trip down life's avenue . . . the tour was such a bore. Take a chance on your mind, you'll be surprised what you find!" ' The voice ripples higher, his face turning back and forth. 'I love Latin music! I got to get some Spanish words for that one!'

On the radio it was announced that Aretha Franklin had been admitted to hospital for psychiatric treatment. Milton turned and said, around the high back of the driver's seat, 'Hey Steve, you know that Aretha's "Respect" sold four million copies?'

'Why they talking about her like that?'

'Huh?' Milton said.

'Why they talking about Aretha like she was something in the past?'

He fell asleep then, his recording-machine on the car-seat beside him. Somehow the sun filtered into the car to form a pool on his face, his quiet lips. All around lay the harbour of Philadelphia, with bright red engines racing to a fire that built its grey forest up into the sky.

Soul is music needing no eyes. There was another blind boy once named Lemon Jefferson, who wandered out of Texas to Beale Street in Memphis, through the crowds. Fat and dirty, he, too, had a voice that could discompose the spirit. His fortune proved less, however, than the boy asleep in the Cadillac. His music grew famous, crying from its ragged room to continuous generations; for which he was rewarded by a white man with a bottle of whisky. He wandered on, to Chicago where eventually he froze to death.

Music is murdered only by definitions. But the birth of Soul belongs to so distinct an epoch that its silhouette gleams, among lesser incarnations, as unmistakable as a grin. It began perhaps a decade ago. Its beginning was the point at which, some might say, the world lost an innocence or, others might assert, we were finally delivered from a blindness of our own. The history of Soul is of one people's determination that they were not, as they had previously been taught, inferior. Blues was the solitary pain of being a Negro. Soul music is exaltation of the state of being black.

'It's a gift from God,' Stevie Wonder said. His face swayed back and forth. 'You only got to express it and enjoy it.'

'I just unzip myself,' said Roberta Flack, 'and let you see.'

For B. B. King, sober patriarch of the concert Blues, a gift of

126

Soul resides even in Django Reinhardt's Parisian guitar. His large brown fingers press the region of his heart in a cloud-coloured silk dressing-gown. Some Blues have travelled far since Blind Lemon Jefferson.

'I've cried,' Roberta Flack said. 'Sometimes in the middle of a song I've really really cried.'

So has B. B. King. 'It's kinda like the note that breaks the glass.'

Wilson Pickett – 'The Wicked Pickett' – guffawed. 'We keep 'em dancin'. We stop 'em thinkin' too much.'

Down in the Chitterling Circuit, the bass-guitarist said: 'We play off the heat the people give.'

Gladys Knight said: 'We celebrate being together.'

Gladys and the Pips have been together for 20 years. Soul is, to many, a belated reward. They are playing an early show at the Apollo Theatre in Harlem. As Gladys sings, she is descanted from the side by the stage-manager, a bass man who reveals his sentimental heart with a remarkably pink tongue. Soul is a theatre, half-empty, sounding as if it is full. She turns into the applause. A big smile joins the curtains of her hair.

'We'd just like to say.'

'— *Rightonbaby!*'

At the Manhattan Centre, a high and horrible New York ballroom, the Spinners, the Ojays, Harold Melvin and the Blues Notes, tread the stage in ceaseless rotation flipping their coat-tails, drawing shapes with their arms. Below, the audience has been on its feet several hours and will be for several more. There are girls with aviator caps fattening their cheeks, with white berets beside their faces, bare shoulders scarcely bound in white; but Soul is also a quality of attention. Many young men, wearing broad hats of grey or green velvet, remain speculatively alone, leaning upon umbrellas. The compere bends down to them and entreats the return of a microphone that has been misappropriated. Another act glides up and back in a sentimental song. A girl's leopardskin arms cradle a boy. Two heads move together in dim clouds, her eyes closing against his shoulder. Not being black is a chilly feeling tonight.

Soul is very rich, where Blues wore rags, and has a proper opinion of itself. The release which it provides is not of anger but that still fiercer thing, self-esteem. In Tina Turner's body, in the enthronement of Isaac Hayes, there is, above all, a gorgeous conceit, able to reach and touch the poorest, palest black: James Brown became their king less for his music's hypnotism than for the strength of his autocracy. Few human beings can now match, in style and hauteur, the beautiful or the affluent Negro. It is fitting over-reaction from the other times, of 'race music' despised even as it was exploited, when Robert Johnson was so humble that he recorded with his face turned to the wall.

Soul is also music reclaimed by its rightful owners. Imprisoned in the Chitterling Circuit, the concert-halls of the ghettoes, they watched for years as white boys were deified who aped their chords and their movements. The very language of Soul, ineptly employed now by all continents of music, dates from servitude – 'The Man', for example, invoked in tones of rolling mockery. The Man, when he ceased to be slavemaster, was the white promoter; and they are unlikely ever to forget him.

'You'd be playin',' Wilson Pickett says. 'You'd see The Man walk out the side door with the money. What did you do?' He guffawed. 'You quit playin'.'

'They'd tell you their wife had died,' says B. B. King. 'Their children had pneumonia. I once had a dude come say to me he couldn't make it 'cause he had four flat tyres!'

'Ike Turner – he wouldn't start to play less they flew a flag to tell him The Man had paid the money,' Pickett said. 'Ike had a safe built in the trunk of his car. Only thing – the car got stolen!'

Most of the artists whose music so evokes a Northern city, a cold and thrilling night, received their apprenticeship in the South. They carry the scars yet, like streaks of chocolate syrup through their flesh.

'You'd get into town,' says Eddie Floyd.

'— Race to get a room in that motel where you was allowed to stay,' William Bell added.

'You'd see them burnin' crosses,' Eddie Floyd said. 'I was

128

The Rolling Stones, back on the road again: ". . . a power of which Jagger, however dominant, represents just one fifth . . . It needs the chords that only Keith can shape . . . It needs Woody's bum notes, Bill Wyman's taciturnity; an impetus that only sorrowful-looking Charlie can give to drums."

The Everly Brothers, 1972: "You're witnessing," Phil Everly says, "one of the great sibling rivalries of the Twentieth Century."

John Lennon, solo performer, 1976. "Suddenly," Yoko says, "I thought, 'He looks so lonely up there.' "

Yoko and John, freshly-shorn,
one of their many symbolic
gestures during the early
Seventies.

Yoko Ono, 1981: "Two days
before it happened,
I remember looking at John.
I said to him, 'Hey — you're
even better-looking than when
you were a Beatle.' "

The Beach Boys: clean-cut
in the surfing Sixties (above),
and (below) in 1977, making
their first appearance with
Brian Wilson after his long
years of breakdown.
''We've discovered harmony
is good.''

Elvis (left) the pouting hip-swiveller who altered the posture of a generation. (Below) the Gracelands recluse. "That he never said or did anything remotely outrageous or even interesting only added to the purity of his myth."

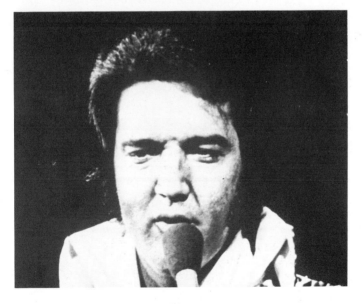

Marianne Faithfull, 1982:
"I know this whole country
still bears me a grudge.
People think I betrayed
them in some way."

Eric Clapton: "He never
really makes up his mind
who he is . . ."

Fleetwood Mac: "They view their current success as small recompense for the years of real pain and genuinely broken hearts."

Ray Charles: ". . . he seems scarcely even to alight at the piano, but kicks and flutters against it like some strange, dusty moth."

Debbie Harry, the Monroe of the Eighties: "Blonde hair we equate with glamour, success, desire. It was just a great hook."

Rod Stewart: ''Music like in public houses, that's what I've always wanted. What we've got tonight we must never lose.''

Sting, alias Gordon Sumner: ''I don't feel I belong here any more than I used to in Wallsend . . .''

Stevie Wonder: "It's
a gift from God.
You gotta express it
and enjoy it."

James Brown:
acknowledged "Soul
Brother Number One":
"That racehorse —
he don't run if he ain't
got no lust."

Suzi Quatro: "The staccato speech expected from a rocker is frequently overlaid by the pleasant self-deprecation of a nice provincial American girl."

Dolly Parton: "Her bosom is as high and prominent as a set of water-wings. Her thighs, barely contained by pink trousers, have some of the same inflated magnificence."

Champion Jack Dupree: settled in Halifax, Yorkshire, he still feels the ghost of a need to ride the boxcars again.

Sleepy John Estes, 1973: a mud cabin in Tennessee is the last resting-place for a Bluesman whose greatest song, ironically, was "Rats in My Kitchen".

Chuck Berry: "... as always he looks sleek but disarrayed, like a man standing under a waterspout ..."

"He would not be Bob Dylan if he did not make us constantly fear the worst."

Ivy Benson: "I'm sure I'll die penniless. But I don't care. I don't care a damn."

Bill Haley

Bryan Ferry

Johnny Cash

Fats Domino

Barry White

Ringo Starr

Bob Marley: "Black
music, once again,
triumphantly private."

Alice Cooper: ". . . he
has further taunted
decent society by
revealing that he wears
neither underwear nor
socks."

pretty young. I used to want to go see what they was all about there.'

'There was places you couldn't eat,' Pickett said, 'and where you could wasn't worth eatin'. Shall I tell you what saved us? Colonel Sanders!

'Dr Martin Luther King wasn't the only one,' he added. 'We was all out there too, gettin' shot at.'

Stevie Wonder had arrived at a motel outside Philadelphia where, instead of resting, he was surrounded by a delegation from the Sickle Cell Anaemia Foundation, to which he had promised help. He passed from Milton's care into that of a miniature white girl named Marilyn, skilfully maintaining her equilibrium below enormous twirls of ashen hair. She led him into the coffee-shop. She mounted his fingers, long and sleepy, on her own, pointed and pale, to sign autographs while he smiled across the booth at her friend Kitty, and all around. No move was made to get food for him, though members of the band sat nearby, occupied with sandwiches on elaborate skewers.

'I need two lemons,' he said to the waitress.

'Lemons?' she echoed suspiciously.

'Two fresh lemons. If it's no problem.'

Milton came in from a soda-fountain across the highway, put a chocolate shake and hamburger down in front of him and disappeared again. As Marilyn laboriously traced out his name once more, for a kitchen-worker, he returned to teasing the other girl, Kitty. She was no beauty. She chain-smoked.

'Hello Kitty,' he said.

'Hello Stevie.'

'Hel-lo Kit-ty!'

In half-an-hour he must leave to do two shows. His cabin is thick with people, including the local black official of the charity, with thick white cuffs, revoltingly bonhomious; a succession of people use his bathroom. He kneels against the bed, coiling and twisting his long body, punching the buttons of the recording-machine, crying out in unison with it but listening, as well, to what the official of the charity is saying.

'Sammy Davis Junior is our National Chairman. Stevie, if we could just use your name . . .'

'That's no good to people when they're dying.'

'Right!' the official agreed hastily. 'You said it!'

'Whenever I want to get in touch with Sammy Davis,' Marilyn said, 'I have to call the President's adviser to find out where he is.'

'If I'm goin' to be on your committee, Jack, you got to hear what I say.' He turned his face upwards, smiling.

'Right!' the official said, rubbing his hands.

'Stevie,' one of his musicians said, 'can I talk to you before the show?'

'Okay.'

'Can you drop by my room before we leave?'

'Okay.'

Marilyn led him into the bathroom. A burst of his voice came out, as if to refresh him. When he reappeared, the official rubbed his hands with no intention of leaving off yet.

'Well, gee, Stevie, I guess you have to eat dinner . . .'

'I don't want to eat.' His smile swayed back and forth. 'I'm gonna die.'

In Seattle, a black woman in a plain red dress faced the empty darkness of the Paramount Northwest Theatre. Her voice climbed into it, bloomed hugely out of it, curving, lazy – then ceased. She turned to the drummer on his plinth. 'Instead of sitting down on that two-and-four,' she instructed him, 'rise up on it.'

Soul assumes that everybody can sing; in particular that every woman can. A power lies in each of them, so it seems, to express for herself what the shimmering girls do with lights on their fingers. For one female voice to gain eminence, a special force is needed; a singularity so immense, as with Bessie Smith, with Billie Holliday, that it has almost a quality of exile. So followed Aretha Franklin, to supremacy denoted by absolute familiarity. One had merely to say 'Aretha'. The voice was rending, but its isolation worked fatally on a susceptible mind. As she is ill now, and silent, gradually they are beginning to speak of 'Roberta'.

Roberta Flack is somewhat of a change, however, from the shimmering girls. She wears sensible brogues. She frets constantly over her appearance, her disposition to be stout; and so undervalues her face, bound in a turban, and her mouth's full, childish charm. This rehearsal was typical of her, in an auditorium sealed off from all bystanders. She is a classical pianist of fastidious training. In a voice which one can desire almost bodily the most desirable thing is, somehow, its breath control.

'You should have played the fifth.' she reproved her bass-guitarist. 'Don't be lazy. Play the fifth.'

'. . . Charles.' She halted the quartet again to address the drummer. 'Charles, just play the groove. This isn't a straight Rock song. When it drives I drive.'

She began to sing a Blues. She is to play Bessie Smith on the screen, although their lives hardly correspond. Bessie, drunken and simple, was an early victim of the road, 'The Man' and her own crying brilliance. Roberta, since her divorce, lives in Washington with her mother. For an entourage she has only a couple of solicitous young white men. As her fame grows, so does a considerable reserve. Only when she sings, when she touches the piano, her face seems to float as if it has been freed.

'*If you treat me right, I'll stay home every day.*'

'*If you treat me right* – Keep those halves open: we've still got four more verses to do – *I'll stay home every day . . .* '

She turned, once more exasperated, on the drummer. 'This is the hand that does the tickling, the caressing,' she explained to him. 'This one is the kicker.'

She began 'Killing Me Softly.' Her voice, tender yet tired, with the sigh of anguish and of meticulous phrasing, stopped again.

'I don't want you to play just chords there,' she told the guitarist. 'That's your little solo. I want you to play something like a crying voice.'

She worked them until the queues for the first performance were collecting outside. Then she came down into the stalls to her make-up man, Vince Nasso, who held her hand. Up on their stools, the quartet offered to try 'Killing Me Softly' through once more.

'I don't want to stay on it,' she said wearily. The doors had begun to rattle at the back. 'I won't have anything left for tonight.'

The Mississippi is high enough to burst. Fields of gliding brown, in which slender forests grow, its breadth exhausts the sight; its bridges seem to race for the farther bank, gambling that they will find one. But the river, like everything of real strength, affects a slumbrous peace. It is the city beside it which is tidal.

Memphis, through all its accumulation of music, was never more than the railhead. Here, people from the dead, hot lands caught trains, or caught freight-trains, out to the dream city, which was Chicago. To acknowledge its share in Country Blues, in Rhythm and Blues, in Rock and Roll, Memphis would have to memorialise too many hoboes; and so, save for Elvis Presley Boulevard, it acknowledges none. Indeed, barely raised over plains of water, the city may well deliberate on its precise identity. It was the birthplace of Holiday Inns. It was the murdering of Dr Martin Luther King. Is it set in a dream then, or a dark age?

Beale Street, to which Lemon Jefferson came, and Elvis Presley, is half-demolished. The swarm has long died; the jug bands and crystalgazers, sharks, dentists and sporting women, of whom only some blackened upper storeys remain a witness. The city still has music in it, elsewhere. There is the Stax Record Corporation. There are session-players, white and black, held to be more brilliant and wealthy than any in the world. This abundance cannot, however, be seen. Memphis music, like all else that America holds precious, has withdrawn behind locked doors; shut in by steel and wire where once it blew out of windows, through skylights.

One thing, at least, did not die. King Hannibal, who sings tonight at the Club Paradise, has travelled the road for as long as James Brown. The difference between them is that after each performance, King Hannibal's suit dries on him. There is always the Chitterling Circuit.

'I ain't knockin' James,' King Hannibal said magnanimously, ' 'cause he made it up there on hard work, but a lot of what James done was prefabricated down heah. You all know the Mashed Potato. He got that from Nat Hendricks, Nat the Cat? Know the dancin' on one leg? That,' King Hannibal said, 'come from a young dude by the name Earl 'TNT' Bragg.'

The Club Paradise is a gigantic and damp barn, illuminated sugar pink. Outside, the night is also as it used to be. Over the plain, marked here with the emerald of a Holiday Inn, there with the emerald of another Holiday Inn, you may still distinguish a single, rushing lamp or hear the cry through the darkness of some endless freight.

In the foyer the bass guitarist from Little Milton's band sits on the rim of a torn plastic bench wolfing a cheap hamburger. Tomorrow night in Vicksburg, the next in Raleigh, will be another sour mouth, beers, further benches, torn; for he is the master only of his four thudding strings.

He looked up warily as the hugely fat proprietor of the Club Paradise passed by.

'They discover your weakness,' the bass-player said. 'If it's speed that bombs you out they give you speed, if it's coke [cocaine] they give you coke, if it's heroin they give you heroin. They put it in your food and drink. They interfere with your environment.'

The fat man paused on the threshold of the Club Paradise. Breathing fitfully, he surveyed that endless pink circle; the tables and steel chairs, the tablecloths, each bearing a fifth of bought-in whisky.

'I been told,' the bass-player said, ''less I sign certain papers – contracts – I'm goin' to lose a couple fingers.'

Beale Street on Sunday morning flaps like torn scenery in river wind. Sand clouds the blue tiles of the Daisy picture-palace; a clump of dustbins is all that commemorates Pee Wee's, where W. C. Handy used to play; Pee Wee's, The Elks, The Hotel Men's Improvement Club are all gone. A solitary pool-hall survives, run by Mr Robert Henry. He points across

133

to the site of the Monarch gambling hall where one day Uncle Ben and Mister Johnny burst out through the swing doors and simultaneously shot each other dead. 'People!' exclaims Mr Robert Henry. 'Crowds! Pussy was 50 cents, a whole night 10 dollars. You didn't able to move down here without sayin'"Excuse me".'

Over the waste ground, behind the blue-daubed windows of the Pentecostal Temple, they are starting a hymn.

'Now,' the choirmaster instructs, 'on that last "Save", I want all o' you sopranos to go on up in the attic and *git it!*'

The Temple murmurs with brilliant pink, the coiled peacock silks, babies tied in ribbons, the white pumps and gloves of the Negro Sunday; yet the choir at its elevation appears more numerous still. In cream and scarlet of many sizes, the choir sings wearing many different smiles. The choir in its surplice is rocking, one foot to the other.

Bishop J. O. Pattison, sleek as a lead-singer, looking sharp in his embroidered cross, leans outward from the pulpit.

'Our sophistication,' the Bishop says, 'has nothin' to do with our sanctification.'

'All right!'

'Our learnin',' the Bishop says, 'has nothin' to do with our burnin'.'

Below him, a fat woman lifts her arms from the full laundry-bags of her breast, raises them up and lowers them again.

'Let everything that has breath—'

'All right!'

'Praise the Lord. *Praise* the Lord!'

The Bishop turns to the choir.

'How are you, Rose?' he inquires. 'How you doin' today, sugar?'

'Jesus I love yuh!'

'She's one of the pretty ones,' the Bishop explains.

'Birds has breath,' the Bishop resumes. 'Let 'em chirp it. Bees has breath; let 'em buzz it. Oxes has breath; let 'em low it. God gave his – what?'

'Only begotten Son.'

'And greater love has no man – what?'

134

'He lays down his life . . .'

'Then he lays down his *life*,' the Bishop repeats, 'Fo' a friend. Say "Praise the Lord".'

'Praise the Lord!'

The fat woman sighs, unwrapping a humbug.

'We're not gettin' it through Black Power,' observes the Bishop. 'We gettin' it through Holyghost Power.'

With motor abruptness, as if held with difficulty in check, the fresh hymn starts; to the top at once, rocking red and white, grinning, a mad, bright wheel. The fat woman dashes her Sunday hat to the floor. She is out in the aisle, eyes shut, arms shaking, arms wobbling, her mouth compressed by ecstasy to a tiny pink flower. Her absence from the pew reveals a tiny lady in a cloche hat, as thin as a jackdaw, doing the Boogaloo.

The Bishop orders quiet. He brings on a visiting dignitary, the Rev. Wyoming Wells of Greenborough, North Carolina. 'We was young men together,' the Bishop explains. ''Course, his hair's gone grey since then while mine's still black and pretty.'

'Yes Lord,' cries somebody in a seizure. 'Yes Lord, yes Lord!'

The bullet head arises of the other Bishop.

'Some folks get grey,' he remarked, 'while some folks' – looking at the previous Bishop – 'gets bald.'

'All right!'

'You folks,' says the Rev. Wyoming Wells, 'ridin' around in your Deuce Coup 25s, your Eldorados, your Toronados, your Mercedes Benzes, your Cadillacs and all the other lacs – read the eighth chapter of Leviticus. Don't read it now, it's too long, but read it.'

'Man!' the fat lady cries. 'I've read it!'

'You think you a big shot and you think you arrived, read it, Man!' the Rev. Wyoming Wells exclaimed, 'I feel good enough to preach this mornin'! Sin is mean! Sin,' says the Rev. Wyoming Wells, 'is the poison in your stomach, poisonin'; Sin is the arrow in your bosom, stingin'; Sin – is – *mean*!'

'Yes Lord!'

'But He died!'

'Jesus I love yuh!'

135

'He died that Sin be forgiven!'

'Yes Lord!'

'They hung Him high, they pierced Him in the side and out of that side came forth both blood and water – He died!'

'He died!'

'Say again,' urges the Rev. Wyoming Wells, 'He died!'

The fat woman unwraps another humbug.

'Stand up all them who wants our prayers! Stand up!' The Rev. Wyoming Wells scans his audience. 'One of the ushers, talk to that young man please. Convince him. Bring him here.'

A young man in sherbet-green clothes, with his head in his hands, is led to the front.

'The sun,' cries the Rev. Wyoming Wells, 'looked down and saw the Son, S.O.N., and got so 'shamed on herself she hid behind the clouds. He died!'

'He died!'

'The dead saints got up and walked. He died!'

'He died!'

'He died, the matchless Son of God – and I'm so glad!'

'I'm glad!'

The red and white choir rocks side to side around the Rev. Wyoming Wells; the tambourines flutter; his hands in supplication clutch a silver microphone; watch me now, he is saying, just like James Brown, I got it. The prayer rises as a heartbeat does. Their God calls to them in tune and they, in chorus, respond.

'I don't know why.

He loved me so

But I'm glad. I'm glad.'

B. B. King has come far from there. The Blues now wear a white suit with sharp tailored shoulders, a narrow cuff falling over the shiny-faced guitar, his fingers lost in the keyboard's silver bars. Intently – for he does not sing and play together – he wrings from it drops and stabs and clusters of notes that make the wax buzz in your ears, the fillings agonise in your teeth. It is for students in New Jersey that he plays. They are on their feet for him and jumping, unmindful of the sacred basketball floor. Possibly the Blues have been passed on to the affluent. He looks benevolently down to a dishmop of hair shaking helpless at his feet.

'You got a pick in your pocket? I'll trade picks with you.'

Gladys Knight and the Pips return to Manhattan from the taping of a television show in Brooklyn. For that, too, the audience was white and delirious. And at the close of their Harlem appearance, a young black band had presented them with trophies; which touched them deeply. The lights of New York appear, as if gold paint is wearing away from the sky. The fat little Pip remarked: 'I always say that's the purtiest sight I ever did see.'

Gladys's brother Bubba sits in the front against the sleeping shapes of his two little boys. 'You know – I never thought how many miles we musta' walked on the same spot in 20 years,' Bubba says. 'You know, I never thought about that before.'

'And Man!' the fat Pip exclaimed. 'Have I got some foot-soak waitin' for *me*!'

In motels all over the surface of the land, people are settling down with a lamp in the same place, and a plastic ice-bucket. Outside Philadelphia, Marilyn and Kitty wait on Stevie's bed as Milton dresses him in the bathroom. His voice cries through the closed door. He emerges, not fed, not rested but smiling, his face turning back and forth. He has not seen his tweed suit and cap, his pink shirt and big bow-tie.

'Oh!' they both sigh. 'Cu-ute!'

'Hey Milton, show 'em the robe I'm goin' to wear for the second show.'

He sways like a long, soft doll up to the plain girl and puts his hands round her face. She smiles too, as if made prettier by the hands.

'Hello Kitty. Hel-lo Kit-ty.'

'Hello Stevie.'

In Seattle, Roberta Flack sits alone on the stage. This after-

137

noon, the rehearsal, the drummer, the road-manager, might never have existed; nor her own body. Her face has parted from it, floating about her closed eyes. She sits in silence. There is silence for each note she sings, and until the sigh of the note has expired.

To begin a new song, that will be high and loving and light, all she says is:

'Stevie Wonder . . .'

And in Philadelphia, a young man is led out into the applause. Into sunlight, warm for all that it is changing beams of red, purple and orange and gold.

John Estes: Sleepy, Getting Sleepier

The road stops at Sleepy John's house, at the top of a ploughed field, outside Brownsville, Tennessee, where the earth is thick and unyielding as old dung and the wind causes skeletons of old newspaper to dance and somersault. There is nothing beyond the cabin, with its mud wall, its strong points of tin and matchwood, poised by some caprice of the weather there against the frigid, threatening sky. It will be the last resting-place for a Blues man whose greatest hit was, ironically, entitled 'Rats in My Kitchen'.

For all its unsteady seat in the wind, the cabin is full. Age and penury, as is often their habit, nourish a vivid colloquy of youth; of children who are mothers, wives who are children still. There is Sleepy John's latest son, intensely dolled-up with patent leather boots, for some imagined night venture across the profitless moor. And home is recognisable, in pieces that can never form a picture. Clothes are washed here somehow, and biscuits cooked. One might imagine mere shelter to have won their submission, but for the look on the face of Sleepy John's young wife Ola. She murmurs, 'It's no 'count.'

Sleepy John Estes is assisted to rise from the blanket upon which, unless interrupted by music, he largely spends his life. He is almost brown bones now, both eyes covered with a yellow blindness, and all over him flutter strange, inexplicable nerves. Hammie Nixon guides him to a chair beside the open door. His limbs subside again to that careless arrangement which precedes their ultimate formality.

For 50 years Hammie has played harmonica where Sleepy

John played guitar, and has borne him company over an infinite number of miles. Hammie, by contrast, is a grizzled tub of good health, robust as the chronometer on his arm. He appears to have married one of Sleepy's daughters now, or entered some alliance in the cabin, designated by a wink. But though Hammie is twice as alive, their relationship remains dictated by the precedence of guitar over harmonica; the beating voice above the melodious descant.

'Old John fooled me you know,' Hammie said. 'He come down and played for one of our country picnics when we was kids, gettin' round two dollars for the engagement. Playin' was awful cheap then. He heard me playin' that harmonica – I had one of those that cost a dime. He said, "Look man, you oughta go to town with me." I said, "Man I can't, you got to see my Mom." She said, "Okay but you got to bring him back tomorrow." So we went on down to Memphis. Next thing I knew, we was in Arkansas. And we been runnin' ever since.'

Sleepy John's guitar is brought out. All in the cabin gather round it, testing and picking. It is a cheap Japanese solid model, unnatural on his aged hip, connected to a board of weakly-glowing valves. His fingers stumble to the frets, fastening there in an eternal chord-shape. His wrist still bears the identity tag from his last sojourn in hospital.

'We went to hoboin' you know,' Hammie said. 'We knowed 'em all. Blind Blake. Barbecue Bob, we knowed him too. Ma Rainey. Memphis Minnie. Blind Jefferson. He could cut a man all to pieces. Take a knife, you know; cut you all to pieces. And man, we had a time! We'd get in them hobo jungles, and they'd have one o' them big pots cookin' and that had ever' kind of meat in there that could be named. We'd set there, man, and get snug and somebody'd go git a bottle. You could buy that whisky for about 10 cents a half – poisoned whisky – and we'd get half juiced-up there.'

Within Sleepy John too, recollection seemed to stir of a ragged firelight.

'I'd sleep all time. Gimme half-pint that whisky: I'd go into the daylight then.' He gave an eerie chuckle. 'Sleepy John: I was Woke John then.'

'We had a jug, you know,' Hammie said. 'We'd blow that jug, too. Ole' guitar, we never did have but five strings on it. Mel Williams, he was R. C. Victor man, workin' for them in Chicago. He walked up. The jug was full. People put quarters and half-dollars in there. "You meet me in my office, 666 Lake Shore Drive, tomorrow, you all too good to be messin' round out here." So we went up and made a record. And from then on, New York City. But we never could give up that habit. All that money in our pockets and we still rode the freight trains.'

They begin. The voice is remote, metallic, as if his tongue has died already; the guitar struggles in a thick fur; the valves on the board glow on and off. Hammie, seated on the bed, is the intelligible Blues, with fingers stuck round the harmonica in his mouth, a stout leg stamping time. But from the reed of the voice, slowly, one yellow eye assumes sight on your behalf, and sees the dreary land, the boxcars passing endlessly over it.

Sleepy John's son shifted his feet and, with the greatest nonchalance, inquired, 'What you all drinkin' today?'

'I couldn't hardly go to tell how long we rode them freight trains,' Hammie said. 'We rode 'em a lo-ong time. Ever' time that R. C. Victor sent us money to come on, we'd get us a pair overalls and catch the freight.'

'– I can go get it down at the beer-store,' Sleepy John's son whispered. 'Just a six-pack of beers.'

'Didn't the railroad guard put you off?'

'Guy caught up with us in Efrin'ham, wasn't it Sleepy? They had Winchester Slim; he rode the trains up from Scarboro' to Efrin'ham, from Efrin'ham into Cairo. He had that Winchester rifle. He was a railroad bull.'

'Special agent,' put in Sleepy John suddenly.

'He made us get off the train,' Hammie said. 'But we was 'terminated to go anyway 'cause we had them people's money, you know, at R. C. Victor.'

'Much money?'

'A few bucks. Just a few bucks and – boom. Gone. Drink and foolishness like that. At R. C. Victor, man, they got rich off of us. They musta' made a couple million dollars off that

"Someday Baby", the one we just quit playin'. A couple million dollars.'

He looked fondly at Sleepy John, who had lapsed once more into his attitude of catalepsy or intense recollection.

'This cat,' Hammie said, 'could hi-ide money. I'd always be gettin' my pocketbook clipped but he'd hide his in his shirt-tails. This guy hid his in his shirt-tails.

'Memphis used to be awful bad 'bout stickin' you up, you know. Confidence. Guys tellin' fortunes on Beale Street there. Oh man, one of the confidencest places in the world! Droppin' the Pigeon. A guy'd come outa' the bank and you'd confidence him outa' what he got. We see all that stuff worked. We was musicians and they thought we was on the sunny side. A slick guy'd come and say "Here's 20 dollars, man, put it in your pocket." We'd get juiced-up, start playin', here they'd all come gangin' around. That was what the slick guys wanted so they could clip them pocketbooks.

'This guy here was awful bad 'bout fightin', you know, when we was gettin' round. He had an ole' black rock he toted in his pocket. He'd get to drinkin' and goin' with some woman and he'd want to bull-do her and some man step in and quite a fight come up there. He'd chonk him,' Hammie guffawed. 'He'd knock devil outa the other fella and then he'd sure take off, man, he's light on his feet but he sure hit you.

'He done been away six or eight months and he 'spects his girl-friend to be the same thing. He say, "Where's all them little clothes I bought you: where they at?" She say, "On the line. They hangin' up on the line." And one o' those bad guys sittin' on the side the bed. He always pushed me in! He'd say "Go on, get the guy, man, go get him." And I was astoundin' nimble at that time,' Hammie said modestly. 'I could really catch the guy and handle him pretty good, 'fore I do too much and have to leave town.'

'How did you handle them?'

'Maybe get to rap a guy with a knife.'

'What was the worst?'

'A boom,' Hammie said.

'Shotgun?'

Hammie nodded. 'He try to hurt me and I boom.'

'Did he pass away?'

'They,' Hammie corrected. 'They passed away, sure.'

'How many?'

'Three. I boom three.'

They played 'I'll Be Glad When You Dead You Rascal You'; Sleepy John's face, against Hammie's buzzing kazoo, fixed by the spectre of a grin.

'I'd get mad ever' once in a while,' Hammie said. 'When we was paid off him and me'd get to cussin' one another. Once when we was cussin' one another, this guy fell plumb in one o' them vats they cooks whisky in! I'd go on, leave that night but he'd always find me at mornin'. I brought him out when he was like to get drownded one time. "Floatin' Bridge", you remember that one? Made that record in 1937. Let's hit 'em a lick of it John.

'There was a bridge,' he explained, 'hangin' up on cables, you see. The high water was there. Didn't have no fences on it. Guy ran us off there in one those A Model Fords. One wheel hang over the cable and the car hang down and water fill up over the windshield. He was floatin' in there like a drownded rat. I bust the windshield and bring him up. His eyes were that big, you know, filled up with water.'

An increase of the wind, a stir in the cabin roof, is a reminder that the journey has not yet finished. There will be no peace for Sleepy John so long as his last breath remains, to the industries of music, a charming discovery. They thought they had starved all the Blues men years ago. He may still expect to be hauled forth, placed in the larger darkness of some auditorium, reverently applauded and returned, once more, to the rats in his kitchen. Now he wants to move on again. When he does, Hammie will go too.

'We been together too long to bust up now. We always run into a good break you know, soon as we get off on our feet. Soon as we start playin', why then we always hit. The trouble with hoboin' now is they got these too-fast engines now. Them ole' coal-burners, you had nothin' to do but get on there. These here diesels, they jerk one plumb off the track.'

'Don't you have a family, Hammie?'

'Well – yeah I have a family. I'm gettin' a family.' He surveyed the women in the cabin and added – 'All the time.'

'You still feel the Blues the same, John?'

His face turned, comprehending, to the light.

'The same.'

'Is it a sad or a happy feeling?'

'Happy feelin'.'

'Sometimes,' Hammie said, 'when I gets to playin' this harmonica, I gets pretty full o' the Blues at times. So then him and me puts the Blues on one another, and that makes both of us feel good.'

Sleepy John was helped back to his restless decline. Hammie took the visitors outside and, apologetically but efficiently, obtained money from them. We drove out of Brownsville and back again, for a briefcase that had been left behind. The cabin was still standing, the litter somersaulting around it, but Hammie's pickup truck had already disappeared. Sleepy John lay crooked on his blanket as if in rehearsal for death. His long hand was alert, however, as he arrested my departure, and the yellow eye suspicious. He looked guardedly towards the door for his partner of half-a-century, and inquired, 'How much was it you give Hammie to give me? I don't trust that sonafabitch.'

144

James Brown: Mister Messiah

James Brown will die on the stage one night, on the moving staircase of his own feet in front of a thirty-piece band; and then who knows what may be unloosed between black Americans and white? In Baltimore or Washington or Detroit, cities where the very peace between them has a quality of angry breathing, merely the presence of Brown has been reckoned to equal 100 policemen. Harlem, on the sweltering night after an atrocity, he can cool by one word. At the end of each performance he sings the chorus 'Soul Power' over and over again with bass guitar equalling a tribal tom-tom in rhythm that locks up the mind; but he doesn't cause a riot, he empties the theatre. The audience dances out into the street.

Oppressed people are the ones who need heroes in the deepest sense of idols that come from among them and can show them a way upwards to release and happiness. James Brown is the greatest American black hero; more than any of their dissenters, more even than Dr King. He is so much to them because of his distance above them as the most famous of all Soul and Rock singers; because he started life far below them, shining shoes on the doorstep of a Georgia radio station; and because this ascent has given him a bulging conceit which, like an itchy ectoplasm, reaches black audiences, somehow transformed to pride that they deserve to feel in themselves but have been denied. He is great, above all, for his music, for never having withdrawn, as the Beatles did, to be cut and issued from record studios by scientific means. After 15 years, every night he is miraculously re-created on the stage of one desperate city or another.

When Dr Martin Luther King was murdered in 1968, the Brown revue was appearing at the Boston Garden arena. It was the televising of his show three times during the following 24 hours that kept streets throughout the Republic relatively clear of the destruction that police and National Guard had anticipated. Brown himself made a public entreaty to black people to contain their grief – 'you ain't going to tear up the streets and throw your shoes in the trash can' – that was afterwards entered on the Congressional Record. Therefore, black politicians sustained by hate say he is an Uncle Tom, just a catspaw of the white law agencies. They monstrously resent Brown for what he does for morale. He has given black people not theories or systems of aggression but a phrase from the soul that they can speak and be uplifted by and yet smile at – 'Say it loud, I'm black and I'm proud.' What can white culture offer to give a glow like that to the spirit?

I first saw Brown sing at the Apollo Theatre in Harlem three years ago; in a winter when the sauerkraut relish from the hot dogs steamed on the breath of queues stretching two blocks either way down 125th Street. And the Apollo audience is exquisitely critical and it has tranquilly watched the decline of many who fancied themselves Brown's equal in soul-size. There was Little Richard, whose stage company finally exceeded any fee he could possibly be paid, who sang flanked by mock Grenadiers and demanded that a carpet be unrolled before him as he walked. There was screaming Jay Hawkins, carried onstage in a coffin (which shut him in one night), and Solomon Burke, who always had the catering franchise. His followers used to sell pork sandwiches and popcorn in wrappers that bore Burke's image wearing a crown.

And then a new generation of perfectly good people, like Sam and Dave, Joe Tex, Arthur Conley, has from time to time produced a challenger to Brown, emboldened by the thought that he was making records in 1965, when 'Please Please Please' sold a million. There have even been tournaments, with Brown and his younger opponent as mailed knights and some gigantic Southern stadium the tilt-yard. Always the

146

challenger has been danced off the platform, roared out of sight, unable to comprehend that Brown has lungs and legs like a normal man.

He could tear down a theatre on his own; yet the turning of a short man of 38 with a perceptible heart condition into this colossus is the product of an organisation as quaint as it is profitable. Brown is a business tycooon and multi-millionaire; a condition that his soul-brothers readily pardon because of the thousands of dollars he gives back to Negro charities and schools. He owns buildings and three radio stations including the one where he was shoeshine boy, and a chain of restaurants called The James Brown Gold Platter, which do quick-service Soul food. His few leisure hours have a baroque quality – in the ornate mansion in Queens, New York, that is soon to become a museum of black history, at his estate in the lushest portion of white Georgia next to the links where they play the U.S. Masters golf tournament, and in a black private aircraft named The Sex Machine after its owner's most characteristic song.

When I reached Washington last month for his appearance at Loew's Palace, the Brown organisation had struck the District of Columbia already. Detailed sheets had been drawn up of exactly how much the four-night engagement should earn, allowing for the usual percentage of children let in at a special rate of 99 cents. The theatre management had received exact, if slightly misspelt, instructions as to the advertisements required, the size of Brown's name in relation to his supporting acts, and how many promotional spots should be engaged on Soul radio stations around the city.

It was only in the wings of the theatre, watching the show for the sixth or seventh time, that I began to appreciate Brown's full size as a star: that is, how many arms and legs existed round him to do their utmost to stop us meeting. There was a U.S. Marshal with white hair, a camel coat and eyes and eyebrows cast into the same dangerous dark nuggets; there were dozens of other acolytes wearing suits and sometimes hats, addressing each other as Mr Bobbit, Mr Hall, Mr Holmes as their employer insists they do – he once corrected

Hubert Humphrey for omitting that courtesy. I was also counselled not to drink to excess, since Mr Brown disliked the smell of alcohol, and told to have faith. In the succeeding 48 hours I must have shaken as many black hands as the Chief Scout at an international jamboree.

The show is Brown – virtually nothing else. Even the three go-go dancers who pump their knees in ghostly red light on a dais behind him seem to have been chosen for perfect inconspicuousness. There is a comic and a supporting group, in this case the Chi Lights, who astonished me by saying they had worked 10 years together. But the band is splendid. Splendour is forced on them. There is an Afro-Rock section, a formal octet of brass and strings, two drum kits, talking drums. Good billing is also deservedly given to an old friend of Brown's, Bobby Byrd, who was in his classic group of the early Sixties, the Famous Flames. Byrd plunged offstage in a glaze of exertion and was at once introduced to me. 'The London Times!' he exclaimed. His hand shot out. 'Talk it up!'

Because of his heart condition, each of Brown's appearances has an element of brilliant suicide: each is like his first big chance or his last, and yet he has probably done two shows tonight already. It is as if he is gripped by demons and poltergeists, themselves in the grip of drums. Hot whips seem to turn him: the eye can only follow him when he stops but he can't bear to stop. 'Get Up, Get Out, Get Involved' with its chorus 'Soul Power' stretches into parts of an hour because there truly is no end to such a rhythm. Brown is wrapped in a cloak which he casts from him again and again, precisely on the drum-roll. Is the only thing he really loves the velvet space he sees beyond the mirage of the stage lights?

Finally at four in the morning I was beckoned through the crowd of supplicants into Brown's dressing-room. It remained, however, difficult to enter, because of the number of black men in suits respectfully crowding the walls. Reverence hung like the smell of an altar. The next thing I saw was some two dozen pairs of boots and shoes, from the 80 pairs Brown wears out onstage each year, in patent leather and piebald and snakeskin, giving the impression of a harbour crowded with picturesque craft. Next to the shoes sat Brown himself, drinking beer from a can. After the way he looks in performance, coiffed and tailored in beige or soft blue, he is a man of surprising shortness and plainness.

He was engaged with a disc-jockey in tape-recording programme flashes for his most recently acquired radio station, in Baltimore. That and WJBE in Knoxville and WDRW in Augusta, Georgia, are among the very few Soul stations in America which are actually black-owned. 'Hi,' Brown said into the microphone, 'this is James Brown. *Hello Brother!* Now,' he ordered the disc-jockey, 'you reply "Hello Sister".'

'Hello Sister,' repeated the disc-jockey.

'Hey no – they'll think I'm some kinda' faggot here. Say after me. *Hello Brother!*'

'Hello Brother!'

'*Hello Sister!*'

'Hello Sister!' said the disc-jockey.

'I think the people are beginning to understand,' Brown recited. 'Get outa' that *bed* and into that *bread!*

'Now li'l brother and li'l sister, if you' on your way to school and you' feeling bad – a education can bring you the things that you never had – so don't feel bad, but say it out loud . . .' Brown produced a variation on the axiom that has passed into the literature: 'I'm going to *school* and I'm black and I'm proud.'

He started to talk, but this was as much to his attendants as to me and his voice, to begin with, was silted up with distrust. 'I'm preaching revolution. Some preach revolution for land and some for politics – I'm preaching it for *awareness*. If I'd of had an education I wouldn't be where I am today, wouldn't know nothing about land, business, but not everyone can have my advantages. Most important teacher I ever had? He was my manager, Mr Bart of Universal Attractions. He was manager to a lot of famous people, Jackie Wilson, Little Anthony and the Imperials, but he told me I had something no-one else had – intelligence. I was a *whole* man. A doctor or an attorney, he's a doctor or an attorney 150 per cent. of the time. How can he satisfy a woman?'

Brown turned to one of his men and said, 'Now Mr Patton, you shoulda' told this young man 'fore he came in here that I was super-hip, you shoulda' primed this man up. I can tell what he's going to ask me 'fore he asks it.'

I replied that this was untrue. For the first time I felt Brown's complete attention settle on me, with a body-weight. There was a little shudder from the door. The interview ended and for the next 24 hours it was intimated at second and third hand that I had blown the whole of it by contradicting the star: he was as a result 'leery' of me and, anyway, I had already enjoyed as much of his time as had ever been granted to *Look* magazine or *Cosmopolitan*. Therefore it was surprising to me – not to mention those of his followers trying to see me off – when Brown told me to go up to his suite at the Hotel Sonesta when he rose in the early afternoon.

Brown was eating a tangerine in a white-carpeted parlour, somewhat complicated by cream-coloured wrought-iron tables and chairs. All the ashtrays had peel in them and the room smelled sharp with it. At first Brown appeared to be by himself: then the soft movements were added of a woman in slacks whom I took to be a chambermaid. It was only when she gave Brown his heart-pill that I realised this was his wife Deirdre. She came back into the room with two of the long waste-paper baskets peculiar to American hotels, and Brown put one leg into each. They were filled with warm water and salts. Then she rubbed his feet with ointment. Sitting beside him on the couch she took one of his hands under her arm and began to trim all the cuticles of his nails. In this apparently servile posture, all at once she looked strong and influential, and Brown not lordly but quite small and vulnerable.

'When I'm on my own on the road I behave just like a teenager, 19, 20 years old – bang, bang, bang,' Brown said. 'I'll eat a hamburger before the show that I won't even finish, but this afternoon I ate almost a full meal with salad and Black Forest dessert. We could get a maid to do all this but she won't have it. People sure like me if Didi's visiting. She salts my feet and rubs 'em and takes the ingrowing hairs out of my nose that I'd cut myself if I tried.

'She gives me a lot of room in the bed. I don't do karate tricks but I have to spread out. If my wife and I are together in bed I'll dream – 95 per cent. pleasant dreams. If I eat late I may dream about an accident and that's not pleasant. And I wake up and see the outline of her there, and I feel like I did sleeping at the back of the aunt I boarded with when I was 12 years old. She gets up to bring me a soda. I drink a little of it. I can relax and feel like my spirit goes and lies on the studio-couch in the next room 'till morning.'

Brown grew up in Augusta; in red clay country where the white word 'Boy' can have the most evil sound in the world. 'It was a country home – water outside. I was nine years old before I had my first store-bought underwear, my clothes having been made out of sacks and things like that. My first memory is unpleasant. If it were pleasant I wouldn't remember it.' His mother left home when he was scarcely walking; his father greased and washed cars and was a sporadic parent. James helped him and picked cotton and gathered coal from railway lines, danced for the soldiers at Fort Gordon or cleaned shoes. 'I'd come home at one or two a.m. and there was nobody there.'

His cousin Fred Holmes, now with the Brown road show, says, 'We'd steal anything – groceries, hub-caps. All I could think of then was that James was going to be a hoodlum.' At 16, Brown was sent to reform school; at 19 he was paroled and became a lightweight boxer. The cleft over his right eye that the stage make-up conceals is a souvenir of that. 'I trained with Beau Jack and all the fighters I was with went on to spar with Ray Robinson. I only ever lost one fight and that was because I was a chicken.' Today, in extreme displeasure, he will still aim a punch at somebody.

When he sang spirituals in a church in Toccoa it was not from any promptings of the soul but because 'I was trying to get a foothold in *anything*.' His early professional years were spent touring Southern dives, he and eight musicians and their equipment all junked into one station wagon. It was that life which gave Brown his extraordinary notions of how orderly and punctual a touring Rock show must be. His employees, as well as addressing one another formally, have to wear suits. Even the road-managers with their filthy nails have to operate in jackets, sometimes with three rear vents. The available females that pursue Brown after each show are used with the same relentless courtesy. Brown himself makes little secret of benefiting from their company. 'That racehorse – he don't run if he ain't got no lust.' According to someone else, 'there can be three different women in three motel rooms but he's polite to 'em; he calls 'em 'Miss' and puts 'em on a pedestal if they put him on one.'

The band is ruled by iron. Rock musicians must forsake their dilatory ways if Brown employs them. He devises each phrase they play and remembers everything. He designs their suits. He is capable of rehearsing them 12 hours at once. With him, recording is not simply a lazy, artful process on individual tracks: he wants everything played straight off as if it were live onstage. He governs by a system of fines: 25 dollars for dirty shoes, 100 dollars for lateness; it can be as much as 1000 dollars for what Brown considers some gross breach of order or courtesy. The astonishing thing is, the bandsmen pay. They believe Brown leads them to play beyond their capabilities.

Possibly his equation of business acumen with pride of manhood is whimsical: even so, it beats political harangues or the vagaries of someone like Chester Himes, the novelist, whose vision is that blacks will engage whites in total war. 'We ain't won,' Brown says, 'until any black man can walk down the street and nobody turns their head to look at him.' But how about looking at his clothes, his shoes or his car? At this question Brown's features parted into a brilliant grin. 'Yeah,' he said, 'right. I put all o' my people into Cadillacs. Miss Sanders my wardrobe mistress I gave a Cadillac Bro'ham. I got a Buick Riviera '71 that there's only seven of made at a time 'cause of the recession, and when I'm sitting in that sometimes I wish I was the car so people would look at me that way.'

By the third night of his engagement at Loew's Palace, a vast number of people had assembled outside his dressing-room. There were several U.S. Marshals now, police and local disc-jockeys, most of whom professed intimate friendship with Brown, and one insufferably earnest white youth from the Boston Philharmonic Orchestra, and the pilot of The Sex Machine. At one point, Deirdre Brown was also there, holding their two-year-old daughter; the child's hair rose up from her face in a cataract and she stared at all the people while her shoulders moved in intimations of rhythm as thrilling to watch as a first step forward.

And there was a preacher named 'King' Coleman with a bald head like a Payne's Poppet and a character named Rufus – 'folks call me Catfish' – Mayfield who was intent on out-preaching him in the small hours, while Brown was still lecturing the band musicians on their night's performance.

'I,' Catfish shouted, 'am the sergeant-at-arms, I am the chairman of the board and the master of my own soul and there ain' no white man on his Ajax horse gonna' come along and say to me "down Boy".'

'Rufus,' King Coleman said. 'You been brained.'

'No I ain't, no I ain't,' Catfish shouted.

'You a militant . . .'

'No I ain't,' Catfish shouted. 'I'm only doin' what J.B. says to do. Get out, get involved and take care o' business.'

At last Brown released his guitarist and bass guitarist and came out of the theatre himself. He was intercepted by two boys, their hair shaved into black stooks, who clamoured that they'd been made to leave their shoeshine boxes outside during the show, and somebody stole them.

Brown gave them a 20-dollar bill.

'Oh – hey, thanks,' said the larger boy. 'I was meanin' to come talk to you James Brown while you was appearing.'

'*Mister* Brown,' Brown said. 'When I come back tomorrow I want to see you here and your shoeshine boxes full of shine. Then I'm going to call you "Mister".'

Fats Domino: Rockin' in Your Seat

Fats Domino is relaxing among his half-unpacked luggage, his glass-heeled shoes, his address-book, his diamonds and his Gideon Bible. He turns out to be less in substance than in legend. During the 1950s, his bulk seemed incredible, undulating over the piano keyboard in a lounge suit that had no end. Today, he is merely stout. He thumps his chest to indicate its solidity. A white vest hugs two wide black arms, one of which wears a small diamond-encrusted antique clock. His face is tiny, oriental and good-humoured, with hair trimmed like the head of a safety-match.

He is now 48. Born Antoine Domino II in New Orleans, the youngest of nine children, his culture seemed to lie, like his whole family's, at 'The Fairground,' the New Orleans race-track, where his father worked the electric starting-gate. Instead, he found work making bedsprings for the Crescent Bed Company and playing the piano at a Club called The Hideaway. His first record, 'The Fat Man', came out in 1949. He was not fat in those days: a mere 140 pounds. It was Creole cooking that expanded him. 'Rice. Pig's tails. Pig's feet. You call 'em pig's trotters over here.'

When the whites took over black music and called it Rock and Roll, his songs were subjected to numerous 'cover versions.' Ricky Nelson recorded 'I'm Walkin'. Pat Boone recorded 'Ain't That a Shame', provoking lively debate as to whether a Christian American boy ought to say 'ain't'. Like Chuck Berry, Fats has stayed true to his material. He hums through his own songs approvingly. 'I always tried to write happy songs the people could remember. They'd always

remember a part of it. Remember "Ain't That a Shame" . . .
you made me cry, you made me sigh. . . Remember "I'm
Walkin" . . . *yes indeed, I'm walkin'.* . . . Remember "The Big
Beat" . . . *keep you rockin' in your seats.*' His version of 'Blueberry Hill' has sold 12 million copies.

He tours for 10 months in every year, carrying 40 pieces of
luggage and some of his diamond collection. Early in his
career, when he had only $3,700 in the bank, he spent $3,500
on a diamond ring. At his concerts, like the one this week in
London, his audience expects to see his fingers clanking with
ornament. He shakes diamonds like ponderous shellfish from
their box. 'This one here's in the shape of a champagne bottle.
There's two glasses in there.' His cufflinks, dusted with small
diamonds, are perhaps two inches long. 'They spell out
"Fats". That's my name.'

He lives in New Orleans, still in the 9th Ward, where he
grew up and where his wife waits with their eight children.
There, for two months a year, he writes music, relaxes, prays
and cooks. 'I fear God plenty. I figure He want you to fear Him
when you're well, not just when you get sick. I got this one big
room upstairs, with a Frigidaire and lots o' electric pots: I lie
in bed there, watching TV, sleep a little, say my prayers,
which I do many times a day; my tape recorder's there; my
Bible. I'm happy.'

Barry White: I'm in a Beautiful Mood

Barry White is the singer who turned black Soul music into a product closer akin to soggy white blancmange. From Manila to Macclesfield his voice can be heard, grunting and gasping in a register of emotions from A to B flat, invariably expressing agitation at the prospect of imminent sexual intercourse and yet sounding as if someone is throttling the vocalist with a pillow. He has become one of the most successful black American solo performers, with 50 gold discs celebrating the sales, and perhaps the uniformity, of his material. He is in England again, playing to rapturous concert audiences of whom few, significantly, are black. With tickets at £7.50 each, the tour represents a major triumph of opportunism over content.

Barry White is a very fat and, it must be conceded, a very good-natured individual. At his last Albert Hall concert, he occupied most of the time in waddling around the auditorium with a microphone and lighted cigarette in the same giant paw, shaking hands with his audience or allowing them to hug his huge and unwaisted velvet frock coat. Returned to us again at an extravagant buffet reception, he greets his media disciples with the avuncular dignity of a minor African despot. He wears a cream coloured tracksuit and a grey woollen revolutionary's hat, which he declines to remove for the cameras. 'It's Barry White's trademark.' The star frequently refers to himself in this magisterial third person.

He was born underprivileged in Galveston, Texas. His mother used to sing in church. He himself sang at services and also conducted the choir. The familiar litany is varied by

156

the surprising admission, that, as a little boy, he had a high treble voice. It disappeared all of a sudden when he was 13, one Wednesday night. 'It frightened me with all the vibrating and stuff going on, and it sure frightened the Hell out of my mother. From then on, the voice was what it is today. Super-class.'

As a boy he had a head for business. His first job in the music industry was as a minor executive and producer for the small Bronco label in Los Angeles, where he procured a minor hit for an artist named Felice Taylor. He implied that he himself was too shy, at first, to go on record. 'They wanted Barry White to sing from 1964 right up to 1972, but Barry White never would. Barry White's first album was an accident.' He filled in for another vocalist who had been due to record, and added some compositions of his own. That was when the glutinous Greatest Hits began.

Most of his songs came from inspiration arising in bed. For corroboration, he turns to his wife, a cosy-looking lady, weighted down with rings and nail varnish, who nods her head with a slightly long-suffering look. All the songs, he maintains, are written from adoration of his wife. 'I don't record in no ordinary studio. Nobody else uses that studio – only Walt Disney and Hanna Barbera animated films. She watches all the time from the control booth. We make it more romantic with the lighting.'

He is now a considerable businessman, with music publishing and film companies and a near-patent on the word 'Love.' Yet he is thrifty. The woollen hats, for instance, come from ordinary cheap stores. 'I spend money: it don't spend me. The name of my best friend is Barry White. Nobody else helped me but him. I've been used, abused, refused, tattooed – so-called friends, even members of my family who told me I could never get a job in Los Angeles. I came through it all professional, unracist, unprejudiced. I know that all people ain't the same. There are some assholes who are black.'

The quickest song he ever wrote? 'It was "Brazilian Love Song". I wrote it in 15 minutes.' He denies that, contrary to the evidence, all his songs are identical. 'If you were a

157

musician and you broke them all down, you'd see that there's a different arrangement on each one. It's the *theme* that's the same. I happen to be in a very beautiful mood and I love to sing.'

Motown: The Gold in their Bodies

Considered together at a party in New York, Nina Simone, the highly political folk singer and Diana Ross, principal exhibit of the Motown Record Corporation, offered a striking lesson as to which kind of blackness is beautiful and which merely vehement. Miss Simone appeared to be dressed as Chief Cetewayo. She wore a skirt of bead-strings through which net stockings, cruel boots and knickers were visible, and her skull was shaved and pulled into furrowed twiglets. As for Miss Ross, with winged eyes, a bunch of curls at the side of her face like wet liquorice, she was the most perfect creature in the room, or world. Her hands as they gestured seemed to have lighted almonds at the finger-ends.

Admirers of Simone's lugubrious style may protest that Motown music, exemplified by Ross, has no soul. How can anything have soul that carries a high-shine handbag or origi- nates, as Motown does, from the crumpled wings of a des- perate city like Detroit? The answer is simple if, with most black people, you define soul as the process of cheering up. Songs like Marvin Gaye's 'Through the Grapevine' or Martha and the Vandellas' 'Dancing in the Street' have all the sharp style of the urban Negro at his best, on holiday in his greatest sharkskin clothes: at the same time the colour of Motown as a political consideration seems as irrelevant as it used to be in the first bands from New Orleans.

In 10 years Motown have issued 600 single records of which about three-quarters have been hits and rather more than less phenomenal hits. Most of them were bitterly con- demned too, in one or other intellectual quarter, as 'white man's music'. Among people who claim to *know* Rock music there is priggishness which says that, really, black artists ought to appeal only to selected connoisseur whites – as the Memphis Stax label does, or James Brown. Such people really loathe Motown: for its profits, for its diamond evening dresses, above all for its infallible trick of assembling hit songs like cars moving on a belt.

It really does – at Motown's headquarters in Detroit there is a department called Quality Control, which screens all recorded material. Quality Control has the power to order changes in the lyric, arrangement, title, or even that the whole disc be put aside – such a thing happened to Marvin Gaye's 'Through the Grapevine', which lay around for years before it was released and one of Motown's biggest successes. The most instantaneously profitable thing they ever did was to record the Jackson Five last year: two multimillion-sellers began in the recording studio simply as a good sounding set of guitar and bass chords; then a tune was added, then some kind of lyric. It practically amounts to building music from kits.

The system all comes from an elusive man named Berry Gordy Junior. Gordy, it is true, rose to his present fortune by way of a job in Ford's Detroit motor plant. However, in his ascent, he also acquired a keen sense of that most worrying portion of the American heritage, committee-journalism. Motown's product may shine and repeat itself like slim limousines: the hierarchy that produces it, in Detroit and Los Angeles, reads less like an auto factory than *Time* magazine or the nightmare 'Writers' Building' of Scott Fitzgerald's Hollywood.

At the top is Gordy himself, surrounded by a considerable family that includes his father and mother. Below that come two white senior executives and one singing black vice-president, Smokey Robinson of the Miracles, and then all the leagues of artists on Motown and subsidiary labels: Diana Ross, the Temptations, the Four Tops, Stevie Wonder, Marvin Gaye, the Supremes, Martha and the Vandellas, Gladys Knight and the Pips, down to such as Edwin Starr and the

Motown Spinners, of whom great things are expected. There is the honoured roster of record-producers and arrangers (who may also be artists, like Stevie Wonder, or members of Gordy's family or both, like Marvin Gaye) and the superior enclave of session-musicians by which the Motown sound is diffused. And below these are the ants – song-writers. Motown has 103 writers under contract, working in pairs, threes or chain-gangs and subject to the strictest editing. The efficiency and success of the system leads many people to a simple conclusion: that Black Motown has been infiltrated, and is now entirely controlled, by the white American Mafia.

Rock magazine in New York is quite explicit. Reprinted in this country by the credulous *International Times*, it alleges that there is really no such person as Berry Gordy any more; he was long ago evicted from Motown by mobs to whom he lost a fortune in Puerto Rican gambling joints, and is now forced to stay permanently at home, surrounded by guards. It is true that Gordy works mostly from his house in the Hollywood Hills and it is true about the guards. However, he insists that he is still in effective control of Motown on every level – he flies around personally controlling the cabaret acts of his chief artists and keeps a hand at songwriting, too, at the head of a composing team named The Corporation. He is deeply involved in directing the solo career of Diana Ross in particular, and she in her turn seems quite bowled over by him. 'Isn't be handsome?' she kept saying. 'Don't you think he's *handsome*?'

No-one has actually interviewed Gordy for years. I was permitted a sacramental few minutes with him at his Los Angeles office. That the company is now directed from Sunset Boulevard instead of Detroit is taken as further evidence that the mobs are in control – yet to have ambitions in films and television, as Motown does, and not to be at the West Coast would plainly be unwise. Also, nobody can blame the Motown Supreme Command for preferring the brighter of the two smogs.

Gordy himself in no way resembles the dynamo, the almost mystic judge of a record's potential that his employees say, and history proves, that he is. He turns out to be a small, faintly hunched, bearded, watchful man in his early forties; watchful in the sense that, after a perfectly innocent question, he will stare at the questioner as if he suspects anarchy and plagiarism in it.

'I have never been approached by anyone that I would consider Mafia in any way, and I know a lot of people in and out of the record business. We have the policy of ignoring rumours.' Of these one of the more persistent is that Smokey Robinson, the singing vice-president, leader of the Miracles and composer of the classic song 'My Girl', has been offered fantastic inducements by syndicate figures to leave Motown. Gordy agrees: 'Smokey has been approached by many people, he's been offered a million dollars cash, he's been offered all kinds of deals to leave Motown; and most of the time he calls me up, or someone connected with the company, and tells us about the offer. We all came up in the same area, what is now called the ghetto, and it would be hard for people to put pressure on us to do anything – but our people have been approached.'

Gordy's sales director, working from Detroit, is Phil Jones, an amicably flaccid white man in a frilled shirt, somewhat resembling a Country-and-Western disc jockey of yesteryear. 'Berry works with a rifle and not with a shotgun,' he says, 'hitting the target in one, not slinging pellets at it, hoping to hit it. Four years ago we were sitting in his office and he made a statement that I thought was ree-dic'lous – he said that one of the most talented song-writers that ever worked at Motown was Jim Webb. Did you know Jim Webb worked here?' Simply from the composition of 'Up, Up and Away', Webb afterwards became one of the highest-paid song-writers in the world.

At the West Coast, Gordy's immediate deputy is Jim White, formerly a lawyer at the influential William Morris theatrical agency, and a man of cobra-like calm. 'I've had what you would say was a classical education – Stamford, clerkship in the Supreme Court of California; before I came to Motown I was offered a vice-presidency at Columbia pictures – and I'm just one of Berry's fingers.' Diana Ross says: 'Berry is the someone else you need, like some of these Broadway shows have dance-captains. They know all the routines; they're the ones that stop you from putting too much in. That last song of mine tonight – "Ain't No Mountain High Enough" – I felt I never wanted to stop singing.'

The Supremes without Diana Ross are still exhibited by Gordy as the essential Motown product; moving from one cabaret or record album to another with the high trot of established bloodstock. This summer they were in the supper show at the Frontier Hotel, Las Vegas, over the parched highway from the Desert Inn, where Howard Hughes had been concealed upstairs for a generation. The new lead singer is Jean Terrell, sister of Ernie Terrell the boxer and formerly vocalist in his group, the Heavyweights – she is the antithesis of Diana Ross in every way, with a face as solemn as an Egyptian cat.

Musically the Supremes are about seven years out of date – still they move in unison, utter breathless lyrics, wear untouchable ball-gowns as heavy as chain mail, as garish as fire drawn by a child. In Las Vegas – a city the colour of colliding suns but tasting of scarcely-defrozen prawns – they are a positive revolution of good taste. Berry Gordy had been there earlier on to write some of the patter for their act, according to Cindy Birdsong. 'He's very intellectual.'

What put the Supremes in ermine in the first place was a score of songs by the Motown writing team of Brian and Eddie Holland and Lamont Dozier: 'Where Did Our Love Go', 'Baby Love', 'Stop in the Name of Love' and others that founded Motown's fortunes in the world market by a music formula very little more complex than pat-a-cake. And Holland-Dozier-Holland did the same for Martha and the Vandellas and for the Four Tops. A year ago, they walked out of Motown after a disagreement: the strange thing was, people commiserated with them and not with the company.

The silence of Holland-Dozier-Holland in the last year is mainly the result of an injunction brought against their musical activites by Gordy (any new song by unknown writers is attributed by wagging tongues to them under pseudonyms) but it deepens the sense of Motown's supernatural influence. One of the earliest of the 600 hits was 'My Guy' by Mary Wells

– Miss Wells left soon afterwards and very little was ever heard of her again. The hypnosis worked in reverse for the Isley Brothers. They were a trio of advancing years who existed mainly on having been the first ever to record 'Twist and Shout' until their million-selling 'This Old Heart of Mine' in 1968, for Motown.

And very few of the people under contract want to leave. They like each other. This is by no means a usual state in a record company or industry where a back doesn't escape stabbing just because it wears a golden coat. Diana Ross has her famous crush on Berry Gordy; Marvin Gaye is married to Gordy's younger sister Anna; Gordy and Smokey Robinson are blood brothers and they all love Stevie Wonder for more than simply being the top-selling Motown performer around the world – or perhaps in spite of it. Such harmony compares nicely with, for example, the members of the Atlantic label's *Soul Together* show which arrived in Britain last year starring Sam and Dave, Clarence Carter and Joe Tex. Sam wasn't speaking to Dave, Carter left the tour soon after it opened and all of them were magnificently upstaged by Joe Tex who at the end of his act announced that it really ought to have been *his* show.

'People don't realise the personal relationships we got – the same that we had in the ghetto,' Smokey Robinson says. 'And the white people too; they came from the white ghetto. The same ties. We all started with nothing.'

Berry Gordy Senior was a decorator and shopkeeper at the Farnsworth-St Antoine junction in Detroit, only a block away from the city's notorious Hastings Street. The family is now almost wholly absorbed into Motown leaving not much room for Mafiosi: Mr and Mrs Gordy Senior do little administrative jobs round the Detroit building; brothers Fuller, George and Robert and sisters Esther and Gwen are senior executives, a niece, Iris, works in Quality Control, and a nephew Tommy, a youth with a wispy goatee beard, does the cuttings in the Press department. But as early as 1948 they had all been singled out for recognition by a black magazine that named them Family of the Year – Esther and Fuller then ran a printing shop and Berry Junior had already distinguished himself by winning something called the Frankie Carle Boogie Woogie contest.

His early business career was erratic. He went bankrupt with a record shop, then worked at Fords to recoup his losses. In the late Fifties he wrote two hit songs for Jackie Wilson and raised the wind for the deposit on his first premises, a two-storey wooden house along Detroit's Grand West Boulevard. Almost his first acquisition was Smokey Robinson whom he met shortly after Robinson had been dismissed by the Western Union company for delivering cablegrams in a hotted up 1946 Ford with white-wall tyres and gold hubcaps, instead of on the regulation bicycle. Nowadays the house has a big sign outside it reading 'Hitsville USA' and worshippers are shown round it in parties to see the bathroom where they had the echo chamber for recording, and the back bedroom where, according to Phil Jones, all the whites were put to work together.

Among the crowds hanging round in those days were four High School girls from the Detroit Brewster Housing Project – Diana Ross, Mary Wilson, Florence Ballard and another one who was left out when Gordy signed them – after they'd pestered the life out of him – as the Supremes. Mary Wilson, the last of the original three (she looks like a pretty Shirley Bassey) says, 'We used to get out of school at 4 p.m. or maybe at 12 noon, and then we'd hitch over to Grand West and beg the writers and producers there to let us do something.' Then, Diana Ross says, 'It would come to snack time and there was a lady named Lily who used to fix tuna fish or pork and beans or hamburgers, and we'd make sure we were all still around there to have a snack.'

Diana was the granddaughter of the Pastor of the Alabama Bessemer Baptist Church, who lived to be 107 years old. She left school in Detroit and started work at Hudson's, the city's one reckonable department store, where she was the only black trolley girl, putting out goods on shelves. Finally they gave her an audition at Gordy's house. 'I was singing "There Goes My Baby," the Drifters' song, and this man walked through and said, "Sing that again". Then he walked through again and said, "Sing that *again*". He looked so *handsome* but he didn't look like someone who was the boss of Motown Records. When we were going to sign the contract, my mother said, "I ain't going to sign nothing with *that* kid." '

In fact The Supremes made 11 failures before the song-writing team of Holland-Dozier-Holland produced 'Where Did Our Love Go?' The Four Tops – arguably the most exciting and original of any Motown group – had an even longer apprenticeship, beginning in the early Fifties when they used to harmonise behind historic figures like Billy Eckstine. 'Berry told us one thing,' Levi Stubbs, the Tops' leader, says. 'He told us, "I can only promise you one thing – that you're going to have hit records," ' They weren't really established until 1967, with 'Reach Out, I'll Be There,' even though their best song was 'Can't Help Myself', made in late 1964. This is the great thing about Motown work – it hardly seems to date at all. 'Can't Help Myself', re-released this year, sounded as fresh as ever. The Martha Reeves song 'Dancing in the Street' keeps coming back and back. 'Tears of A Clown' by Smokey Robinson and the Miracles, which did so well in England last summer, had not even been released as a single in America (Quality Control didn't think much of it) and, indeed, had been recorded so long ago that Robinson himself could not remember the occasion.

Another of Gordy's innovations – which has since lapsed – was a school within Motown to instruct his artists in manners, posture and deportment. One of the early pupils was Stevie Wonder, who was signed with Motown at the age of 12. One of the charm school's failures, according to a Motown writer, was a fat girl named Oda Barr. 'She was in Vegas and they had the tapes on her in Detroit and went wild about her. They brought her up here and she weighed like 240 pounds but still they put her on a diet, they even sent her to reduction parlours. Then one day somene was sent up to the hotel to her and in her room she had . . . a *whole box* of Hershey bars. She ate herself right out of that contract.'

At the moment Motown's biggest dollar-earning investment

is the Jackson Five. These are a quintet of little boys from Gary, Indiana, whose first three records this year all sold over a million, with stupendous orders for the fourth. On the strength of that, Jim White, Motown's Los Angeles vice-president naturally claims that they will rise higher than the Beatles, a claim that cannot be accurately judged until six to eight years from now. What they undoubtedly have done, with a lead singer who is only ten years old, is unstopper a fresh, great market for Motown – unleash that phenomenon, the purchasing power of the American child. Also, there are special problems in dealing with the female admirers of a ten-year-old heart-throb. One pert girl rang White's office and said she had to have Michael Jackson's private number because she had just been cut off from talking to him – his mother caught him using the telephone in the bath and made him hang up.

It seems curious that a dry, blond white man, an ex-lawyer, is responsible for shaping the destiny of these little nuggets, but Jim White appears to be warming to the task. 'I went with Michael and Marlon Jackson to the beach and it was the first time they'd ever seen the ocean – they didn't know anything about the little sand crabs you see on the beach. We were all there shooting an album cover and my girl friend fixed things to eat; a couple of months later they told me it was the first time a white woman had ever cooked for them before.'

White's close associate is the Motown Press Director, the bearded Junius Griffin. His former occupation was helping to write the speeches of the late Dr Martin Luther King. The composition of simple handouts for Motown and its associated companies Griffin approaches with the same earnestness and, occasionally, abstruseness. As well as the Motown and the Tamla and Gordy labels ('Tamla-Motown' is just the British export name), Gordy has started to venture into acid rock with an imprint called Rare Earth and to sign up uncharacteristic people: they include an English band, Toe Fat, and Sammy Davis Junior's own record label named, with startling originality, Ecology. Griffin also has to write Gordy's

167

speeches with the right sort of plum in the mouth; and he has been put in charge of Motown's first serious attempt at black politics, an issue of albums of the speeches of Stokeley Carmichael, Dr King and other dissenters. 'Music,' Griffin says, 'is the only form of communication – revolutionary communication – that is non-violent.' With a canyon-top bungalow and access to hundreds of free records, it is a style of revolution that appears to suit him.

Diana Ross is, of course, the Empress of Motown. I saw her solo cabaret performance in the supper room of the Waldorf-Astoria Hotel of Fifth Avenue New York – a gilded place in which the horrors of American mass-dining, so faithfully imitated by the English, all converge in the odour of the gravy. Vast chandeliers overhead give the illusion of breadth and space while below, each table not really large enough for one man with elbows is occupied by four bleached stenographers from Yonkers. Cuffs on the head are frequent as panic-stricken waiters rush to and fro.

She has a voice that was finally wasted in the Supremes, a voice with a kind of sleepy snarl in it, or else the pitch and faint breathlessness of a nervous girl singing for dimes. Dancing, she is like a wildly animated clothes horse hung with quickly-changing gowns and silly hats. She stretches upward with long arms, the palms of her hand out flat as if feeling the finish of the sky: the living embodiment of a truth that beauty is style, and blackness may not be enough. Afterwards, in the 97 degrees ironically called Indian summer by Manhattan, she flings herself over a sofa, covers her face with her hair and says 'My God I look awful.' This was the party attended by Nina Simone and a great many soft-shelled white people, some in periwigs, some making notes of the titles of Motown hits.

She had named her own act *The Can Diana Ross Make It Alone Show*. 'I've been criticised. People say "Oh she acted like she was doing a Broadway audition." I could have leff' out the hats, I could have leff' out the Famous Stars imitation and then maybe someone else would have said "She looked like she could do something else." There's so many people with Motown and they all got their different things – people say it's Motown telling them. But it's people doing what they really enjoy and what the people like.' What does she read? Rather sweetly she produced a bound volume of *Classics Illustrated* comic.

Detroit, for all the dinginess of the hand-towels in the Motown building, is still the corporation's artistic capital. European producers are flown in by relay to supervise the dubbing of material into other languages – only France resists the sound and France has no music in it funkier than operetta. Quality Control is here too, and a computer room that is the only one with decent air conditioning. Office conditions generally are quite horrible: some floors are fitted with corner mirrors of the type that discourage shoplifters in supermarkets; the only employee-catering is by a dire little automat – Lily now being Smokey Robinson's maid – and only the most select offices are equipped to make telephone calls to numbers outside the buildings. The lifts are ancient, cage-clanking devices passing by; with musicians in them they look like miners' cages on their way down to some impossible masquerade.

Presumably because they are not bound by house-regulations the artists regard this ex-municipal authority building as rather more of a spiritual home than the luscious premises on Sunset Boulevard, Los Angeles, with its oatmeal and claret decoration and executive pool-room. *Rock* magazine also claimed that Detroit had a grim-faced security department, given to following visitors for hours after they leave the building. In fact, the least-serious department deals with security; the women giggle as they arrange your head for photography in a special plastic identification card. There is also a uniformed guard in the front hall. Every time I saw him he was eating.

The Motown Spinners had just had their first real hit with 'It's a Shame' – so they were still humble enough to be appearing locally, in a bar called Casino Royale in the city's North-West section (Detroit seems more brooding and miserable than perhaps it really is because it lacks warm-sounding suburb names). The Spinners have been in the company for years, famous principally as imitators of other Motown artists. On this night they even did an unkind impersonation of Stevie Wonder's blindness and it was warmly applauded by a crowd that remained attentive even in the brief instant when a fight broke out and someone flew dizzily along the surface of the bar.

The Spinners having had a hit, there was a perceptible shiver among the 103 songwriters to be able to provide their next single or, for their choice, their next three. The analogy between a Motown record and a piece of journalism is genuine – unless you are of the Diana Ross size, you are held to be only as good as your latest chart-result. At this moment the Spinners were being made more of in Detroit than David Ruffin, brother of Jimmy who makes all those mournful records about Goodbye; than Otis Williams of the Temptations, who one morning emerged from the primitive elevator-gates wearing a grey curly brimmed hat trimmed with ribbons of Catholic purple.

In the higher leagues of Motown songwriters, with teams like Whitfield and Strong who wrote 'Through the Grapevine' and Ashford and Simpson who wrote 'Ain't No Mountain High Enough', there's an English woman named Pam Sawyer, formerly of Romford, Essex. She had a hand in, among other things, the Supremes' 'Love Child'. She sat upstairs in the Detroit building with her latest collaborator; a little black girl called Laverne whose hair was so frizzed out at the sides that she seemed to have placed her head between the paws of a gigantic bear.

They had co-written a song called 'I Can't Forget the One I Love'. Pam Sawyer produced the lyric and the music and test vocal came from Laverne; so did the best line – 'I can't forget you/Not even the size of your shoe.' 'It came from a guy I knew once,' Laverne said. 'He had tennis shoes, kinda' *ree-al* raggity.' Pam Sawyer was cautious. 'I'm worried,' she said, 'about that "whoo-hoo" bit. They'll say, "It isn't Motown." ' Altogether, the scene was like any whispered little conspiracy in the *Time-Life* building. Only Laverne, of all the 103

170

song-writers, seemed not to think it should all be taken seriously. 'I don't aim to make a million,' she said. 'To make a million you got to write a million.'

Champion Jack Dupree:
Travelling North

Around 1920, Champion Jack Dupree left the Coloured Waifs Home for Boys, New Orleans, and started walking. He had nobody. His father and mother were burned in their house by the Ku Klux Klan. 'All my life, from six years old,' he says, 'I wanted to work and save up enough money and git enough emmunition and catch *them* in a meeting and spray them and let 'em spray me – 'long as I could lay down dead in the field with a few of them I'd be happy.'

He walked to Missouri or rode the blinds – clinging danger-ously to the boxcar couplings. From St Louis he went to Chicago, where Police Model A Fords could still be out-distanced by the fleet-footed criminal. In New Orleans again, a barrelhouse pianist named Drive 'em Down taught him the Blues. Considering the roar of the speakeasy all around, it was a subtle, beautiful style, pecking and light. But Jack became a prizefighter before he turned to music. He knocked out Battling Bozo in the eleventh. Nor did he stop walking, nor saving in a corner of his head for that machine-gun, until he reached Yorkshire.

The very last of the New Orleans barrelhouse piano-players lives in a council house with its side door constantly open, as is the way in those parts, to admit the children, neighbours and large-tailed dogs peculiar to small dwellings. Champion Jack is 61 now; an age at which the past may begin re-weaving itself on the mind with today's clarity and colour. From his scrap of front hedge he can see Halifax and her encircling hills – he can also see New Orleans at Mardi Gras time. There were Creole gangs whose Cherokee blood per-

172

mitted them to decorate themselves like Indians. Champion Jack ran as scout with the strongest of them. At first light they stood and drank around bonfires in the street; feathers stirring with the breath of the fire and raw cold.

He says that sometimes he still feels the ghost of a need to ride the boxcars again; to be with the hoboes cooking red beans and rice out in the woods, or drinking and jamming it up all night with his greatest friend Brownie McGhee. Or he broods about Drive 'em Down and Blind Lemon Jefferson and all the others whose only reward for creating the Blues was the privilege of dying of bad drink on the street. His white wife Shirley says Champion Jack can be difficult at times. 'He'll hurt me by saying "Oh you white folks is all alike." But he always finishes up sorry. I tell him while he's doing it, "You know you'll pay for this, don't you?" and he does. I got a new pair of shoes out of him last time.'

Shirley is half his age. She calls Champion Jack 'you lousy cow' yet treats him as if he were the younger one, as if he were beautiful. They hold hands – hers with work-chipped pink varnish over his black ones, the joints mapped and lightened by age. Into his left lobe she fits the single gold earring he wears – 'Hold your head still, I haven't got rubber arms.' It's hard to make it stay. Champion Jack's ears were pierced so long ago, when the habit survived from tabulation of cotton slaves.

They met when he came to London in 1959 and Shirley worked in London at a club. ''Took a week for her to kiss me,' Champion Jack says. Shirley pretends to belt him one. They had originally planned to settle in Rugby but then a business associate broke a promise to lend him half of the £400 deposit on a house. Shirley was furious, but, to Jack it was merely another example of the world's conspiracy to keep Blues artists on street corners. Out of 200 albums he thinks he has cut – the rarest of them for the famous Okeh label in Chicago – he is paid royalties on about the last five. What supports him now is work on the Continent, in countries known equally for their welcome of music and of black men. In Finland, in Germany, or Yugoslavia, he can fill a sports arena. In this country he occasionally plays a club.

Shirley goes with him if it's local, her eye kindling for anyone trying to do him down. So does her Dad, Leslie, who is just two years younger than Champion Jack. Leslie conducts one of those truly beautiful relationships that a man can have with the highlights of a pint of beer – 'He's only here for the beer,' Champion Jack says. Shirley's mother stays behind to look after their two children, who are the colour of perfect honey.

Champion Jack is having his wash in the kitchen. He still has the cabled muscles of a fighter with old scars darkly glistening among them. Half a heart is tattooed on one arm. It was begun by a fellow prisoner in Indianapolis where Jack once served 30 days for raiding oranges. The other man's execution unfortunately interrupted the design. In the kitchen, too, his and Shirley's little girls are eating Soul food with a view of gasholders; ham, string beans and rice. Though the house is cramped by cots and small, drying socks and Jack's own thousand pennants, souvenirs and stage photographs, a system of order finally prevails. A notice on the living-room wall proclaims: 'All the paying books is here.'

The discotheque in York that had booked him is like any other; its disc-jockey as sad a figure as any other, from one pound a week to five hundred. The disc jockey utters his confused sentences about 'Champion Jack Dupree the Living Legend' while the Living Legend sits on one of the plastic banquettes drinking a lager with a brandy chaser. In New Orleans, if you drank yourself into the grave, at least you sometimes did so by an unconventional mixture – Scotch and milk, or the beer and white wine together that the stevedores favour. However, some of the other Blues men, like Sleepy John Estes and Big Bill Broonzy, never liked to see Jack touch strong drink. They always thought of him with his innocence intact and the big dimples he had when he first came from the orphanage.

At home he is at times a rather solemn man of the house; wearing spectacles to fix Shirley's electric hair-rollers; inclined to be strict about letting his daughters stay too long with neighbours. At the piano keyboard, sideways to it sud-

174

denly he becomes impish. In the barrelhouse in the Twenties, Drive 'em Down's particular trick was to keep the thumb of the bass-playing hand locked below the other fingers so the bass jumps, the treble jumps and chops like a dancer – Champion Jack does it too. His white pumps on the pedals bounce as softly as tennis shoes. Suddenly he looks round. His dimples have come back again.

At first, the young discotheque crowd seems puzzled. They are not accustomed to music so quiet. But by the second song, they are captivated. They shake their long hair back and forth across their faces, singing along with songs written half a century before their birth. 'Oh, oh baby – come here quick. This old cocaine's makin' me sick . . .' 'Wine, wine, wine,' they sing in tune. They sing 'The Sheik of Araby' with Champion Jack's saucy descant: 'At night when you're asleep – *with no pants on*, In-to your tent I'll creep – *with no pants on* . . .'

For an evening no one will forget, he is paid £50. There was to be a percentage, too, if the gate money went over a certain amount. It cost 50p at the door: later a representative of the management fights his way through the pack of suddenly joyful customers to say he was sorry but only £82 had been taken. Champion Jack is accustomed to this tone of regret on the part of managements; it still angers Shirley. After another engagement recently, where she believed he was badly used, she told the impresario, 'You're the lowest of the low, and you know what that is, don't you? It's a snake that crawls in the grass.'

When they were married she had never been out of the country before. The wedding was in Copenhagen, then for a year they lived in Zürich. 'At first I was a bit – well, you know, shocked at the language I heard, because when these musicians get together it's mother-this and mother-that.' Later she was to discover for herself the satisfaction, especially in dealing with club-managers, of such words from outside Halifax as 'sonofabitch'.

Though he mends her rollers and cooks for the girls, Shirley can still see traces of his old violence. Rather, it is the

175

imperviousness to violence that a musician will develop by continuing to play as bar-customers have pistols emptied into their faces and the shells clang on the foot rail; as horsemen ride upstairs to celebrate Jessie James's anniversary, shooting at the lights.

Jack is slow to anger. 'Then,' his wife philosophically says, 'it's always "Shirley – hold my jacket".'

'In Switzerland they call me Mister Pasquale 'cause they say I got the nerve of an Eye-talian. In France one time I was going to get a man's head off.'

'That's right, he was,' Shirley interjects.

'I was playing the pinball machine in this place. Some man there talking all about the South – and he was in the wrong place to be doing that. He says out loud, "Ah the niggers is all the same," and when he say that I swung round from the music-box. I had him up at the bar with his head up, my knee in his stomach, my knife 'cross his throat. The people there was shouting, "Cut it off" and the manager shouting, "No, no, no". The blood was running down my hand from where I broke the skin. I said, "Breathe loud and I'll pull your dam' head off." '

Other Blues people always thought of him as the peacemaker. If Big Mama Thornton, for example, is provoked she will at first say, 'Jack – talk to this guy and 'splain to him 'fore there's any trouble.' Big Mama weighs almost 20 stone and wears men's shoes and dungarees with a razor in one pocket. Once, Champion Jack saw a bold man hit Big Mama with a chair, and she was unmoved. Then she threw the man through two sets of shut folding doors. But she is fond of Shirley, whom she calls Little Mama. Shirley remembers asking, 'How many eggs for breakfast Big Mama, one or two?'; whereupon Big Mama looked at Champion Jack and said jovially, 'Jack, 'splain to this bitch that I got to have six eggs for breakfast'.

Sometimes Brownie McGhee comes up to see them in Halifax. Though more celebrated for his partnership with Sonny Terry, Brownie did a lot of work with Jack. Once, the two of them were engaged to play at a party in New York, where they noticed a buffet table covered with nothing but lemon meringue pies. Champion Jack adores cream pie and was hoping to take some home with him. It turned out, however, that the object of the party was neither to hear the Blues nor eat the pies – it was to throw the pies. One got into the hole of Brownie McGhee's guitar. Then they were riding the Subway together and both fell asleep. When they awoke the train was in the marshalling yards. Brownie's guitar had been stolen from under him as he rested on it. His face was still supported in mid-air by his folded hands.

In obedience to the wish of Blues players of two generations, Champion Jack still drinks very little. He remembers the passion with which Big Bill Broonzy dashed a glass of gin out of his hand in 1938. In his arsenal of a cocktail cabinet, the Canadian Club whisky and Old Grandad bourbon is just for the guests. After a night's talk with Brownie McGhee, the house is likely to be disturbed only by preparation of Southern fried chicken and potato salad as the sun comes up over Halifax. He may, of course, have the occasional lapse. Shirley appears equal to coping with it.

'Oooh' – she gives him a reproving look. 'One night in Denmark he were real paralytic, he should have been ashamed of hisself. He comes up from the hotel lounge when the birds are singing. I'm trying to get him undressed and all the time he's on the move round the bedroom. When I get him to his underwear he says he's been invited to a party in the room down the hall. I says, "Do you want to go?" and he says, "I want to", so I put him outside in his pants and vest.'

Jack points out that one night she was a little tipsy herself.

'Oh, in Stockholm, that's right. Yes, I was so bad he wouldn't walk with me back to the hotel; and it were a steep hill and all. Then of course not being used to it, I was up and down all night, running you-know-where. When I finally got off to sleep . . . I wake up and Jack's getting in bed with me. He'd been reading the book *Dracula*, and thought Dracula was coming to get him.'

Of course the Blues do not necessarily come to an end in Halifax, even with good in-laws and the neighbours, immensely proud of Champion Jack and the parking of his gold-lettered station-wagon with lace curtains in the rear windows. Halifax will probably hold on to him. He likes the racing at York. A gipsy selling lace at the back door has told him that now at last he is going to make the money he deserves. Besides, one of his little girls is handicapped; although she is so exquisitely graceful that it gives her movements only the merest obliqueness. Anyway, you can't ride the blinds from here: trains are too erratic.

He remembers anyone who ever showed him kindness. There was the Italian priest at the orphanage who got him his first piano, and Drive 'em Down, who let him sleep on the floor of his room, and the 'sporting women' of St Louis who gave him a dinner he can recall flavour by flavour: stew, rice, three hamburgers, pie and a 'jumbo' of pop. It was only after he left the orphanage and began his travels that he discovered he had a sister living in New Orleans. He met her; she gave him an address to go to that night, saying it was hers. It lay eight miles out of the city and when Jack got there, it was the home of the Police Chief. 'He came out to me with his gun up here. But when I told him, the Police Chief coulda' cried himself, that my sister done that.

'. . .Christmas, nobody give you anything. I used to go to a show on Christmas – sit up in the show 'til everything was over. For me now Christmas just like today or any other day.'

Shirley chides him, 'Get on. You know you enjoy shopping for the children as much as I do. You say, "Oh we're not going to spend as much this year", and end up spending £40.'

'I don't get nothin' for Christmas.'

The finish of the Blues.

'Oooh you lousy cow, I bought you them earrings.'

He is mobbed when he has finished playing at York, and when even sitting down again he has the guitarist from the local supporting trio kneeling in front of him. The guitarist could not fully comprehend the sounds that Champion Jack left the piano to produce on his instrument – produced only by kipper-flipping his hands on the guitar fretboard.

It is his sixty-first birthday that Fourth of July. He has just heard of the death of another old Blues friend, the guitarist Bukka White immediately following a European tour; '– and Otis Spann; he came over, went back and died. Sonny Boy Williamson came over, went back and died. And little Walter ... Bukka White. Scaring me to death, these cats, with all o'their dying.'

Leslie, his father-in-law, winks at the colours of his pint of ale.

'You only die once,' he remarks philosophically.

Part Three
The Middle of the Road

Joe Loss: The Upfront Man

The waiters in their raincoats were piling chairs on tables in the ballroom, talking about the dance the night before. Seven pounds a ticket for dinner and the Joe Loss Orchestra, and it had been a good night, they said: it was a pleasure to work late. The waiters' voices died away among the colonnades as the orchestra boarded the bus for its all-day journey, from Liverpool in the top left-hand corner of England, down to Ipswich, somewhere low on the right. Liverpool receded, and all its numerous satellites. By four o'clock the light had vanished, together with all consciousness of where they were; how far they still had to go. Most of the musicians went to sleep, with stockinged feet stretched across the alley between the seats. A stage suit, in its zip-up container, swung gently from the bolted sun-roof, like a corpse left long on the gibbet.

Joe, alone, did not drop off. He remained awake and watchful all afternoon in the seat behind the driver and the big front window where the crooked wiper beat time ceaselessly to the fits and squalls of rain. He was remembering Liverpool in better days, when the Adelphi Palm Court really had palms in it. He remembered playing with his orchestra there during Aintree week, and how he would get tips from the owners, the trainers, the jockeys; and usually disregard them all. England is full of cities, and of large hotels, which Joe Loss can remember in better days. Even so, he, too, was satisfied with last night's engagement. In his wallet he carried a scrap of paper scribbled hurriedly at a moment between dances. Somewhere near Birmingham, he took it out and studied it again in the swaying half-light. 'They've asked us back again next year. November 18, they want us.' He took out his diary. 'I think that falls on a Friday.'

The journey from Liverpool to Ipswich by road takes six hours, crossing England on a perverse diagonal known only to commercial travellers and dance-bands. You leave the North and skirt the Midlands, and eventually cross a bridge into the lighted Market Square of St Neots. You head out of St Neots towards East Anglia, across a flat and lowering landscape. Even among these scattered towns there were few in which, at some time or other, he had not appeared with his band. He had played in Cambridge for the May Balls. He had played in Newmarket at the Jockey Club. He had played in Colchester, in Chelmsford and Bury St Edmunds. 'And we once played in a little place named Soham. That's somewhere around here, isn't it, Sam?' He consulted his deputy in the orchestra. 'S.O.H.A.M. Soham.'

Even if you did not recognise him, you would guess that Joe Loss led a dance-band. His back is concave, his cuffs are prominent, his hands small and clean and his feet small and pointed. Both his shirt and his tie are pink. His voice is slow and fruity with the hesitant precision of numerous announcements made from the bandstand. Though he wears his hair a little longer these days, the physiognomy is as it was in the 30s, the 40s, the 50s, the 60s: the eyes crinkled up, the prominent nose, the smile, like the smile of a turtle, covering the lower part of his face. This is his 46th year as a bandleader and he is as busy as ever.

He recollects his career with loyal and legitimate pride. 'Three Royal weddings we've done. And Christmas at Windsor – the staff dance. You'll see the Queen there, dancing with a footman or somebody of that sort. Miss World, the ballroom-dancing championships. We've done them all. The QE2 world cruise. British Road Services: we played for them at a function a few weeks ago. We carry over 1000 pieces of music – the boys do. One night, you see, we might be asked for "Boomps-a-Daisy". The next night, it might be "Rhapsody in Blue". We can provide both.'

184

'I should have retired 20 years ago. But it still gives me a thrill: going to a town, and people come up and say. "Joe, I heard you play a tune, I went to my wife and told her that's our tune, and married the girl." I'm accepted as a native of whatever town I happen to be playing in. I brought in 17 Hogmanays, I had to be flown specially back from Arnhem, in the War – A.R.N.H.E.M. – so that I could bring in another Hogmanay.

'You ask me what sort of music I like. The music I like is what the people like. You talk about educating people with music – imposing things on them – well, I've never carried on like that. I weave about, you see. What I've always played is just music *for the occasion*.'

On records, his following is enormous. The rise of Pop music, which killed off most of the big bands, has ensured his triumphant survival. This is because each new pop craze, devised for audiences ever younger, trails an older audience in its wake. For these more cautious millions, the bandleader remains a comforting figure, interpreting wild sound in a familiar way, rendering it into a familiar tempo. The latest of his albums on the EMI label – to which he signed 40 years ago – features such characteristic items as 'Match of the Day Samba'; 'Bridge over Troubled Waters Rumba'. His appearance in the Top Twenty has been by no means infrequent.

His overheads are small. He has never diversified, as his fellow bandleaders did, into the entertainment 'industries'. For the past 40 years, his office has been in Morley House in Upper Regent Street, suitably near to Broadcasting House. You go in through a gap in the shop-fronts and ascend to a dim region of wholesalers and exporters in a smell of wood polish and soap-suds. 'Joe Loss Ltd' is on the fourth floor. A small outer office contains a secretary in a pink jumper and numerous clippings of the current Top 20. A small inner office contains a desk, a desk-set, net curtains above a thick-bodied radiator, and Joe's wife Mildred, who takes care of things while he is on the road.

One visitor to the office today is a tram-driver from Blackpool Promenade who follows the Loss Band to its engagements all over the country, in a checked hat, carrying a briefcase.

'This gentleman,' said Joe, 'knows more about all the bands than I do – who was in them and which year. How long have you been coming to see us, John?'

'Thirty-seven years. I'm 56 next birthday, all being well. I always get along, if I can, to see where The Maestro's playing.'

'He's got all our records.'

'In here,' the tram-driver said, patting the briefcase. He added confidingly, 'We're doing very well in Australia. Very, very well.'

As the office door closed behind the tram-driver, Joe's smile became a little bleak.

'He's come all the way down from Blackpool today, and he's going all the way back again, just to spend an hour in the office. You can't just say "Hello and goodbye." If I was to say I was in a hurry one night, at a stage-door or something, it might ruin that boy's life. It frightens me sometimes when I think about it.'

Joshua Alexander Loss was born in 1910 in Spitalfields – 'S.P.I.T.A.L.F.I.E.L.D.S.' – in a Jewish community proud of its foothold on the City of London. His father had fled from Russia in the 1890s to set up in business as a cabinetmaker: the name Israel Loss still commands respect, he says, in the office furniture trade. The older son went into his father's business, and in Joshua resided the hope of cultural advancement. He was put to study the violin, first from a local teacher named Kaplan, afterwards at the Royal College.

He was drawn away from his classical studies at the age of 17, when he got a job as a 'repet' ('R.E.P.E.T.'), a junior violinist in the pit orchestra at the Coliseum cinema, Ilford. The orchestra wore evening dress, although concealed by a curtain, and played airs appropriate to the silent film on the screen. Talking pictures arrived almost immediately, removing the demand for pit orchestras. He went to Blackpool, despite his mother's protests, and played for a season at the Tower. He played in the Chinese Café, near the top of the Tower. During the intervals, sheet music was taken round and sold, and he used to creep downstairs, down many flights, to the balcony of the Tower Ballroom. Below him he saw a vast mosaic dance floor and a magnificent orchestra, led by Bertini ('B.E.R.T.I.N.I.'). At the beginning of that season, his only ambition was to sit among the violins in Bertini's orchestra. At the end, he had vowed to lead an orchestra like Bertini's.

He became a prodigy. At the age of 20 he led a band playing second on the bill at the Astoria ballroom, Charing Cross Road. He called it Joe Loss and his Harlem Band. He thought Harlem was in Holland. He played with that band in the afternoon and by night was musical director at the Kit Cat Club in the Haymarket. He used to wear a black cape and a top hat that collapsed. His suits came from Hall and Curtis. On leaving the bandstand, he always took his trousers off and hung them up until it was time to go on again. His memory of those West End nights is like a code for which he alone remembers the key. 'Buddy Bradley did the routines. Wonderful girls. Wonderful shows. Wonderful shows at the Troc', too, and Ciro's. Hutch was on at the Troc. Hutch might be on at the Kit Cat.'

In 1935, he made his first broadcast. To be heard as a band-leader over the BBC then could lead to inconceivable fame. It had made national heroes of Jack Hylton, of Jack Payne, the dapper Roy Fox, the supercilious Ambrose. He was given his own show on the Light Programme on Saturday nights. It lasted one hour 40 minutes. He introduced it with the words: 'It's dancing time for dancers – roll back the carpets and dance.' He was too ebullient. The BBC decided that his voice was insufficiently refined. For one Christmas band show the continuity had to be spoken by an announcer from Gaumont-British News. His voice, on the BBC, is long since emancipated. But the memory of that early snub still fades his smile a little at the corners.

His band has given a start to many singers down the years. There was Chick Henderson ('H.E.N.D.E.R.S.O.N.') who died

187

in the War and who might have been as great as Al Bowlly; there was also 'a little girl called Vera Lynn'. He decided that her wages were too expensive. Eamonn Andrews, even Spike Milligan, owe some of their success to an early chance on Joe's bandstand. In his cupboard at Morely House, two big ledgers give the history of his music in newspaper-cuttings, rectangular or T-shaped, covering the paste-thickened pages: a thousand one-night functions in Corn Exchanges, in Assembly Rooms, when, at his coming, Runcorn or even Cheltenham might legitimately claim to be 'the rhythm capital of Europe'.

Now it was the turn of Ipswich. In the darkened bus, he switched on his overhead light and studied a piece of paper which gave particulars of the venue.

'The Corn Exchange Centre, Ipswich. It's one of those new leisure complexes, I believe. It's only been open seven weeks. Do you know anything about it, Sam?'

Sam, the band-manager, came and stood on the step inside the coach-doors. He is a plump man with spectacles, bright yellow hair and a small, crisp chin, who also plays trombone in the band.

'You'll never guess how to spell my name,' he remarked. 'It's Whatmough. W.H.A.T.M.O.U.G.H.'

'Do you know anything about this place, Sam?'

Sam did not.

'It's a leisure complex, I believe. It's only been open seven weeks.'

It was not a leisure complex. It was a Corn Exchange, dating from the 1880s hidden in a labyrinth of dark streets. A man from the Corn Exchange was swung aboard the coach to pilot it to the door. He piloted it to the mouth of an alleyway 50 yards from the door, at which point his ingenuity seemed to be exhausted.

'You'll get her round all right, Colin,' Sam said.

'Yes,' the coach-driver agreed drily. 'She's only 40 feet long.'

Inside the Corn Exchange, the dancers were already

waiting, in evening gowns of green or turquoise, in white shirts and lounge-suits and bow-ties, their tables around the floor staked out firmly with pint beer glasses and small gilt evening bags. A raft of coloured spotlights, suspended from the ceiling, did little to soften the chill formality of a sterner brickwork era. It was shortly before 7.30 p.m.

The band assembled, leaderless, in the little modern restaurant for soup and cottage pie. Some other musicians and the three vocalists had come up from London by car. The three vocalists sat apart: Tod Miller, just out of his teens, and the dark-eyed Rosa Loveband, a little further out of hers, and Larry Gretton, no longer anywhere near his, an avuncular man with upswept golden hair, who chaffed the waitress, and chaffed the other waitress and then chaffed both waitresses together.

Gretton and Sam Whatmough and several others have been Loss employees for 20 years. Others, as their facial blemishes proclaim, have been with him only a few months. He is strict with his 'boys', enjoining punctuality and courtesy, disliking them to drink before the engagement. His parting shot, before going to his dressing-room, is, 'One thing I would ask: please don't talk to them about wages.'

With so complex an organism as a 12-piece band, it is wise to employ the principle of divide and rule. Executive duties are shared between Sam and the trumpeter Vic Mustard, a little Tynesider, long emigrated to London, who is 'deputy leader'.

'I always have to spell my name,' Vic said. 'But it's just the way it sounds. M.U.S.T.A.R.D.'

None can imagine working for anyone else.

'Who else is there?'

'There's no-one, is there?'

'And we always get a fantastic welcome, even if Joe isn't with us, through being ill,' Sam said. 'And if he is with us, it's fantastic. In Wales once, after we'd played The Queen, the audience sang "We'll Keep a Welcome in the Hillside". And in Scotland they sang "Will Ye No Come Back Again?" '

'Can we take our coffees up with us?' Vic asked the waitress.

She considered.

'All right then. If you promise to bring the cups back.'

In his dressing-room, the bandleader was almost ready. After all these years he still suffers nerves before taking the bandstand. And there was a 'sub' in the band tonight, who had never played with them before. 'One long face on the bandstand and that's it.' He murmured other axioms to himself as he drew the comb sideways across his head. 'Twice late, and my organisation wouldn't last a week.' He wove and crossed over the plump black bow under his chin; he cannot bear a made-up bow. He looked at the programme. 'I think we'll start off with "American Patrol". There's a few old ones out there. Then into "Gentle on my Mind".' He took up the black dinner-jacket with its black plaid satin lapels. 'I think John Michael have made a very nice job of this, don't you?' He bent before the mirror and sprayed lacquer from a tall canister over his head.

He appears to the overture strains of 'In the Mood', his signature-tune for 30 years. On the Corn Exchange stage, a screen of pale blue satin hangs behind the band, so that one hardly notices the organ-pipes on the wall above. The opening band did not play beneath this screen, but only from one side of the stage. The applause continues after he has arrived at the microphone. His greeting is long and heartfelt. The band, in pale blue jackets and in black bow ties, wait behind their little desks, shouldering instruments of bright gold. The bassist and drummer wait, and the pianist with his back turned. The vocalists wait offstage, next to the switchboard. The dancers wait, massed below him, for their instructions.

He raises both his arms. He brings them smartly down in front of him, then pushes them out sideways as in the breaststroke. His body grows terribly alert, as if rods are being thrust at all angles through his coat. His head retreats into his collar, his cuffs, as he extends them with the trombones, are fully revealed. The music is instantaneous, confident like a bellow. Its tempo is beyond a doubt. He conducts with the energy of a one-man show, pointing, beckoning, flattening, lifting, waltzing up and down. A piece of hair is dislodged: he quickly replaces it.

190

'American Patrol': the B.29 bombers pass over Ipswich Corn Exchange. 'Gentle on my Mind' is sung by Larry Gretton. When Larry Gretton comes on, he does a funny walk. His voice is drawling and rich, from the Midlands' deep South. The three vocalists come and go from either side. Larry Gretton always does his funny walk. 'Pennsylvania 65000'; 'Snoopy and the Red Baron'; 'Wheels Cha-cha'. For the latter item, the bandleader joins all three vocalists in a movement reminiscent of skating uphill. Meanwhile, John Grainger, his road manager, has set up a little stall at the foot of the stage, selling Joe Loss record albums. While the vocalists have the microphone, he comes and signs autographs. He bends down first to ascertain the purchaser's name. He signs the record, holding it against his chest. He does not stint the message.

At the side of the hall, a lady in a green wild silk dress, disclosing large amounts of her collarbone and scapulae, opens her evening-bag. A lipstick is revealed, and a large, round, pink sponge. She peers closer inside. Her lips, silenced by the music, utters a stricken exclamation.

The message is carried swiftly among the dancers. The bandleader waves the music peremptorily to a stop.

'A lady's brown purse has been mislaid. A small brown ladies' purse. If anybody . . .'

A man, seated next to the lady, spots the purse under his chair, and sets off with it, through the waiting dancers towards the bandstand.

'Look at that! Oh, look! Thank you! Thank you so much, my dear Sir!'

In his dressing-room during the intermission, he takes off his trousers and places them carefully on top of his open portmanteau.

The band come to the door, one by one, to be paid. Their money is ready for them in pay packets. Sam Whatmough comes in last to receive his, and agrees that the audience, so far, is a little slow. When Sam has gone, Joe settles down, at last, to his own dinner. He sits at the dressing-table in his little striped bathrobe and his pointed suede shoes, drinking his pale green soup. He says he will be seeing his grand-children tomorrow.

191

'I've got rather lazy, you know,' he says. 'I'll show you how I used to be until a few years ago.' He puts down his soup spoon. He gets up and stands on tiptoe, his hands in his bathrobe pockets, so that his calf muscles bulge forth. 'Every night I used to spend three hours on the bandstand like this.'

For the second half, he wears a dark green jacket. The band wear jackets of light green. His back stiffens, his cuffs shoot out: 'Y Viva España' is followed by 'La Paloma Blanca', 'Hold Me Close', 'Tiko Tiko', 'Tie a Yellow Ribbon', 'Blanket on the Ground', 'Sweet Gipsy Rose'. And gradually, throughout the Corn Exchange, a feeling takes hold that it is stranger *not* to dance. More and more people drain away from the tables, leaving their pint glasses and their vanity-bags behind. The new dancers clasp one another, stare glassily in front of them and move off. The unskilled walk; the skilled rush to and fro recklessly, like speedboats among sailing craft. They dance together, or facing one another, nodding their heads up and down. An elderly couple in evening dress dance the Shake. A 12-year-old couple dance the Tango. All dance the Samba, waving their arms above their heads. The hands of the Corn Exchange clock pass 11.30; the two bars pull down their shutters. Now, the band plays 'In the Mood'. Below them, the floor is one single, concerted movement, proceeding rapidly clockwise: a straight-backed gentleman, a swan-necked lady and, clasped by his hand against her back, a Joe Loss record album.

The final item of the evening according to his programme is 'The Queen – in full'.

At a little after midnight, the crowd has vanished. The spotlights have died; the floor is empty. The waitresses are putting glasses on trays, talking about the good night it has been: £1.50 for dancing and the Joe Loss Orchestra. It was a pleasure to work late, they said. Colin the coach-driver moves rapidly along, picking up the music-stands, piling them one inside the other. Vic Mustard takes his coffee cup, as he promised, back through the foyer to the restaurant.

There is still a little queue at the corner of the stage. They are holding Joe Loss record albums, waiting for his auto-

192

graph. He stands above them, clutching an album against his chest. He does not stint the message. He takes another album and leans down towards the final couple in the queue.

'Who shall I sign it for? Cynthia? And Cyril? That's C.Y.N.T.H.I.A., is it? And C.Y.R.I.L.?'

Lionel Bart: How I Helped Bertrand Russell

Lionel Bart has been keeping busy. He intimates as much, walking into his office with a pained, unseeing, somnambulistic step. He was up all through the night, he says, writing songs. He is short but powerfully-built, dressed in precarious-looking clogs, a red neckerchief, coyly-knotted, and a great deal of bulging blue denim. A large denim cap is pulled down over eyes set remarkably close together. Their expression alternates between the dreamy abstraction and the devout glare of a Soho strip club bouncer.

Lionel Bart is bankrupt no longer. The composer who was once a byword for giddy heights of success has become newsworthy again for getting his chin just above water-level. Last year, he finished paying off debts of around £150,000, accruing largely from *Twang!*, a musical of a calamitousness still remembered 12 years after its premature death. His creditors satisfied, Bart is free to plot a comeback to the West End. He has also been signed up as solo singer by the record company which had arranged our interview, apparently without the great man's knowledge. 'You won't *believe* what he's got in the pipeline,' a publicist said exultantly, if ambiguously.

Life has changed since the days when *Oliver!* and four other Bart shows ran concurrently in London's West End. His home, during the bankrupt years, has been a small mews house in South Kensington with a plastic seagull perched enigmatically on the window ledge. His office is furnished with an upright piano; some sheet music, ostentatiously scored; photographs of Alma Cogan and Noël Coward ('To Li from Noël'); and editions of classical literature, already dissected to make Bart musicals, or awaiting possible future dissection. His personal retinue is equally modest. He is attended by a young man whose blue denim is better-fitted, whose clogs are white and who is sent out repeatedly on small and often humiliating errands.

With trembling hand, the composer drew towards him a desk diary with heavily-annotated pages, indicating his renaissance. 'Today at 12 noon, I'm due at the dentist. The management of a show will be meeting me at the dentist.' Here, a telephone buzzed under his desk. Bart answered it in a voice transformed to raging Cockney. ''Ello 'Erb! 'Ow are you, doll! 'Ow's it goin', doll? Yeah, okay. Tea? For you, doll, a bloody samovar full of tea!' He replaced the receiver. 'I've got musicians working here,' he explained, resuming the hushed, poetic tone.

He seems to find his early life wearisome to discuss. Poverty? He was one of a family of nine. Stamford Hill – he's a *real* Cockney. Not like that Michael Caine. He studied art at St Martin's, then joined he RAF and spent nine months painting a mural on the NAAFI wall. Then he was around Soho; he played the washboard in skiffle groups, met Tommy Steele. The memory of this epoch appears a particularly strong irritant. 'You can look all this up, you know mate. It's all ancient history.' From his desk drawer he took a half-bottle of brandy and drank, at one swallow, possibly a third.

From the success of *Oliver!* to the ignominy of *Twang!* Bart regrets nothing about his career. 'I set out to be a millionaire. I became one. I wrote songs with Richard Rodgers, after Hammerstein died. In the end, I told him he should write his own lyrics. I did a musical with Bertrand Russell. He rang me up and asked me to do it. I sent out to Christina Foyle for a truckload of his books. I didn't read them all the way through. I used to go down at weekends to his house in Wales. In the end, I had to tell him that his essay "Satan in Suburbia", which he'd written when he was only a young youth, had the same premise as a show called *Damned Yankees*.'

During the years of failure, he kept on writing. 'Just look in that drawer. You'll find four shows and about 400 songs.'

Things were bad, but he was helped by his many dear friends in show business. 'I've got 48 godchildren. Thirty-five nephews and nieces.' Why did Noël Coward like him so much? 'Because I was sophisticated at the same time as being genuine.' He says he never lost confidence in himself or thought he was written out. 'Nobody's ever written out. I'm not a butterfly,' he said, with demonstrable accuracy, 'but I never repeat myself. I never make love the same way twice.'

He is working on three shows, from sources freely borrowed, as of old. The first is based on *The Hunchback of Notre Dame*, the second on *Gulliver's Travels*, the third on the early life of Golda Meir. There is also a show in preparation called *Li*, based on his own early life. Li is the name he is known by to all his dear friends in the business.

He intends to be a millionaire again soon. For the present, he is hastening to the dentist. He wraps his blue denim body in a safari jacket, adjusts his cap to a more villainous angle and picks up a dowdy umbrella. 'This is the name of the book, mate. To succeed, you gotta want to. Get it? You gotta wanna ... Jerry,' he said to his attendant young man. 'Go back and get that extra packet of fags, will you? And that little comb of mine?'

'Sure,' replied the young man meekly.

Ivy Benson: Music From the Pie Factory

The new girl stood at the edge of the dance-floor, nervous in the daytime twilight, among the firmly-shuttered bars. She wore a blue blouse; a grey skirt, sensible shoes. She had travelled down that day from Bridlington to Caister, near Great Yarmouth, where the Ivy Benson All Girl Orchestra was appearing at the Holiday Centre. Before her audition, she was to hear a couple of numbers, then spend an hour 'blowing through' a repertoire not familiar from her college studies. Ivy spoke to her in the brisk yet comforting tones of Matron on the first day of term. 'Let's have a look at this, you lucky girl.' The recruit opened her music-case to disclose a saxophone like welded and clotted gold doubloons.

'I borrowed the money to buy it from my grandmother.'

'Never mind, love,' Ivy said. 'You'll soon earn it back.'

Ivy Benson is an inspirational figure. She is little, red-headed, with arms covered in bangles, a neat shape in see-through blouse that causes young men around the holiday camp to look at her with more than filial interest. She can seldom remain still, either on the bandstand or off it, flicking and twirling to an unheard tempo, occasionally giving a more extravagant backward skip and hop. She is 64 years old, and has been leading her All Girl Orchestra for 35 years. It is a long time to have spent as a novelty, providing jokes for bad comedians. Now, at last, it seems as if she may become a star.

She was born in Leeds 'on the eleventh of the eleventh', 1913. Her father was a musician who had played in both the Leeds Symphony Orchestra and the pit of the Leeds Empire, as well as in a variety act named the Ten Loonies. He put her

197

to learn the piano at the age of three. At the age of nine, she won a talent contest organised by Florrie Forde at the Empire, singing 'Yes, We Have No Bananas.' She learned the clarinet at the British Legion Club. She worked at the Montague Burton suit factory and saved half a crown each week to buy her first saxophone. She auditioned, and won a place in Edna Croudfoot's Rhythm Girls. There were numerous all girl bands in those days, but little musicianship was expected of them. 'All you had to do was tootle.'

It became her ambition to lead a girl orchestra who *could* play. Her opportunity came with the war, when depredations among the male bands forced the Mecca company to give her a residency at the Ritz ballroom in Manchester. For £9 per week, she provided musicians, music, instruments and clothes. It was the beginning of an unbroken struggle against discrimination expressed by poor payment, the contempt of musicians and other bandleaders, even arrangers who provided scores with deliberate mistakes. She has always been her own agent, organising bookings, costumes, auditions, even training girl musicians from the very beginning. 'I took a girl from a pie factory once, and made her into a bass guitarist.'

There have been numerous casualties. Especially when they were playing at American bases in Germany, the girls were always running away with GIs. This is why a girl band can never be as good as a male band, Ivy says: their attention is only ever 50 per cent on the music. One member of her present band has been with her for 15 years, another for 10 years. The rest are very young. The bass-guitarist, with her T-shirt, and cloudy yellow hair, is only 17. At the edge of the ballroom sits a German youth, politely predatory, who has followed the vocalist across from the Continent. 'I had one girl – beautiful piano player she was – she said "I just want to go across and have a word with Skip". I've not seen her from that day to this.' In Germany recently, as befits the age, a girl from the band ran off with a girl friend.

Ivy has brought her 84-year-old father to Caister with her for the summer. They live in a self-catering flat, provided by the management, with an archetypal grey poodle named Pepe. She enjoys the Caister season, despite the Hokey Cokey she had to play for a company in wheelchairs, and despite Friday nights, which are a little rough after the kitchen staff have been paid. Her hobby is learning languages. She likes to bet on the horses, and is drawn against her will to the fruit machine in the Neptune ballroom.

For the first time in 35 years, the band has made an LP record. 'I've sacrificed two marriages; I've had four major operations; I sometimes ask myself why, for God's sake, do I do it? I'm sure I'll die penniless. But I don't care.' She gave a sudden little skip, with her handbag on her arm. 'I don't care at all. I don't care a damn.'

The Café de Paris: Faces Older,
Feet as Light as Ever

You enter the Café de Paris, like Edward VIII and Mrs Simpson used to, down a staircase disguised as the entrance to a Caliph's harem. London was once full of such staircases, lighting the rich and indiscreet to their pleasure haunts underground. Here, in Coventry Street, remains the last unclosed loophole into catacombs of glamorous night, never more alluring than at three o'clock on a weekday afternoon. You descend, through tent-like, parchment folds, into a twilight region where the Ladies' room is called *Mesdames*, and the walls were lined with painted footmen, proffering dusty gilt candelabra. Somewhere beyond, at the volume of a football crowd, a Tango is just beginning.

It was a faithful reconstruction of the SS *Lusitania*'s Palm Court lounge that opened here in 1924, originally named the Elysée supper club. Twin stairways, twisting to an oval floor, served at the first to exhibit only the Café's own clientele and, later at night, the greatest names from the age of supper club cabaret. Below, massed between the two bottom steps, sat the white-bibbed orchestra of Ambrose, Roy Fox or Sid Roy and his Lyricals. A commemorative plaque records the date – the very time: 9.30 – when a German bomb scored a direct hit among the shirt-fronts and 'Snakehips' Johnson, the orchestra-leader, perished.

The Café's daily tea-dance – London's last surviving one – begins at 2.30. No-one is there at the very start but a few unaccompanied males. Each table round the balcony has a red-shaded lamp, a tea-tray and a single spectator, anchored aloft by one elbow, watching the descent once taken by Noel

Coward, Marlene Dietrich, and Liberace, listening intently as if to catch the echoes of their ovations. On the quilted ceiling close above, balloons wait in wrought-iron clasps to be let down on the heads of the evening crowd. There are also old-fashioned propellor fans which, in a few minutes, slowly begin to rotate.

Dulcie sits up here by herself, two or three afternoons a week. She is expensively-coiffed, hazily-scented and, like most daytime customers, anxious not to discuss her identity. A piece of black chiffon crumples and twists inside her hand. Let's just say she has a little part-time job near Great Portland Street. Her eyes, in tinted glasses, search the darkness, wide with their anxiety to smile.

'I've had some nice partners here. One gentleman from Seattle – several nice foreign gentlemen, in fact. But most who come aren't the sort I like to mix with, if you know what I mean. A lot of waiters from the restaurants come in during their afternoon break. The trouble is, you can't be friends with a man these days without him expecting you to be immoral. I've had two proposals of marriage here, but not from my sort of man. One pot of tea, and they all want the ultimate thing.'

Dulcie is a widow. Her husband took her to all the tea-dances once. 'The Savoy – Strand Palace. Oh, he was a handsome chap. Six feet tall. And I've got the most wonderful son – he's six feet tall as well. Not one of those longhaired things. He's always had an executive appearance. I don't tell him I come here in the afternoons. He'd think it was too degrading.'

At 3.30, the dance band records are replaced by a piano quartet, playing behind gilt music stands that resemble faucets on the bath of an Edwardian millionaire. In the balcony, another habitué finds his usual seat among the shadows. He is a retired Naval officer who spends the morning at one of his two clubs and comes in here each afternoon for tea. A confirmed bachelor, he hastens to say. 'They'll never get me, old boy!' A little later, a figure goes to sit by him. His fingers creep round a shoulder with a thin strap.

A dark-skinned woman, thumbing a bass guitar,

summarises with husky disinterest those numerous reasons why the lady is a tramp. The floor is now full of circular movement, extravagant but careful, like speedboats in some precision display. One bald man, urging his partner zestfully backwards, contrives to bend a leg outward in a bow shape. Another bald man and his partner begin to hop across unseen stepping-stones. Another, perceiving the end of the number, drives his partner to a standstill with so many supernumerary feints and flourishes that her yellow hair flies up and down like a lid.

These dancers retire to chairs and tables close to the foot of the staircase where Marlene Dietrich and Noel Coward once concluded their descent. Hereabouts is now the preserve of the Café's Monday and Friday regulars – the women who change their dresses to dance; the men who have troubled to shine their shoes. It is undoubtedly a clique, difficult to penetrate since its members have been acquainted for years, back through other halls such as the Astoria and the Paramount. Even when all are dancing, something in the pattern of the chairs attests this to be private property.

Doris Gordon comes up regularly from her flat in Lewisham: she, for one, does not mind giving her name, or her age. She is 65. She has close-fitting ash-blonde hair, impeccable posture and a laugh like a string of bubbles. All her life she has been crazy about ballroom dancing. Even World War 2, when she joined the fire service, seemed to Doris to be one long dance in uniform. If the siren went, they used to dash back to Control clinging to the open engine they called the old red pump.

Doris is a widow. She has been married twice, and would not at all object to trying it again were it not for her second husband's rather complicated will. So on Tuesdays, Doris goes to the Rivoli, Crofton Park: on Wednesdays, to the Riverdale Centre in Lewisham. As many of the Café de Paris regulars turn up there, too, she seldom wants for a partner. 'They all know me. The face may be getting old but the feet are as light as ever.'

'This is life to me now. From Friday right through to

Monday, I don't see anybody. I live in a tower block, sixth floor – the neighbours don't want to know. I used to keep in touch with my widowed friends, but you don't like to, do you, the phone bills are so high. This is always a tonic to me. I *am* lonely,' she admitted with a little laugh. 'But tonight I'll go back on that three minutes past six train, and I shan't mind the empty flat. I'll settle in perfectly happy for the evening.'

The supply of male dancers within the group is limited. The uninvited sit picking their gold bracelets apart from the wrist-tag given out by the handbag depository; cardigans over chairs make a wall against unwelcome advances. A lone male with corrugated black hair, formerly in the balcony, has reappeared at floor level. Table by table, he seems to be stalking something through the twilight.

Muriel happens to be sitting this one out. She would rather sit and watch, she says, than walk round the floor with an indifferent dancer. Muriel, too, is a widow, prone to that fond trance which eventually fills up the cracks of bereavement. Her husband was an accountant. She met him on her first day at work – he showed her how to use the decimal point. He's gone, so she must live again: a little. 'I sometimes meet a friend in here.' And elsewhere? The question earns a playful slap across the wrist.

The quartet has now embarked on a Rumba. 'That gentleman over there is the manager of a club. That little man, going to and fro, comes in every afternoon for an hour. He works locally, and takes his lunch and tea-break all together.

'Well – my friend's gone, so I think I'll be off.' In the footsteps of Marlene Dietrich, Muriel began to ascend the staircase, carefully balancing the precious burden of her hair. As she climbed higher, an emboldened voice spoke up. 'Did you hear that?' she gasped. 'He says he likes my hairstyle!'

At the edge of the floor, Una sits watching from her usual table. She is 72, tiny and clear-skinned, in a pearlised costume and silver grey beads. She still loves to dance, although there are not many partners to suit her these days. 'Two have died – I must have worn them out. Still, I like to come for the music, the life. The antics. The Waltz, I like. The Tango, not the Rumba. My legs haven't got the spring any more. Do you feel sorry for me?'

The other love of Una's life was motorbikes. She used to be a dispatch-rider for the Cable and Wireless company. Until 12 years ago, she still had her Matchless 350.

She has often tried to persuade her husband to come with her to the dance. He could have tea and watch if he didn't feel like dancing. He prefers to spend the afternoon at the library. 'The other thing I love is swimming – but he won't go into the sea. So I have to swin alone.'

Michael is a young City insurance broker with ambitions in competitive dancing. Twice a week he comes here to partner Rose who, despite a difference in their ages, has taught him more in four months than most studio teachers could in a year. Michael and Rose are the first to take the floor and the last to leave it – he matador-straight, she, in orange frills, lying back like somebody levitated. The sternest critic in the clique by the staircase is forced to admit they are immaculate together. An Italian girl came down from the balcony once, interrupting them to present Rose with a flower.

Rose, who would prefer to be called 'a professional person', holds the highest amateur ballroom trophy, the Alex Moor 10 – Dance Marathon Award, with honours. That was how she built herself up after a car accident had put her into a wheelchair for three years. 'I nearly died – in fact, I *was* dead. God decided to save me, though I wasn't much loved then. Ever since, I've tried to do a little bit of good, if I can, somewhere every day.'

The quartet strikes up again. Rose lies back in Michael's arms. 'I love this place,' she says. 'I'd like to die on this floor and be cremated and have my ashes scattered here.'

Sandie West: I Will Fight Back

Sandie West is a cabaret singer on Tyneside. The region stretches in a ghost-grey plain below the back garden where Sandie is shutting out her three dogs, preparatory to an evening appearance in Newcastle. A group of plaster gnomes huddle together against the colliery wind that blows up over South Moor.

Working men's clubs in north-eastern England are as numerous as pit-head lights – 3,000 between Morpeth and Middlesborough alone. Sandie West performs in an average of four each week, often at two the same night. Her hasband Ray drives her and sets up her sound equipment. Her usual fee is £20 – something less than the rate for a mediocre comedian.

Sandie West's real name is Gwen lves. She is a slender woman in a tall wig, her complexion between the curls flushed with nervousness and with a skin allergy that has not stopped her from accepting club work. At one place, she had to sing in reading glasses to conceal her swollen eyes. Ironically, she says, that proved to be one of her more successful nights. The club welcomed her, despite her allergy and reading glasses, as if she was Shirley Bassey. Many other clubs make her feel like something less.

'You know when you're doing all right – that's when they're not walking out. Around Sunderland are the hardest clubs. If they don't like you, they start selling housey tickets during your spot. They'll start playing pool while you're singing, right near to the stage. Usually I'll lose my temper and think "I *will* fight back." It happened while I was singing "Make Me

An Island". My husband said, "Eh, you were biting the words off in that one".'

At working men's clubs the entertainers often face conditions which working men themselves might not tolerate. For a dressing room Sandie is frequently shown to a nail in the wall. She is accustomed to changing into stage clothes among piles of beer crates or in cubbyholes so small that she literally cannot turn round. Often she will be in earshot of the Committee Room, and a club chairman debating which acts in the cabaret shall be paid off at half-time for half-price. A comedian, thus discharged, may wonder how a coal-miner would regard such a proposal.

Sandie's professional career has been dogged by ill luck which she now considers irreversible. As a teenager, she was noticed by the bandleader Lou Praeger, who promised to feature her in his next television series but died before he could do so. Her bungalow is scattered with miniature trophies, won in talent contests at Butlin's holiday camps. Talent scouts have liked her voice; then, always, they fall ill or neglect to telephone back. For 10 years, she has regularly passed the audition for the talent show *Opportunity Knocks* and has regularly been left out of the current series. She relieves her disappointment by writing poems, one of which she sent to Hughie Green, the show's lovable compere. Back came the form for another audition.

Fame would mean, above all, the luxury of a full orchestra. For the present, she is accompanied by just an organist and drummer, different at every club. The organist is frequently unable to read the music score Sandie hands him, so he simply follows her, changing key as she does. At one club, the organist was blind, and she had to sit beside him, calling out key-changes. Experience has taught her, among other things, that it is unwise to complain or take the mickey. Club chairmen are the most sensitive and volatile of men.

Her stage preparations are not elaborate. She has two dresses, one yellow, one blue gingham, both made by herself, and three operational wigs. Tonight she chooses the yellow dress, although the hem is still unfinished. Her husband Ray

206

drives her from Carmel Road, Stanley, down into Newcastle through indigenous fog and rain. In the city centre, their car bumps another. While the drivers confer, Sandie goes ahead on foot, carrying her bright red suitcase.

The Hofbrauhaus beer keller is not busy on Tuesday nights. At any other time, we are told, 1000 people would be in; tonight, vacant tables and benches for 1000 extend into cavernous gloom. A Tyrolean band, villainously bare-legged, is providing oom-pah music for a score or so of scattered roisterers.

Sandie is greeted near the bar by her agent, Herbie Butchert, a pink-faced, fragrantly-perfumed, smiling man. His partner in the firm happens to be compere at the Hofbrauhaus, exhorting the scanty customers to swing their arms, see-saw back and forth on their benches or rise for a Conga interlude which renders the whole place temporarily deserted.

Sandie West is billed as 'surprise cabaret'. Her dressing room lies behind a substantial-looking antique door. The size of a generous sentry-box, it contains lockers for the band, a selection of hula hoops, bubble-blowing mixture in bottles, a blonde wig, a broken mirror, the compere's trousers and the heavy stopcocks of the central-heating system. As dressing-rooms go, it is not the very worst. 'We had a five-piece band changing in here the other night,' the compere remarks. Sandie, unperturbed, opens her case and spreads a sheet of plastic on the floor to protect her yellow skirts.

The performance does not go as badly as she feared after her three-minute band call with the Tyrolean organist among the central-heating pipes. Her style is Country and Western, her manner self deprecatory, her voice as warm and strong and accurate as many better-known singers. Towards the end, the band's exposed knees are bumping up and down in a less Teutonic manner than before.

Her big finish is 'Keep On Singing', a number that reminds her of her father. It was he who first encouraged her to sing, at the age of eight, back in Upton-on-Severn. The organist comes in too fast, and is dissuaded by an arm, vigorously shaken behind her back. The lyric echoes what her father always told her. 'Keep on singing, just keep on singing. You'll be a star some day.'

At the end, she bows her tall, curly head. Herbie Butchert's partner jumps on to the stage, levering up the thin applause with his arm, shouting into the microphone. 'Thank you, Miss Sandie West ladies and gentlemen, come on! Sandie West! Thank you, come on ladies and gentlemen, Sandie West, Sandie West ladies and gentlemen, come on! Thank you! Sandie West!'

'You'll notice she put in a lot of Country stuff,' said Herbie, her agent, glancing benignly around the untenanted benches. 'She knows they're looking for that kind of thing here.' So long as a German beer keller can contemplate putting on a Country and Western night, there is always another chance for Sandie West.

New Faces: TV's Star Chamber

There is a television monitor set in the producer's room, faithfully transmitting everything that happens below on the studio-floor. Next to rehearse is a 15-year-old boy, playing a grand piano. The boy's suit is heather-coloured and the piano is white; his image shifts and slips a little as different camera angles are tested. He plays the 'Warsaw Concerto', then he plays 'Dizzy Fingers', the theme from *Love Story*, Chopin's 'Impromptu', then he plays 'Honky-Tonk Train', smiling from time to time. He has a ready smile upon which the whiskers of adolescence may faintly be detected. His name is Freddy Anthony: in this edition of the *New Faces* TV talent show he will be the youngest contestant.

The show is recorded on Tuesday for transmission the following Saturday. The six acts have already spent two days in Birmingham, staying at the Holiday Inn across the plaza from the ATV studios, getting the feel of what, for most of them, will be their first appearance on television. Nevertheless, the morning is a jittery time. Singers pay frequent visits to the nurse for throat medicine; the stand-up comics loom around, mutttering distractedly to themselves. It is the humane practice of Les Cocks the producer to allow them, during rehearsal, to tell all the blue jokes they wish. But for the show itself, even ambiguous material must be expunged.

On this very subject, Les Cocks is conferring in the producer's room with his scriptwriter Phil Parsons.

'It's just here,' Parsons murmured, 'Where Lew says "I'd like to do Raquel Welch . . . I'd like to do Raquel Welch but she won't let me." I've mentioned it to him. But he does say it

209

humorously, you know, like Bernie Winters.'

New Faces is an astonishingly successful television talent show, networked by ATV. Its success is sharpened by its having arisen from no new idea but from a theme as ancient as exhibitionism itself. For years, every television company has dreamed of such a programme, popular as a human spectacle yet genuinely influential in the promotion of new entertainers. And for years there has been only *Opportunity Knocks* on Thames Television, presented by Hughie Greene. *New Faces*, after its first series, could claim an equal audience of some 40 million at the Saturday evening peak viewing-time.

In form the two shows are quite different. *Opportunity Knocks* is avowedly an amateur affair of bagpipe bands and faltering sopranos, judged by the sentimental gauge of studio applause – registered on an instrument called The Clapometer – but providing a forum, above all, for Hughie Greene's own sententious personality. *New Faces*, however, is for professional and semi-professional entertainers. All its contestants must belong to the Musicians' Union or to Equity, the actors' union. The judging is done, not by a Clapometer but by a four-man panel, recruited from show-business or its fringes, awarding marks for 'presentation', 'content' and 'star quality'.

It is this panel, as much as any individual discovery, which gives *New Faces* such a hold upon its 40 million viewers. Its transmission in the early evening tends to catch families at home all at once and to bind them into panels of their own, hotly challenging the judgement given on the screen. The public controversy over the high marks awarded a child singer called Melandra Newman became front-page news in the *Sun* newspaper. And the memory still haunts the production-team of a ventriloquist who threw his voice into an orange monkey, though at times it did seem as if the monkey was throwing its voice into the man. Clifford Davis, the show's most fastidious panellist, awarded the ventriloquist no marks out of 10.

'Actually,' said Phil Parsons, the scriptwriter, 'he was

210

billed as "Ken Graham and Family". His wife did a vent' act as well. He told me before the show that his wife wouldn't be appearing because she wasn't such a good vent' act as he was.'

'He got work at all the big clubs after that, you know,' Les Cocks said. 'He was on at the *Talk of the North*, the *Talk of the Midlands*, the *Talk of the South*. All of them except the *Talk of the Town*.'

'But you raved about the monkey, didn't you Les?' Phil Parsons added. 'You thought the monkey was great.'

Les Cocks is a pug-like, friendly man with straight silver hair whose appearance betrays little of his airless, windowless, complicated life. Single-handed, he conducts the 14,000 auditions which go to make up one series of *New Faces*. All over Britain in the auditioning season, Les Cocks sits in hired cinemas and halls and clubs, watching an interminable, at times unbelievable, cavalcade. An elderly lady in a fairy costume; a ventriloquist performing with the aid of a dead fish; a man who exhorted his silent mynah bird to 'say what you said to Russell Harty' – these are some of the entertainers to whom Les Cocks has had to break it that their act would not do. His private life is filled with would-be performers, playing musical instruments to him down the telephone or hastening beside him, holding cassette-recorders up to his ear. One woman recorded her son as he sang in his bath, and sent in the tape, explaining that the youth was too shy to audition on his own account. The tape was extremely splashy. Through all this, Les Cocks somehow remains freshly-shaved and rubicund, ever hopeful that something good must turn up next. Only when a stand-up comic is telling jokes, the producer's lips may be seen moving silently in unison.

On the monitor-screen in front of him, Freddy Anthony the boy pianist has finished playing 'Honky-Tonk Train'. He rises from the piano, picks up a grey bowler hat and, turning his face to the ceiling, he balances the hat on its brim at the bridge of his nose. With several little jerks of his head, he makes the hat rotate in a full circle – indicated by the movement of a spot on the brim – and, finally, tip backwards on to

211

his head. This accomplished, he bows to left and to right again, smiling his ready smile.

Les Cocks, in his room, is delighted by this unexpected finale.

'We found out he was brought up in circus – his mother and father do a speciality act, and they've taught him balancing. I think that bit's great,' Les Cocks says. 'I told him to leave that bit in.'

The contestants sit among the empty audience seats, watching as the studio-floor is made ready.

The rewards will be great – and not only for the winner. Each Saturday, a growing number of variety-agents, club bookers and record company men tune into *New Faces*, hoping to beat the others to another Sweet Sensation or another Nicky Martin, perhaps the most successful of the programme's numerous alumni. The winner will appear again on a special winner's show; should the viewing audience vote for a different act, this will be brought back on a viewers' winners' show. Simple association with *New Faces* can generate work: at best in the programme's own tours and seaside shows; at worst in better billing at one's own club appearances. But it is at the moment when hope should be highest that hope is often lowest. In these early afternoon hours, how much preferable to be one of those carefree men with long poles, pushing lamps among the forest of metalwork in the ceiling.

The ATV studio staff, to their credit, understand this. Floor-managers, with small instruments in their ears, listen sympathetically to anxieties over the positioning of this or that. Phil Parsons the scriptwriter moves about, his checked coat full of lozenges for ever-failing voices, and wardrobe and makeup departments play an indulgent, sedative part.

Every *New Faces* bill includes at least two pop groups. This afternoon, a white band called Rabbit is watching the rehearsal of a black band called Tropical Harmony. Rabbit are small and dark and Latin-looking, from Lancashire, sitting with a number of friends and relations, anxiously passing

212

cigarettes and sweets among themselves. Tropical Harmony close their act with a limbo dancer. He passes under the pole, touching the ground with his shoulderblades, his toes moving busily and tinily like centipedes. The floor staff all applaud loudly. The members of Rabbit look on with glum faces.

Their manager joins them: a pink, portly child in drooping moustaches and a waistcoat.

'Where's Liz?' he asks.

'Washing her hair.'

'Liz?'

'Yes, she's gone to have it blow-waved.'

Elsewhere, Mitch T. Mitchell, a male ballad-singer stops to exchange a word with Jeri Benton, female ballad-singer. Both of them – and also the beautician whom Jeri has brought with her – have hair lacquered into spun yellow fabric, woven stiffly beside the two men's ears; dressed in weighty scrolls which encircle Jeri Benton's face like the cowl of a monk. They are examining a bottle of ultramarine liquid in Mitch T. Mitchell's hand.

'It's for me streaks,' he explains.

Higher up in the rows, a slender, quiet, wispy, wistful-looking man sits by himself. He is Trevor Wallis, the stand-up comic.

Higher still, Freddy Anthony sits with his bowler hat on his knees. On one side of him sits his father and on the other side, his mother. Next to his father sits his agent: a military-looking man. There is a faint smile, reminiscent of his balancing-act, on the boy pianist's face.

The atmosphere quickens with the arrival on the floor of the programme's compere, Derek Hobson. He is well-known, to Midland audiences at least, as a newscaster on local ATV. He wears a jacket of cream and light blue tartan, dark blue shirt, a cream-coloured tie, large-knotted and decorated with floral sprigs; pale blue trousers and black slip-on shoes upon which he moves with a curious, rolling gait, like a Wild West gunslinger.

A final dress-rehearsal is carried out, linked by Derek

213

Hobson in the judges' alcove, at his desk beneath the score-boards. At a longer adjoining desk, two members of the week's panel are already in their places: Martin Jackson, the television editor of the *Daily Mail*, and the record producer Jimmy Henny. In this run-through, scrupulous impartiality must somehow be maintained. Nothing in Derek Hobson's continuity must imply that one or other contestant has taken an even hypothetical lead over the rest.

For Lew Lewis, comedian and impressionist, the big chance has come quickly. He is a stout young man in a yellow suit and blue shirt, wearing a yellow guitar. A week ago, he resigned from the Royal Air Force after 15 years' service. 'The only way you can get on in there is by creeping. I wasn't going to do that. I had more O-Levels than my Flight-commander.' His large grin disappeared for a moment. It returned, valiant and toothy, above his plump velvet bow tie.

Mitch T. Mitchell, the ballad-singer, cherishes fewer illusions. He has appeared with a show band and has worked professionally in America; his blue blouse and lighter blue jump suit has seen some little service. The song which he will sing on the programme he has already recorded. 'I'm not being big-headed – believe me I'm not – but I don't regard this as an appearance on a talent show. My record comes out next week. Forty million people watch this show. If 20,000 of them buy my record, I'm in the Top 50.'

Jeri Benton wears a gown composed of her shoulderblades, her spinal column and prominent bosom, separated by some thin sashes of a grey luminous substance. Her fingernails are pointed and extremely red. She is to sing 'I Who Have Nothing'. Her face, within the aperture between her golden curls, looks anxious.

'I can't remember those flipping words,' she murmurs to Lew Lewis. 'I've been singing that song for 10 years and I *still* can't remember the flipping words.'

Before the recording, Les Cocks and his production team collect in one of the green rooms off the main vestibule. There are pieces of fried chicken, cheese cubes on sticks, and various intoxicants. And the third of the four judges has arrived. It is policy to have a funny man on the panel to render expert advice to aspirant funny men. Some weeks, it is Arthur Askey. Other weeks, it is Ted Ray. This week it is Ted Ray.

He sits on a chair in the centre of the green room. His hair is white and his legs are small, with socks of pale grey. His face is round and rich, as if suffused by the humour of all the jokes he knows. His voice has the resonance of a wisecrack capping all others, even though he is at the moment talking normally about golf. It is as if impending wise-cracks teem like spirits in the air round his head. One feels the urge to laugh and applaud, even as he desires the girl to replenish the glass in his hand.

The last judge to arrive is Tony Hatch the composer, most dread of all *New Faces* panellists, both for the influence that he wields in the music business and for the candour – many say, unkindness – of his remarks. He makes a point of missing all rehearsals in order to keep his mind fresh. He is of modest height, dressed in a black and red checked sweater, carrying cigarettes and a smart gold lighter, and yet, for all that, still faintly resembling the sort of boy at school whom everybody else used to kick.

Derek Hobson, the compere, is deeply occupied in memorising some cards on which the scriptwriter has typed biographical details for each of the acts.

'There could be something here for you, Ted,' he suggests. 'one of the acts is a golfer.'

'Which one?'

'One of the comics. He won the Bud Flanagan Trophy.'

'The Bud Flanagan Trophy!' cries Ted Ray in his comedian's twang. 'What's that? A fur coat?'

Outside the green room, Trevor Wallis sits by himself on the long plastic bench. He has unveiled his stand-up comic routine for the first time at the final rehearsal, then gone by himself for a coffee in the ATV canteen. He works for an office-supply firm in Bolton.

His manager approaches, with an auburn toupee gingerly perched on the top of his head.

'Here's a telegram from Bruce,' the manager says cheerfully.

215

Trevor's hand shakes as he studies the coloured greetings telegram.

'How's your Mum? Have you had a word with her, telephone-wise?'

'Aye – just briefly, like.'

'They said you was very good,' the manager continues heartily. 'And clean, you know, which is ideal. Hey – we just went into a special room, with Mister Hatch and all.'

'Aye?'

'Had ourselves a whisky, we did.'

'Aye?'

'Anyway, how are you feeling, old son?'

'You're either living or dying, aren't you?' Trevor answers bleakly.

The studio audience has now been admitted, and are now receiving their instructions from the 'warm-up man'. He is a club comedian named Keith, whose qualification for this particular job is that he has extremely large, flat, broad, loud hands. With these he instils into the audience the principle that they must break into clapping upon the slightest signal from himself. Keith looks tough but his voice has a fond, lingering cadence; he wears a grey suit, with pronounced rear slits, from the pocket of which he brings Polo mints and Rolo chocolates to offer to those members of the audience who seem most restive. It is necessary work, but frustrating. Keith complains that nobody knows him as anything but 'Keith'.

The contestants line up behind Derek Hobson inside the studio door for the opening sequence. It is a moment, despite all their acclimatisation, of pure panic, as the huge lights descend on them. Jeri Benton murmurs some words to herself, touching her silver, rolled curls. She has changed her dress since rehearsals. This one is green. It gapes. But is it right? Their managers are now ordered to the side. Rabbit's manager forgets that he is a manager and kisses the girl singer in her rabbit fur pinafore. 'Do your best: you can't do more.' The title music and announcement can be heard, then fierce applause from inside the studio. A camera dashes towards them, adjusting each face to a smile of ghastly radiance.

216

The show itself is a little masterpiece of television's particular hallucination. It is the paradox of the television studio that nobody really sees anything save through monitor screens, which makes them no more privileged than the viewers at home. The judges are hidden from the performance by the scoreboard: they view each act through small monitors on their desk. The performers see nothing, except by monitor, from their prison in the wings. The audience perceives the illusion and its imbalance, yet is forced to condone it by the crashing hands of Keith the 'warm-up man'. Only the camera is omniscient, binding blindnesses into sight, cutting back and sweeping sideways. It elevates the little judging alcove into something Olympian. It stretches the little sets into long, glittering cloisters from which glittering talents must surely now come forth.

Rabbit, the Lancashire pop group, are the first to receive judgement. Tony Hatch remarks acidly that their harmonies were off-key. Martin Jackson and Jimmy Henny express guarded approval, befitting their uncontroversial status. Ted Ray declares that, if they are called Rabbit, he would be reluctant to put two of them together.

Each panelist in turn registers a number of out of 10 for 'presentation', 'content' and 'star quality', to be computed on the board above Derek Hobson's head. 'A total', Hobson says, 'of 88.'

Lew Lewis, the RAF boy, is next. The first three on the panel do not like his comedy or his impressions. They find his face appealing. His face appears on the monitor-set as they say this, smiling with a terrible geniality.

It remains for Ted Ray to comment.

'Arthur?' says Derek Hobson.

'Who the hell's Arthur?' cries the comic in anguish.

He looks down at his notes as if he cannot quite read them. 'Well, unfortunately,' he jokes, 'this boy didn't tell us which impression was which . . .'

Rabbit are now sitting around a small sofa in the wings, watching as Lew Lewis's marks appear on the board.

'A total', Derek Hobson says, 'of 68.'

'That Mickie Most slated us, didn't he?' whispers one member of Rabbit to another.

'That was Tony Hatch.'

'Oh.'

As a further complication, the boy pianist Freddy Anthony does not appear in person, being below the legal age for performing at night. His act has been pre-recorded; he himself is shown only during the judging, holding the hat which he has balanced, smiling his ready smile.

The panel is captivated – although more by the piano-playing than by the balancing of the hat. Tony Hatch congratulates the boy on his manager. Martin Jackson and Jimmy Henny are eulogistic in their turn. The camera moves to Ted Ray.

'Arthur?' says Derek Hobson.

'You're ruining my life!' Ted Ray cries.

Lew Lewis has now joined Rabbit in the wings. His face is wet with perspiration glueing his hair against his forehead. He has not appreciated that Ted Ray was just joking. 'What did he want to say that for?' Lew Lewis gasps. 'He couldn't tell the impressions apart!'

He looks balefully at the smiling face of Freddy Anthony on the monitor screen as very high marks are registered on behalf of every panellist. 'A total,' Derek Hobson said, 'of 102.'

'What did he want to balance that thing on his nose for anyway?' Lew Lewis murmurs. 'Bit like a ruddy performing seal if you ask me.'

The boy pianist himself arrives to join them in the wings.

'Well done mate,' Lew Lewis says, patting him between the shoulderblades.

On the monitor, Jeri Benton is now smiling uncertainly between her silver curls as Tony Hatch attacks her rendering of 'I Who Have Nothing' for its 'pseudo-funky beat'. Martin Jackson's opinion that 'with a few jars inside you, she'd be tremendous' does little to moderate the brutality of the adjudication.

'A total,' Derek Hobson says, 'of 81.'

In the wings, they are adversaries no longer. They are united, in hatred of Tony Hatch.

'– and have you seen *his* club act?' Lew Lewis gasps in fury.

They look on in real concern as Trevor Wallis, the comedian, appears on the monitor-screen, insouciant and shy in his white suit.

"Feller cooms out of a wedding-reception,' Trevor begins unsmilingly. 'And he's sick all over a Pekinese. He looks down at it and says, "By – I don't remember eatin' that." '

The only judge who matters here is Ted Ray – his name is remembered this time by Derek Hobson. The camera alights upon the veteran's rosy face, whose eyes, a little moistly, return its scrutiny.

'His timing,' Ted Ray said, 'was – excellent.'

'– 'Very fair man, Ted Ray is,' Jeri Benton whispers emotionally.

'A total,' Derek Hobson said, 'of 88.'

Mitch T. Mitchell wins praise and high marks for his ballad – 10 out of 10 in one instance. As the marks go up on the board, the girl from Rabbit slips an arm around Freddy Anthony's shoulders. 'You could still have cracked it, kid,' she whispers.

'A total,' Derek Hobson says, 'of 100.'

Tropical Harmony, the black band, have been chosen to play last. Their opening song changes to the limbo dance, and the boy with a spiked bar in his mouth, wriggling on his back. But, if you are manifestly not the winner, to play last is to play with a sense of time running out.

'And if you think,' Ted Rays says, 'that I'm going to tell that gag about getting under toilet doors . . .'

'A total of 88,' Derek Hobson says.

On the board above Hobson's head, among the six names, Freddy Anthony's name begins to flash on and off. The others, assembled on the podium, turn and congratulate him with warm, bleak smiles. The applause, orchestrated by Keith the warm-up man's hands, grows still louder. The boy advances from the podium into the spotlight, bowing to right and left. On the monitor screens high and low, he stands alone in the spotlight as the programme credits arise in front of him, and receives the ovation with his slight, faintly-whiskered smile.

The moment of fame is brief. In another moment the lights have gone out. Studio workmen are ripping out the scoreboard and desk and replacing them with the scenery for ATV's nightly soap opera, *Crossroads*.

Part Four
Outings and Adventures

Radio Fun in Roswell

Close to Albuquerque, New Mexico, as we hung motionless on the streaming white trans-America road, the voice on the radio-dial faded and returned in yet another different form. The voice, which identified itself as that of Radio KBIM, Roswell, seemed to belong to a tetchy, rather intoxicated old gentleman.

'Okay,' it said, 'now I got two tickets here for the Late Show Friday night at the Del Monte Drive-in here in Roswell to see *Twins of Evil* and *Hands of the Ripper*, both rated 'R', which I'm gonna give away to the first person who walks in to KBIM with a grilled cheese sandwich. With two grilled cheese sandwiches,' the old gentleman amended. 'One for me, one for Parker.'

Roswell proves to be a tiny town, huddled round a Main Street of gas pumps and motel-signs, in desert country famous for having developed the Atom Bomb. Its only landmarks are a clothing store with a life-size horse on the roof, and an old-fashioned military academy. Its only claim to orginality – our reason for pursuing that tetchy old gentleman's voice – is that Roswell, with a population of less than 20,000, is served by five different radio stations.

It is less strange if you consider the categories into which American radio, as American life, ruthlessly divides. Of the five Roswell stations, only two are directly in combat: KBIM and KKAT, both designated for continuous Rock music. Each of the other three may thus guiltlessly claim to be foremost in its field. KRSY is the Country and Western station and KSWS the 'easy listening' one. Finally there is a Spanish language station for the Mexican populace named, with some appropriateness, KRDD.

Along the sunny Main Street, dominated by 'The Store with the Horse on Top', Jim King commences his calls upon Roswell's advertisers. Jim King is manager of KBIM. A pleasant, clean, clerkly man he is celebrated in the town both as announcer at the station and also for having married its proprietor's daughter. He is accepted everywhere. As he passes, even the bullet-proof visor of the drive-in bank can produce a ghostly 'Hi Jim'.

King's next call is a stationery store. 'Hi Zeke,' he greets the man behind the counter. 'Is Thelbert in?'

Thelbert is out, but pleasant moments pass nonetheless.

'What's new?' the manager – and News Editor – of KBIM inquires.

'The radio isn't on,' says one of the ladies behind the counter.

'I turned it off,' the other lady says. 'I didn't want to hear all of that cowboy mess,' she adds loyally, referring to the Country station KRSY.

'Let me just tune it in to the right channel there.' King reaches up to the set on the wall. After a moment, out of its loud-speaker, a stern voice says, 'KBIM First Team News!'

There is a fanfare. The voice resumes:

'Police reported no burglarisation in Roswell last night . . .'

Zeke says, 'When are you going to let me put a good typewriter in that front office of yours, Jim?'

King answers that he'll think it over; meanwhile he needs a refill for his ball-point pen. The two men stroll to the wall displays. More pleasant moments pass, concluding with King's selection of a blue refill and a red.

'Charge it,' he says, 'to KBIM.'

Of all five stations KBIM has the best situation right on Main Street. It is also the most variously-equipped, with both AM and FM transmitters and a television studio providing exiguous continuity for programmes that flow in on the networks. Outside it has a large shop window from which is broadcast every night the record show of Jerry 'Boom Boom' Parker.

KKAT, its rival, is more modest. A bungalow on a deserted avenue, it was acquired bankrupt by its present owner Jim Tally for the sum of one dollar. Tally is confined to a wheelchair, with an energy that shames the merely walking. His challenges to KBIM are numerous. Once he stole all of their disc-jockeys. He has brought KKAT's advertising rates so low that it is possible to engage a spot for as little as 50 cents. Should a tradesman book one spot, Tally may give him several dozen more free of charge, without the tradesman's knowledge. That way he will suppose his increased trade to come from a single advertisement.

KBIM grandly affects not to notice these subterfuges, Indeed, it acknowledges KKAT's existence only in one oblique way. Both stations carry, for support of their parish newscast, the same nationally-distributed bulletins. These, joining coast with coast, arrive hourly, simultaneous at each station. KBIM's master-stroke, however, is transmission of their identical portion, not on the hour as is customary, but at five minutes to it.

'KBIM-NBC News!' Jim King's voice proclaims. 'Five minutes sooner! Worlds better!'

The music director of KBIM enters the studio in which Randy Seiler's midday show is in progress, and awaits an opportunity to speak. This is Jerry 'Boom Boom' Parker.

Randy Seiler's was the voice of the old gentleman soliciting a grilled cheese sandwich among the winds of Route 66. He is 21 and not without blemishes. 'Pardon my breath,' he apologises. 'I been eatin' those lousy tacos again.'

'Can anyone lend me a cigarette?' inquires Boom Boom. 'Just till I can cash my pay-check.'

Different indeed is Randy Seiler's situation from the teenage blimps who play Pop music over the BBC. Where they are pensionably secure, an American disc-jockey walks with fear; the diminutive 'jock' expressing best the marginality of his existence. Randy broadcasts from a standing position. For three hours his arms are violently employed, among turntables, cartridge-playing machines, bleeps, flashes, temperature readings, the low and the high, even as with another hand he winds the next record round to its beginning, at terrible cost to the record, so that never shall there occur what every jock on every station fears most – the sound of no sound whatever.

Nor is it only music which engages Randy Seiler's attention. Though KBIM is a Rock station, its prosperity derives from courtship of all levels of the community. Therefore, it opens in the morning with items of interest to farmers and with a talk-show broadcast from Denny's coffee shop farther down the street. Randy and the other jocks are also taxed with devising pretexts to dispose of gifts donated by local stores – vouchers for tacos and milk-shakes; redundant LP's; Fostex pimple-packs.

While Randy works, he is cheerfully hampered by Bill Austin, a cherubic youth who conducts the morning record show and who has not yet gone home.

'Randy!' He adopts the mongoloid voice of one of their most constant callers-in. 'Randy! Randy!'

There are scuffles while the red light is off, and sometimes while it is on.

'The fire wagon just went by!' Boom Boom cries.

'It did!' Randy is on the telephone at once to the Fire Department. Each News bulletin about a fire is sponsored by the Roswell glazier.

A three-hour show is not as bad as at KKAT, where the jocks work for six, leaving the studio only to read a thermometer in the scullery. Now Randy Seiler hands over to Jerry Vee, recently filched by KBIM from KKAT in dignified retaliation for its own earlier poaching of jocks. Jerry Vee is a discovery; a voice deep and large, laden equally with wisdom and fortified wine. He still attends High School in Roswell.

Randy in fact is leaving KBIM; which might have been divined from his boisterous treatment of the studio equipment. He is to join a larger station in Eldorado, and can by now scarcely conceal his jubilation. 'Pardon my breath,' he adds. 'I been eatin' those dam' onion-rings.'

Blown thus among the thousand airways that enmesh the land, jocks have a sort of liberty. But for Howard the deputy

226

manager no such promise remains. Howard is a thin, white-armed man in short sleeves; a man who does impersonations all of which, even the humorous ones, serve only to emphasise the melancholy of his disposition.

It is Howard who signs on KBIM in the early morning for the New Mexico farmers. He assists Jim King in the talk-show broadcast from Denny's coffee shop. It is also Howard's voice today which exhorts. 'The Gibson Discount Center offers genuine whitewood toilet seats for only $2.99.' He has lately recovered from a breakdown caused by overwork, yet would be content, in a pessimistic way, but for one thing: 'If I could only make,' he says wistfully, '$20 a week more.'

He and Randy are in the gift-room, with all the undistributed Fostex pimple-packs.

'Randy!' the mongol cries from the corridor. 'Randy! Randy!'

Howard says, 'I'll send you on some promo' spots for your new show.' One radio voice endorsing another, instead of the voice being compelled to endorse itself, is something akin to a testimonial in the world of disc-jockeys.

'Maybe in my Kentucky Colonel voice,' Howard says. Not varying the solemnity of his face between its large ears, Howard assumes a Kentucky Colonel voice. 'Son-of-a-gun!' he wheezes. 'It's that Randy Seiler, boy!' He returns to his own voice. 'I'll send you on the tapes,' Howard promises sadly.

'Well, I'd be flattered,' Randy says.

When Howard has gone, Randy muses, 'It's got to be fantastic working on that Eldorado station, Man! Seven cart-machines [cartridge-players] they have there. And my new employer has even found my wife a job.'

Randy ponders a moment.

'I'd better watch it, though,' he adds. 'Young as I am. And cocky as I am.'

From the loudspeaker in the corridor issues a sudden thunder of drums.

'KBIM,' a stern voice says, 'First Team News!'

Roswell has a story today. It remains undetected, however, by First Team News. This is both compiled and broadcast, in a deep, crusted voice, by one florid-faced child whose costume brings together numerous previously incompatible coloured stripes. The story is by no means secret. Indeed, it is put out every few minutes over the Country station KRSY; but the KBIM newshound disdains to monitor his competition. Had he done so he would be aware that tomorrow KRSY intends to give away, not milk-shakes, not pimple-packs, but $1200 in cash.

This Olympian attitude on KBIM's part has left KRSY as somewhat of an unknown in the struggle for the ear of Roswell. Its young manager is plump but lively. He once challenged KBIM's jocks to a taco-eating contest; an invitation that was rather stiffly declined. Nor have they yet pardoned KRSY for getting one of its employees humorously arrested by the Sheriff so that a record-show might be transmitted from the jailhouse. And KRSY possesses a fallout shelter. On Doomsday there would be no question which was top station.

Now its manager has engaged somebody to walk about Roswell wearing an iron mask, the key of which is hidden somewhere in the town. Its finder will receive the $1200. At KRSY, they are debating at this moment where to hide the key. In the ear of the horse on 'The Store with the Horse on Top'? In the flower tubs that stand outside the foyer of KBIM itself?

'There was a slight traffic mishap today in Roswell,' thunders KBIM's First Team News. 'Wilson was slightly shaken up by the crash,' it continues sternly, 'but did not require immediate medical attention. The Gillespie woman,' it adds, 'has received a Police citation for failing to obey a "Stop" sign.'

The evening brings an habitual demonstration by Roswellian youth. They drive in their cars up Main Street, almost to the Military Academy; then, past KBIM to an illuminated hamburger stand, they drive back again. This is called 'dragging Main'. It continues for several hours. They pass and are passed in their turn, and from time to time sound their horns.

The record-show of Jerry 'Boom Boom' Parker looks forth upon this noisy but predictable display, being conducted from

228

actually inside the KBIM front window. By day it is too hot for the purpose. Boom Boom's show lasts from seven to midnight, the peak hours of 'dragging Main', so he has conquered any reserve he may originally have entertained. 'When I first came here, Man, I was embarrassed. "Hey, there's a dummy in that window, Man – moving!" '

Boom Boom is small, with a ginger moustache. He walks in a curious rolling manner derived either from some displacement of the hip or from cowboy boots a little too high. But the voice! Again, the voice is unlike the speaker. It is elegantly dry, as if directed to beautiful, attentive girls. Borne even the few feet from its lighted window, the voice seems to create in the repeating traffic some other night, filled with promise and softness.

A head screams from a car, 'Do I get an album?'

Along the pavement comes a boy wheeling a bicycle. He pauses and regards Boom Boom, leaning in the silver antlers of the bicycle, crunching the ice from a soft drink cup.

'That's my brother out there.' The boy points into the stream; then he is unsure. 'That's my brother's car. We have six cars. No – that's my brother,' he says, pointing. 'There on the motorcycle.'

'Who's driving your brother's car?'

'The guy he traded the cycle with,' the boy answers.

Suddenly, from the other end of Main Street, come jogging a group of lanky youths. Each wears embroidered on his chest a capital letter R; all move in strange, disconnected unison like one large creature that attacks by bouncing on the soles of its feet. Bouncing thus, they reach Boom Boom's window and, before it, assume the form of a Medusa, or some Hindu deity, waving arms, waving heads, many voices crying out 'Hey, Man!' 'Hey, Man, what's happenin'?' Then, bouncily as they come, they move onward. Each wears, too, on his back the capital letter R.

'Who were they?'

'The tall guys on the basketball team,' the boy says raptly.

KBIM remains active after dark. A television announcer arrives to read the News, which he will do from a standing

229

position, and jovially leg-wrestles the boy before passing within. A silent youth sits by the automated FM system. One of the secretaries is also still there. A preacher's daughter, curvaceous to the point of overtopping, she prefers to stay in her office watching television rather than to go home to her apartment.

'I can get you a girl, Man,' Boom Boom says. 'Which car do you like? The Gremlin?' Boom Boom addresses his audience, still rushing past without respite. 'I got two English guys with me here, Man, they keep talkin' to me 'bout a Gremlin, I don't know, a purple Gremlin they say, Man. . . .'

From out of the traffic a Gremlin immediately detaches itself and stops outside the window. A Gremlin is a car resembling a slice of cheese.

We continue driving up Main Street; Sherry behind the wheel, and her friend Ann. Sherry proffers a bottle of strawberry wine in a paper bag, cautioning it must not be sampled as we pass the police car that placidly watches from a recess.

'We have good police here,' Sherry remarks. 'They'll let you chase them at 3 a.m. or ride on the street-sweepers. We get a lot of murders, but that's the Chicanos. Well . . .' she says. 'This is "dragging Main".'

We turn and head down again towards KBIM. As we pass another car there is a loud explosion.

'A firecracker,' Sherry explains. 'In summer we throw water balloons too.'

Her friend Ann remarks, 'This is my night off.'

'From your boy friend?'

She nods. 'Every once a week, I have a night with the girls and he has a night with the boys.'

'What's he like?'

'He's real sweet,' she says.

'What does he do?'

'He does nothing.'

'Where is he tonight?'

Ann points to the next car at the drive-in.

'He's in that car.'

Boom Boom's wife has appeared in the foyer of KBIM. They

230

married two months ago and are awaiting a divorce. She stands chatting with the preacher's daughter, who from time to time goes and firmly repulses those outside whose desire for a free gift causes them to approach and rattle the glass front doors.

'I haven't been in my bed since I moved to that apartment,' the preacher's daughter says. 'I'm so terrified of prowlers, I always go to sleep on the couch.'

'You should buy a knife,' Boom Boom's wife says. 'A big butcher-knife,' she added with relish.

The young newsreader emerges from his FM room. 'Hi, how are you?' Boom Boom's wife greets him.

'I'm not feeling too well,' he tells her.

'Go get something at the Pharmacy.'

'I'll soon have enough money,' he says. 'I'm going to get me a shot of penicillin.'

Should you tire of 'dragging Main', Roswell at night offers little else. The preacher's daughter is escorted by a taciturn engineer from the television-studio out to Motel Six, the town's only night-spot. In a large room at the end of a bar, a Country and Western trio somnambulistically performs, its bass-guitarist leaning against the wall. Around the floor, middle-aged men wearing stetsons dance with middle-aged women in very short skirts, knee-boots and lacquered white wigs. The trouser cuffs of each male brush his heels. He dances ardently close to his overripe partner, but also pumps their two arms conscientiously. The floor is filled as with people trying in vain to pass through one another. The bass-guitarist's head slumps lower on his chest.

Suddenly the beat changes. The bass-guitarist awakes, into New Mexico's approximation of Rock and Roll, and so does the preacher's daughter. She kicks off her shoes, which skid independently across the floor. She is dancing – yet not dancing, since it bears no relationship to her partner's slightly awed *pas-seul* – with arms stretched up, hair flying, eyes open, she is alive and dancing to the point of back-somersault.

At almost midnight, abruptly, Main Street empties. Boom

Boom continues his show in his window, but with darkness increasing round him, and the wind of a forsaken place. One car passes. It stops below the hanging red light; it goes away. Perhaps, after all, there will be no beautiful, attentive girls.

'I didn't have any luck all last summer,' Boom Boom says. 'Maybe this summer. . . .'

Boom Boom tells them, 'You got 20 minutes left, Man. I know it's kinda' cold out there, Man, about 30 degrees, but you got time, Man – this lunar module model-set, presented by Radio Shack, I'm going to give away, I'm going to give away, Man, I feel like giving something away, to the first chick, the first chick who comes down here, Man, to KBIM wearing a swimsuit.'

Dylan and the Angels

He would not be Bob Dylan if he did not make us constantly fear the worst. We feared it three years ago, when he returned to Britain after a gap of almost a decade. We expected the stubble-faced, curmudgeonly figure who had snubbed his audience in 1969. We saw, instead, a genial, almost perky Dylan, playing his old songs in breathtaking new arrangements – 'Tangled Up in Blue', for instance, lengthened to a super-charged Odyssey which, for many who heard it, still haunts the girders round Earls Court.

We feared the worst before his current tour because Dylan is now a 'born again' Christian, and because his last album, *Saved*, while attesting to the euphoria of his newborn soul, collectively musters not one-tenth of the poetic power in a love-song like 'Sarah' or a pamphleteering lament like 'The Hurricane'. We shall always fear the worst since Bruce Springsteen, a month ago, altered for ever the principles of Rock performance. Dylan, however brilliant, gives concerts only as a favour. Springsteen, like Chaplin, seems to have no existence other than in the rapt eye of his audience.

Dylan's opening Earls Court concert on Friday began with slackness perhaps intended to show his disregard for such comparisons. Half an hour's wait led to nothing more than a pink-robed, gold-hung, quickly tiresome Gospel group. When Dylan himself appeared – not in the breezy white trousers of three years ago but drab and preoccupied – it was to launch without apology into two heavy anthems proclaiming his conversion. Then, suddenly, with scarcely a beat's hesitation, he was singing 'Like A Rolling Stone'. In every chorus, a dozen cross-hatched searchlight beams rose up behind him. The audience, in the presence of this more familiar divinity, sighed deeply as if truly saved.

Born again or not, Dylan recognises his previous existence as an avid generation's Pied Piper and troubadour. Yet again on Friday, he demonstrated his uncanny ability to cut and shuffle anew the epochs of his music – whether 'Maggie's Farm' transformed into heavy metal, or 'Mr Tambourine Man', its tempo unchanged from 1965, yet each phrase, each inflection subtly reconsidered. With him he brings a mature, straightforward stage band, steeped in the tradition of Country and Rockabilly, agile in following the new designs which Dylan weaves out of them. 'A Simple Twist Of Fate', poised between warm words and cool guitars, will be the echo left behind this time.

And yet that pink-robed, quickly-tiresome Gospel group is, unfortunately, never far away. The songs from *Saved* and *Slow Train Comin'* admittedly sound better on stage, set about by bass as thick as the walls of Jericho. But Gospel music, though it has many tunes, has only one mood. Not even a Dylan, using all his powers, can hide the monotony in continuous exaltation. The eyes, that look inward to see such visions, look upward to behold a tableau with no surprises. He is telling a story the whole world has already heard.

His audience on Friday night continued forbearing, even after it became clear that 'devotional' songs would dominate the closing hour. They simply listened, leaping with desperate applause on the scraps of his old self Dylan threw them – the first jangle on acoustic guitar; his belated first blast from the harmonica he now prefers to conceal.

When, at the end of another electronic sermon, he abruptly left the stage, it seemed that the worst had happened after all. Matches flared in the dark, begging him to return. He did so, to sing 'Blowing in the Wind', putting the choir in its rightful place at last, and then 'Don't Think Twice, It's All Right', alone with his guitar, his harmonica, his undisputed genius, and not an angel in sight to spoil it.

Dolly and Tammy and Carl In The Wembley Wild West

The gunfighter walks alone, staying close to the side of the street. His clothes are black and faintly luminous. His hat is tied insolently under his chin. His six-gun is tied challengingly against his lower thigh. For him, the thoroughfare is empty. He pays no heed to the crowds around the 12-inch hot dog stall, the stall which sells sheriff badges and saddles, and the single, free-standing telephone-kiosk. He passes the dais where Jim Reeves' widow is signing autographs behind a hedge of entreating hands. In the 12 years since Jim's death, only she, and a business corporation, have kept the memory alive. Grief and valour are permapressed into the widow's face; her deep mourning is relieved by an embroidery of silver studs.

This is the eighth annual British Festival of Country and Western music. George Bertie Clark has been at most of them, travelling with his wife Doris up to Wembley each day from Ipswich, where he works on the railway station. He saves all year, works through all other holidays, in preparation for the outing. Doris likes Slim Whitman, but George Bertie likes them all. He likes Dolly Parton and Vernon Oxford and Jim and Jessie and, especially, Marty Robbins, the singer of 'El Paso' and 'Devil Woman'. Doris and he are complementary, like figures in a weather-house, with long raincoats and small stetson hats and bootlace ties and badges, and extensive hand-luggage to sustain them through the hours before the concerts begin. In the busy concourse that encircles the Empire Pool, they are by no means the most conspicuous figures.

235

On the first of the three days, Tammy Wynette makes a personal appearance. Her songs 'Stand By Your Man', 'D.I.V.O.R.C.E' and 'Jesus Put the Yodel in My Soul', have placed her in the forefront of queens of Country. Her appearance on the CBS Records stand is the occasion of a minor riot. The cardboard stetsons converge like a crowd in an old photograph inspecting an aviation disaster. A block of three men lift up a fourth, and his camera-bag, on to their shoulders. He wears a leather slouch-hat, pulled down over his eyes, and shoots and shoots in frenzy with an Instamatic, crying, 'Up, Up!' A public address vainly pleads with the crowd to stand back. The stand is beginning, palpably, to tremble. Those who have secured their autographs batter their way to the rear. A man from Darlington shakes hands emotionally with a perfect stranger whose hair and moustachios appear to be coated with fine, grey dust. 'We formed a scrum, didn't we? Thanks, mate. See you again, I hope.'

Even in its eighth year, the Festival remains the object of some disbelief. How can the sentimental songs, the mawkish native instruments of rural America draw so deep a response from the recesses of urban England? It is less surprising to the Country music industry, which long ago appreciated that in America, too, the music has its strongest appeal among city-dwellers. It is as conservative, as self-sufficient a myth as the Wild West, legitimising costumes and mannerisms that once were the subject of private yearnings in cinema darkness. Nashville, with its reconstructed Grand Old Opry theatre and its prowling tourist buses, is the Country and Western capital only in a strict commercial sense. Wembley at Easter, with cherry-blossom and ticket-touts in bloom, can claim, at least, equal kinship.

The hunger in Europe might have remained unassuaged but for one man of the entrepreneurial class. His name is Mervyn H. Conn. There is strong evidence to suggest that he selected the surname himself. He is a small, dapper man of East End parentage who hides his comparative youth behind a close-fitting, rather truculent beard. It was Mervyn Conn, in the late 1960s, who realised that no one outside America was promoting Country music, and who assiduously set himself to repair this omission. The Wembley Festival, bigger and longer than ever before, with a satellite festival in Sweden, testifies to his extraordinary prescience. Last night, there was a banquet for the chief artists: three courses and Confederate flags beneath the harsh chandeliers of the Hyde Park Hotel, that banjo-pickers' home-from-home. Mervyn Conn, in a black and gold shirt and a white bow tie, welcomed his stars with a heart-felt testimonial to the virtues of free enterprise. Today, he is at the Festival in person, inspecting the contents of his cash register. He has the air of a man blissfully employed at his vocation.

The perils in promoting a major Country and Western festival are less than attend the smallest celebration of Rock or Soul music. There are 30,000 people at Wembley, easily contained by the small, miraculously civil staff of uniformed porters. Country is mothers' and fathers' music, it consummates marriages and commemorates anniversaries; it gives a special joy and freedom to the handicapped. One of its lesser heroes is Tex Withers, a man who, although physically deprived, has created for himself a widely-envied life as a cowboy in Sussex, singing, compering or cooking out underneath the stars. His voice is overlaid – almost – by a deep Montanan drawl; sheer style elevates him among the tallest and broadest of men. 'I got me a little house now, down in Sussex. Me and the wife, we saw up logs and bring 'em in for the fire. The name of the house is only called 28 Eastdale Road. I'm thinkin' of changin' it to something like "The Wikeup".'

The gunfighters represent a small, radical minority. Roy – 'think of Roy Rogers' – Hawks, a security training-officer from Slough, maintains he would feel naked without his replica Navy Colt revolver at his hip. His friend, Tony Girle, cannot yet affort a gun-belt, so Roy is going to try to have one made up for him in Majorca next holiday. But to Country purists, the gun replicas are both unnecessary and undesirable. At some clubs, one is required to check one's replica at the door.

237

Tammy Wynette (pronounced Wine-ette), who has sung so many songs dear to the heart of Country music, is a woman admitting to 30, with pale blue trousers and obligatory heaped golden curls, and a certain thinness and wanness. Long ago, her private life and her public existence as a Country queen became indivisible. Her divorce from George Jones, which prevented her appearance at last year's Festival; the 'major surgery' which she underwent in November; her leisure pursuits of 'bowlin', cookin', fishin'' – all are as public as an album-sleeve, intoned with the familiarity of a school lesson. As she speaks, she constantly refers to a large plastic bound almanac of her own engagements, for months to come. Wembley, to her, is merely a further stop between Jacksonville and Tulsa, scarcely noticed in the endless road, the bleak, unchanging luxury.

One by one, the Festival stars are brought down to the Press room, an airless subterranean chamber, to be quizzed by journalists from the specialist music press. Tammy Wynette yields place at the baize table to Carl Perkins who, as the original singer of 'Blue Suede Shoes' and 'Honey, Don't', not to mention 'Glad All Over' and 'Matchbox', embodies some musical history. A large, dark, patient man, wearing middle-aged denims and a Masonic watch, he inclines his massive profile obligingly towards each inquisitor, from Victory Radio (Portsmouth) or Radio Sunderland; he delivers the same reply, time after time, into the cassette-recorders thrust under his nose. He doesn't mind. 'If I wasn't sittin' here, I'd be sittin' somewhere else.'

Last in the queue is a small, wild-headed youth in a green and wordy T-shirt.

'Carl – er, sorry there isn't time for an interview. Can you just read the words on this card?'

All the Country stars, in addition to giving interviews for local radio, are pressed to read cut promotion 'flashes' for this or that station so that some disc-jockey, be he ever so vile, may bask in second-hand glory. An excusable response would be to break the tape-recorder over the child's importunate head.

238

'Sure.' Carl takes the scrap of card and reads: 'Hi, this is Carl Perkins. Wherever you are, a Merry Christmas and New Year.'

The ice-rink is hidden under a vast counterpane of hard little red seats, binding it into the walls of hard seating which ascend to the roof of the silo. Johnny Gimble, the fiddler, is using the stage for rehearsal, his musicians enclosed by a necklace of television apparatus and bright blue, critical pilot-lights. The solo is passed from Johnny Gimble to Lloyd Green, the pedal steel guitarist, a clean-shaven, short-haired man, clerkly for all his multi-coloured shirt. Whatever Lloyd Green does is watched by the other pedal steel-players with almost physical hunger. The music swoops and slides through for the benefit of the camera only, and a little block of Wembley porters. It says much for the law-abiding nature of the fans that none would dream of crossing the flimsy barriers which divide them from their dreams.

Into the rehearsal area, a single intruder has been admitted. He wears a stetson and two guns, and even spurs, which snag on the ground behind him. His name is Frederick. He works as a cleaner at Heathrow Airport. Three horseshoes, embroidered in silver on his back, glimmer eerily in the semi-darkness.

Dolly Parton awaits him in her dressing-room. She is possibly greater in status among Country queens than Tammy Wynette. The badge stall, on the very first day, had sold out of Dolly Parton badges. Her bosom is as high and prominent as a set of water-wings; her thighs, barely contained by pink trousers, have some of the same inflated magnificence. Her mouth is red, and very talkative. Her silver wig is as lofty and as pendulous as the wig of Louis XIV.

'Hi,' she says to the gunfighter. 'What's yo' name?'

'It's Butch,' he replies modestly.

'Okay, Bootch, let's see yo' body.'

He removes his suede bolero and his blue silk shirt. His stetson remains on his head. He pulls up his trousers to cover the elastic of his underpants. His back, from scapulae down,

239

is covered by a tattoo of Dolly Parton. It is executed in several colours, copied from the sleeve of one of her record albums. He has requested her to sign it. The autograph, in its turn, will then be tattooed.

'Wow!' she says, perhaps a little faintly. 'That's sure . . . somethin' different.'

'Fourteen hours, it took,' he tells her proudly.

'What's that on your chest?'

'Jesus.'

'No girls?' she inquires jovially.

'On my leg.' He pulls up a trouser cuff and turns down the edge of his cowboy boot. There is a Geisha girl tattooed on his leg.

'That's real pretty.'

'Not as pretty as you,' he says.

Uncle Mick is in charge of the hospitality marquee and the VIP enclosure, immediately adjacent to the stage. The seats in the hospitality marquee cost nothing: at the bar, one has to pay. All functions under the weighty custodianship of Mervyn Conn's Uncle Mick. He has two other celebrated nephews, Mike and Bernie Winters. He is the scion of a boxing family, formerly licensee at the old Bodega in Brighton, a stout, suspicious man in gold-rimmed glasses, smoking a thick cigar. To watch Uncle Mick greeting the VIPs is to understand the quality which makes our British pubs what they are today.

'Up along the *back* row, please.'

'Can't we sit at the front?'

'It's reserved for Mr Conn's private party.'

'What about the second now?'

'That's reserved for Mr Conn's private party. Now I've offered you a seat. Take it while it's going.'

Tonight is the Festival's climax. True, there remains one further day, but that is for 'contemporary' music: the gun-fighters and cowgirls will disperse before the more sardonic eyes of Rock fans. Tonight, there is Skeeter Davis; there is Marty Robbins; there is Dolly Parton, garrulous in her

240

colossal Versailles wig. There is the fiddle, played by crouching, grinning men, and the pedal steel played as it ought to be, remorsefully; and 'Jolene' and 'El Paso' and 'The End of the World'; and children and dogs and simulated Rebel yells; all the 'old virtues'. In the foreground, the silhouette of Uncle Mick watches his nephew's interests, indenting for any hospitalities on a looseleaf notepad. Behind Uncle Mick rolls the applause. From the lighted faces in the front rows to dark multitudes on high among the Exit signs, all are under the same hypnosis of delight.

Gene Autry was scheduled to be here to present Country music awards. Better that the ancient cowboy is indisposed, and could not come. For a new star is born tonight. Out into the crowded stage, among the women in gowns and clean-shaven men, steps an official of the state of Tennessee. In one hand he bears a framed certificate. In the other he flourishes a five-string dulcimer. He brings a message to Wembley from the Governor of Tennessee himself. From henceforward, he announces, among the people of that state, April 18 will be known as Mervyn H. Conn Day.

Reviewer's Blotter

Chuck Berry
Rainbow Theatre

It is more than 20 years since the world first laid startled eyes on a young man with a crouching gait and a skinny guitar who sang songs about High School, about girls called Maybellene, and Cadillacs and Coup de Villes. In all that time, Chuck Berry has remained the greatest uninterrupted exponent of Rock and Roll music, preserving his original gift as carefully as he watches over his petty cash. He is in Europe again on yet another triumphal progress: on Wednesday it was the turn of Finsbury Park to share his continuing rejuvenation.

He is, despite the millions which he has husbanded, miraculously unchanged. As always, he looks sleek but disarrayed, like a man who has been standing under a waterspout; he looks, at the same time, epicene and salacious, the white flannels gripping his waist as with drawstrings, the lounge-lizard's moustache decorating a grin of irradiant self-satisfaction.

And how he works! For rhythm he employs only drums and bass, and the bass-player finds himself largely superfluous. The classic Berry guitar solo – the solo which introduces 'Johnny B. Goode', 'Sweet Little Sixteen' and most others – is a one-handed duet, leaping from half-chords to the middle register, bending notes so cheekily that you think he has missed them entirely, which, indeed, he sometimes has, as he hops and struts; as he kicks and genuflects above his audience and their entreating arms.

Satire and self-mockery now play a part in his performance. 'You Never Can Tell' is done in an effete tango style. He will toy with a dreadful Pop song in order to torment us with impatience for his hits – a process in which we willingly acquiesce – or, in full flow, he will suddenly stop playing, to the obvious surprise of his own musicians. By his Rainbow audience, especially by those wearing cylindrical coats and cowlicks, such aberrations were instantly pardoned. One of their dreams, at least, is uncorrupted. The house lights turned on could not quench the happiness that was created.

Frank Sinatra
London Palladium
The emergence of Frank Sinatra from retirement has become as regular a ceremony as when Lloyd George or Churchill used to be wheeled out on parade, enfeebled in physique but, for past attainments, still the object of fear and wonder. In recent years Sinatra's taste for regeneration has, if anything, increased. At the Palladium on Thursday night one felt less a sense of gala than of familiar religious obsequies, with hair-oil, nylon frills, white furs, a small, noisy fountain in the foyer and a rich smell suggesting that, in the Havana cigar trade, there is still no recession.

Rites of welcome were offered not merely for Sinatra but for two other heavyweights of that genre. To the tuxedo-wearing soul of the Swing fan, Count Basie's band and Sarah Vaughan come very near to the top of perfect rapture. But to a lover of Rock – wearing, perforce, a ready-made bow-tie – certain heretical questions occur. Is Basie's the most won-derful band in the world, or the most wonderful instrument of remote control? Basie absents himself from the stage almost immediately, leaving his boys to their symphony of fits and clever pauses. As for Sarah Vaughan, she has a beautiful, oboe-like voice. Why does she choose to dissipate it on feeble songs which have been recorded by the Carpenters?

And so we arrive at the greatest question of all. What is the secret of the hold that a 60-year-old man, a self-confessed toupee-wearer, of anti-social, occasionally aggres-sive tendencies, has managed to maintain upon two whole generations?

After so many exits, how can he ever make another entrance? He is revealed on the bandstand just as an execrable (and possibly masochistic) comedian takes a final bow. It is the star's quaint humour to ride in on the applause for someone else, and to transform it into his own ovation.

How can a statistic so vast as Sinatra everbe realised as a mere human being, a suit, cuffs, shoes, socks? Yet, in the shrinkage of vision, it is all terribly simple. He possesses, and cannot lose, the power in voice and gesture to make every song he sings privately his own. The power keeps him still at pistol point, although the gestures are not careful and the voice sometimes drops away, exhausted. At times he seems physically appalled by the necessity of singing. As well as sighing with pleasure, the audience rustles with amusement over his mistakes. It is not altogether a happy state of affairs.

Alice Cooper
Wembley Empire Pool
Alice Cooper started the week by releasing a balloon effigy of himself to float above the River Thames. The reported cost of the balloon may give comfort to anyone who believes Pop music to be affected by the economic blizzard. Last night he moved on to the Empire Pool, to perform the stage version of his LP *Welcome to My Nightmare*, this time enjoying the involuntary assistance of London Transport. After I had spent nearly an hour on the Bakerloo Line, Alice's nightmare promised only comparative horror.

I trust it is not necessary to explain that Alice Cooper is the alter ego of Vince Furnier, an American clergyman's son, who has grown famous as a Rock performer by harnessing in his audience a seemingly widespread predilection for being nauseated. Boa constrictors, live chickens and plastic babies rent limb from limb have all been numbered among Alice's stage properties in the past, and he has further taunted decent society by revealing unabashedly that in private he wears neither underwear nor socks.

Mr Leo Abse, M.P., who campaigned against Alice on a

previous visit, will be pleased to know that in this production the singer has forsaken snakes and dead babies for terror of a more socially acceptable kind. He is propelled to the front of the stage standing on a brass bedstead, a strangely school-girlish, knock-kneed apparition in red tights, cringing away from the dancing figures who issue from a toybox at the side of the stage: mutants and demons and sheeted ghosts, some of whom I, at least, instantly recognised.

If I sound supercilious, I do not mean to do so. I like Alice Cooper immensely. It is good to find a Rock star who is consciously, rather than unconsciously, monstrous. He has exchanged the weary conventions of superstardom for the slightly more unexpected ones of Punch and Judy (as I write this, a gang of skeletons are actually putting him into a toybox). Although both his publicity machine and his audience strive to overlook the fact, he is rather a good singer and a gifted composer.

Later in the show, the bed is withdrawn. A large spiders web appears, with two spiders climbing in it. The spiders also dance. It is time for 'The Black Widow', featuring the voice of Vincent Price. I left Wembley in a contented frame of mind. I had not missed the panto this year after all.

Bob Marley
Lyceum Ballroom

Bob Marley and the Wailers reached the Lyceum two nights ago, in some style. By early evening, long before they were due to appear, the foyer was impassable and a queue stretched from under the portico into Covent Garden's hinterland. Across the road stood a double row of police vans with many constables, shirtsleeved and sceptical. Clearly, the gravest fears were entertained for this home of the quickstep and foxtrot at the hands of the kings of Reggae.

It is unnecessary, I hope, to repeat that the Wailers are adherents to the Rastafarian faith, worshipping Jah in the person of Haile Selassie ('recently deposed', as their press handout candidly admits) and believing in their spiritual repatriation, some day, to Ethiopia. For the present, they

245

remain in Jamaica where – aside from periodic jail sentences – they have existed for 12 years, idolised, plagiarised, yet dreamily resisting the demands of world fame. Their last concert tour of Britain was curtailed because it began to snow.

I do not think that they could complain of the temperature this time. I have been in hot places before, but seldom in a place as hot as the Lyceum ballroom, just before the Wailers appeared. It was like breathing through a sodden blanket. Presently, it became like wearing one. The dance floor was a human swamp; the red lamps, on the balcony above, burned with the unearthly brilliance of equatorial flowers.

In such circumstances, the performance itself had something of the quality of hallucination. It seemed that two stout figures in robes and turbans, for all the world like the favourite wives of some ancient chief, swayed and side-stepped and played pat-a-cake together. On one side of them, Marley himself, with hair standing up in the waxy plaits called 'dreadlocks', threw his arms wide from an untouched guitar; on the other side, a little kneeling group seemed to be enjoying a quiet game of cards. This, at least, was what I saw through a press of bodies, radiant with heat. There was a curious odour in the foetid air which I could not identify. It reminded me somewhat of newly-pressed shirts.

In these frightful days of Barry White, I love Bob Marley and the Wailers. It is not merely that theirs are the first and the best versions of 'Stir it Up', 'I Shot the Sheriff', 'Guava Jelly'. The slow bass, the slow drum, the unrepentant idleness, the matronly figures stepping and gliding – all are visitations from a world which whites in the audience, bobbing ardently but fitfully, cannot hope to comprehend. Through them black music is, once more, triumphantly private.

Ray Charles
Royal Festival Hall
Occasionally, amid the bloated exaggerations of popular music, we remember the true revolutionaries. These were performers so far ahead of their time yet so obviously brilliant that they could pass unchallenged long before the bar-

riers were erected against their imitators. Ray Charles, perhaps more than any other, embodies genius taken utterly for granted. He appears in no album-charts or publicity sheets; he is absent everywhere save in our subconscious. We are reminded of him only as his concerts approach, with joy but with a little guilt.

At the Festival Hall on Saturday, he was forgiving, both of our neglect and the mighty ovation with which we sought to expiate it. One is unprepared for a figure so slight or uncoordinated, bowing low as if unstuffed from the waistband up; beatifically turning his head, and the blank flashing glasses which have read the hearts and seen into the souls of three generations of white people.

The breadth of his achievement almost beggars definition. The way he sings 'Georgia' has passed into our judgment of any Soul ballad, yet is there a fledgling of Rock who can afford to overlook the way he sings 'What I Say'? Our first understanding of Country or Gospel is infused by his voice, even as the voice itself defies any classification between its rapture and the trembling reed of melancholy. The man within the voice is almost frighteningly insubstantial. He seems scarcely even to alight at the piano, but kicks and flutters against it like some strange, dusty species of moth.

The programme was executed in obedience to those fitful movements, shadowed with unerring skill by an excellent conventional band. Perversely, the best moment came not from any well-loved standard but from the ballad 'Till There Was You', as it was never sung by Peggy Lee or Paul McCartney. Then he moved into a region where even the band could not follow, twisting his arms and head and shirtfront into weird, gasping knots for an endless Blues introduction as he tortured the keys of an electric piano.

But the Blues never came: it was as if he drew back at the last moment. Instead, we met the Raelettes, and, soon after that, the smooth-talking compere; he left the stage in a bright Las Vegas finale which could not obliterate the gasp of disappointment in the audience. Now that he had won them, why could he not take them all the way?

247

The Cold, Cold Heart of Country Music

For all that Country and Western hopes nothing will change, its heroes die horribly fast. Jimmie Rodgers died of tuberculosis only hours after he had turned railway brakemen's songs to art; and Hank Williams, coddled in the rear of a Cadillac, managed to die of the cold. Immortality is counted in relics at the Nashville Country Music Hall of Fame – Jim Reeves' red shoes, Patsy Cline's orange wig. These died in aeroplanes: many more do on the roads. Or they sink to drugs by the agency of diet-pills named Great Speckled Birds, or simply have nervous breakdowns.

How, then, has Ernest Tubb the Texas Troubador endured? A grandfather in a lime-coloured bolero suit, he is still, to his worshippers, a dream made flesh. The flesh may be pickled and tanned somewhat against flashing rhinestone but – he smiles. That is what has never changed. A million miles of travelling cannot wear it away. Under the stetson brim, his eyes turn down like tadpole tails; the corners of his mouth turn up to meet them, giving the Texas Troubador the look of a cathedral gargoyle as he exclaims, 'Why – bless y'r hearts!'

The smile must be fastened on with pins. Past midnight on the Strip, the rain tumbles in pink snow through its magical illuminations. Buddy, Jody and Jimmie Bee, who live in Nashville on hopes of stardom and weak beer, have gone back to the final humiliation the city can offer – their apartment. Luckier cowboy kings are asleep in ranch-style mausoleums. But for the Troubador this is the second show this evening: he came back today from three weeks on the road and is leaving again shortly for Adaca, Ohio. No matter how long the reputa-

248

tion of a Country giant, it still depends on remorseless caravanning between State fairs across the continent.

Already his band, who in their velvet somewhat resemble cowboys from *Faust*, are re-packing the bus, pushing through the crowd to the pink-lit rain, never neglecting to say 'Excuse me'. But how can they watch *him* go? To see him they have driven from the pale cities of the North, bringing with them an even deeper kind of American Conservative: their children. They have waited hours for him, stale and packed behind the window of a record-store; the song which the Texas Troubador sings through his nose contains all the fresh air they desire.

He goes among them, brilliant bird-green under a ten-gallon hat, with a 'Thank y', thank y', Ah prishiate it, *so* much.' A fat woman's camera misfires. Fat women love Country music. So do men with bare, pale arms, with sunglasses in their pockets and Spiro T. Agnew in their hearts: so do all the homely folks that bought a million copies of 'Battle Hymn of Lieutenant Calley'. A Conservative's only demand of his idol is the opportunity to shake hands. It takes the Texas Troubador half-an-hour to reach the street. He smiles at the fat woman. 'Y'need a new flash there, Hon'.' Before leaving, to drive through the night instead of going home to his grandchildren, he picks up his guitar and turns it round to show a reverse side lettered 'THANKS'.

Any music-making city ought to be loved; which is why some even love Detroit. Had Nashville given birth to her product instead of annexing it, even she might have inspired affection; then perhaps kinder songs would have been written of her. But the music came raw from the South all around, fiddled and beaten against jugs through every state where people own front-porches. Nashville merely amplified the violins. Elvis Presley is Country and Western's most famous foundling, and he got his feeling over in Memphis. They brought him to Nashville to fix the contracts.

Buddy Harris is from Arkansas – Johnny Cash country. He came into Nashville, like Johnny Cash, with a guitar over his back. There the resemblance ends. Buddy's hair falls down from his old black hat in oily ropes; his eyes, from incomprehension or perhaps from weeping, are permanently half-shut. His mouth was made not to speak but to yodel, and at the age of 27 he has reached the limits of genius available to yodelling. Down on the Strip, in Music City Lounge, he stands up against the lights of the pinball game. He howls his soul empty to just a line of drunks twisted on bar-stools. He can carry every note in 'Mule-Skinner Blues', every impossible scroll of notes. His reward is what the drunks toss him in small coin.

Buddy is lucky. He hasn't pawned his guitar yet. At least he isn't a tourist, endlessly climbing the hillside of tenement hotels in the belief that Country heroes exist behind their effigies outside cafeterias. He is young enough – just – to believe he will be as great as Presley, Johnny Cash, Hank Williams – and will one day follow them in playing on the stage of the Grand Ol' Opry theatre. He has a girl named Jody ... 'Uh, uh,' she giggles. 'Really it's Jo-Anne.' From her tiny child's neck and ears arises an immense, pointed, yellow pompadour. She seems to live in the hollow of Buddy's slack body, covering it constantly with kisses.

Jimmie Bee has none of this, however, and not even youth on his side. Jimmie Bee admits to 30. Poverty has already laid belts of middle-age around him, imparting to his movements that painful formality which comes from wearing, for months on end, the same pair of trousers. In Music City Lounge, while Buddy sings, Jody collects the dimes in a cigar-box and Jimmie Bee waits in the booth for stardom to descend, without warning, upon himself. Already he has waited two years. He does not even so far sing for tips. Yet his body, spirit, impossible hopes and dirty cuffs are bound miraculously together by a homespun and wise manner, borrowed from his idol, the late Jim Reeves.

The contents of his wallet, too, give Jimmie Bee happiness and release. 'Did you ever meet anyone that had designed their own house?' He begins to sketch it – the mansion he will build when he is a Country and Western star. 'The structure alone will cost a minimum of 150,000 dollars. These units, like flying-saucers, they make out of aluminium for people at the lake resorts. I plan,' Jimmie Bee says, 'to have 12 of 'em all joined up by passages. You watch on closed-circuit TV. If you don't want the fans, you tell 'em to go away. The house – and my clothes – will be all one colour scheme. Blue. That was Jim's favourite colour. And grey. And out back,' Jimmie Bee says, tranquilly folding his hands, 'I plan to have a perfect replica of Le Mans for me to play in.'

If only he and Buddy, and all the faces at the windows of excursion-buses, had consulted a street-plan first. It would reveal to them that the part of Nashville they all haunt is contiguous, in the matter of a dream, to absolutely nothing. The Strip is no more than a hundred yards of light, spreading, wheeling, withdrawing. The Grand Ol' Opry at least is nearby, at the foot of the hill. If Buddy cannot reach the stage, he can see and hear it, and Jody keeps a piece of the brick-work for a talisman. The true, cool beauties of Nashville, however, are somewhere else.

They are physically higher; a dozen blocks nearer the stars, on Music Row. Set upon the trim grass befitting stern and self-centred industry, this is the Nashville they all dream of but cannot touch. It is walled off from them by palisades of sun in the glass.

All the record companies are here, and their ancillary activities; a sizeable portion of Nashville's 500 millionaires occupying themselves in the lullaby of air conditioning. RCA's building, where Chet Atkins has his office, seems delicately carved of wedding-cake icing. Opposite, in an affectedly simple shanty, a tailor sews coloured glass into cowboy suits, the lowest price of which would feed Buddy and Jody for a month. Here, the cash rolling into Nashville with the road shows and rodeos accumulates with a soft, golden click.

Music Row history dates not from the birth of Country music but from that of Rock and Roll. At his death in 1953, Hank Williams had already recorded 'Move It On Over', which is 'Rock Around the Clock' almost note for note. It was

251

left for Presley to ascend in his place, to astonish the world with pink coats such as old Country musicians had been wearing on the stage of the Grand Ol' Opry for years. And homely boys like the Everly Brothers found themselves turned to figures in a revolution: the quiet Carl Perkins, playing in the open air, suddenly saw his audience obscured by dust – they had started to jive.

Nashville is ruled by a brotherhood of session-musicians, as close and exclusive as Japanese Samurai, carving the studio work between them with the sharp sides of their guitars. One of them, the Spider, begins his day at 7 a.m. on the Country music television spectacular and, on the Opry, plays into the succeeding dawn with not so much as a grin of fatigue. It is the session-men, not single stars, who diffuse the Nashville 'sound', steely and exquisite, a sort of barrel-organ of banjo and strings, proceeding not from the heart but from ferocious dexterity and lasting not one second longer than it has been booked.

To grow rich, however, your heart need not beat in tune. On Music Row the biggest figure in every respect is Buddy Lee, a gigantically fat man with violet-encircled eyes. Buddy Lee's original occupation was wrestling, and encouraging midgets to do so. Arriving a year or so back, he seized the opportunity to direct the career of the immortal Hank Williams's son. That pugnacious-looking youth at the time seemed to promise little of his father's waif-like brilliance. Today he pugnaciously smiles down from the billboard of the restaurant outside the Opry theatre itself, and Buddy Lee is about to build a skyscraper.

Outside Buddy Lee's office the 'Mourners' Bench' is full – the queue of young men, and some not so young, entreating a similar transformation for themselves. Beyond the office is an apartment furnished in hacienda-style. Here Buddy Lee himself sits, in his new world of tailored buckskin and sentimental melodies, silent but for the stertorousness of his breathing.

Tiny against the pleated bulk of Buddy Lee, his assistant

Oscar Davies outlines the achievement of the corporation. Since his most recent stroke Oscar can do little beyond fetching the beers from the icebox to the bar. But what history there is in his dry bark and harnessed frame: an Odyssey not of music so much as the endless ways man will devise to make his fellows pay gate-money.

It was Oscar who first discovered Elvis Presley, singing in an airport lounge. At different times he has managed Eddy Arnold, Buddy Holly, Eddie Cochran. It was because Oscar was called to the other side of the room that Jerry Lee Lewis so far forgot himself as to confess to having married his 14-year-old cousin. Oscar, in the 1920s, wrote the publicity of Tom Mix, the cowboy hero. In the 1930s, he promoted dance-marathons. He was, they say, the first man to make a million dollars in Country music. Then, they add, he lost a million-and-a-half. He brings out another beer, gasps for breath, then tells you that Buddy Lee is a remarkable, remarkable man.

The money up here is sometimes ridiculous. Mel Kilgore, composer of 'Wolverton Mountain', has a gold-plated telephone. Hank Williams Junior's Cadillac is hung with firearms that fire; his house with wrought iron musical notes. Loretta Lynn owns an entire town, Hurricane Mills, including the ghosts of a troop of Confederate soldiers. The city divides into those rich in Country music and those broken by it, or about to be broken; with a Greyhound bus gliding uncomfortably between.

But the application of those millions is apt to take on the wildness of the fiddler's arm. A star is, of course, obliged to build himself a palace, like Hank Snow's Rainbow Ranch in which the odours of cakemix and polar-bear rugs curiously commingle, but what then? The safest is to put it into catering; since those who are drawn by a dream do not care what they eat, into horrible catering. There has been Minnie Pearl's Chicken, and Tennessee Ernie's Steak 'n' Biscuits, and the Conway Twitty Twittyburger, and Hank Williams Junior's Barbecue Pits, and Tex Ritter's Chuck Wagons. I have an enduring memory of him: America's Most Beloved Cowboy. He is saying, 'Now, jest you take a look inside that

Superburger.' I could not.

No Mourners' Bench is busier than outside Chet Atkins's
office in the RCA building. As well as being the most famous of
all Country guitarists, Atkins is RCA's chief talent spotter. As
well as touring and recording, he also designs guitars for the
Grecht company. 'My face got so tired today, I thought I
wouldn't shave,' he says apologetically. 'Last night I fell
asleep playing guitar.'

He is so dapper and laconic, it is difficult to credit what
personal insecurities he had to overcome to attain his reputa-
tion, such as sweating at the palms. And asthma, and a
stomach ulcer caused by his dealings with the lugubrious
RCA star Jim Reeves. Years after his death, Reeves still sells
in millions, and he is Jimmie Bee's great idol and model.
Jimmie Bee cannot know what a vexation 'Gentleman Jim'
was to those about him – 'Poor Jim' as Chet Atkins calls him.
'He tried so hard to be great that in the end he was.'

Buddy's apartment is only a few streets away, at the top of a
broken, grey wood house where the sun comes through the
window mesh like yellow point lace and an old-fashioned propellor fan roars from the linoleum. Buddy and Jody have the
bed and Jimmie Bee occupies a space on the floor. His manner
intimates 'I've slept rough out on the range many times'. His
dignity is unassailable, even as Jody hands to him the bundle
of freshly-washed rags that is his underwear.

Country music did not originate in the Grand Ol' Opry any
more than on Music Row. When the first Opry show was
played in 1923, Vernon Dahart had already won a gold disc
for 'The Wreck of the Old '97'. Nor has the spectacular
always been in its present hillside theatre, somewhat like a
small Albert Hall. Originally, it was just a barn-dance on the
radio, executed by a single fiddler. Subsequently he was
joined by a zither-player named Mrs Cline. A half-crazy
steamboat captain increased it to concert proportions and
brought it to where it now is. Though Jody with her talisman

254

from the brickwork does not know yet, the hygienic forces behind the Hall of Fame are planning to abandon the old dark, poky theatre in favour of a new, air-conditioned 'Opryland'.

While the old Opry lasts, it has a heart. It must, if even Jimmie Bee could get backstage. Or perhaps the Opry atmosphere comes from conscience, an atonement for those silver-coated cars and guitar-shaped swimming pools; for the greatest star who appears on it receives, as Buddy would get for his first show, a flat rate of 29 dollars. From this altruism, only the session-musicians are exempt. Their rate is even less, but they are paid for each appearance they make. They are onstage all night, accompanying every act.

It is still a radio show, promoted by the National Life and Accident Corporation over its station WSM – We Shield Millions. Smaller manufacturers sponsor parts of the programme – wild fiddles and choirs of pedal-steel by courtesy of pile-ointment or bacon guaranteed not to shrivel in the pan. The audience sits in encircling wood pews, cooled only by souvenir paper fans, obedient to every signal for applause. The compere is the same, supernaturally-wrinkled old gentleman who officiated at the Texas Troubador's midnight jamboree. At his lighted lectern, the old gentleman grips one ear and, in tones of sternest realism, praises Goo Goo Almond Clusters. 'Goodness gracious, they're *good!*'

Jimmie Bee moves about the wings unchallenged: it is an Opry tradition to welcome all visitors. Friends and relations may wander through from the stage door, and even out in front of the audience: there is a constant shuffle at the edge of the music, a popping in and out of the pantomime backdrop for Martha White's Self Rize Flour, and through the door leading through to Tootsie's Orchid Lounge. Free coffee is provided backstage, and lemonade and cola. Old men tune fiddles. Children play games. Every man's suit, when it left the tailor, seems to have had a guitar attached. As Queens of Country and Western walk through, their blonde hair crackles. Patterns of instrument cases lie underfoot, spilling forth silks of blood and burnt orange.

Here are Lester Flatt and Earl Scruggs, solemn and quiet.

Here, chubby with wealth, powdered with benevolence, is Roger Miller, in town to overlook the running of his King of the Road Motel. Here is Marty Robbins, who sang 'Devil Woman' and 'El Paso'. He is unrecognisable, his hair dyed yellow after a stock-car racing mishap, but they recognise him. He is willing to shake hands with a whole audience.

Here is Hank Snow with a toupee like a moustache on his tiny skull, who carries himself as one irresistibly handsome. He will pass into legend, not for 'I'm Movin' On' but for letting Elvis Presley depart from his payroll. The kid, according to Oscar Davies, was upstaging him. Here are fat girls and gingham boys with bells on their knees, dancing – to the angriest Conservative, nothing in Country music is suspect. Here, with his winged eyes, is Ernest Tubb, the Texas Troubador and his cowboys from Hell. Here, briefly reclaimed from the world of the superburger, is Tex Ritter, America's Mos Beloved Cowboy.

He is like a bullfrog with a headband, 49 years of hats having pinched a line about his skull. He is dressed in cream frogged with green, the beauty of the composition threatened by ash piling off his cigarette as he says to his drummer, a boy named 'the Squirrel':

'Gimme a number.'

' "Just Beyond the Moon",' the Squirrel suggests.

'Nope.'

' "The Boll Weevil".'

'Okay.'

The cigarette-ash falls to scatter down America's Most Beloved Cowboy's cream and green coat-lapel.

'Now,' the Squirrel cautions, 'you ain't goin' to stop in the middle of it are you?'

The Beloved Cowboy is another very old man; but the cardboard Wild West he represents has proved to be imperishable. In the confluence of the stage lights, his legs unsteadily ride their high heeled boots. He does 'High Noon'. They love him for singing it. Not well, for it sounds like a phonograph running down, but the way he always sings it. He is the soul of Country and Western, of white America, whose Soul music this is. He is a happy ending. The applause and flickering fans spread out to form a continent in the darkness.

Down on The Strip, Buddy is playing to the drunks in Music City Lounge. When Jimmie Bee can make his single beer last no longer, he walks along to another bar called The Wheel. It is the same as Music City Lounge – the same empty barn whose muted jukebox has little to do with the scrawl of violins released out on the street. A hag in white topboots dances with the solitary customer, pumping his arm conscientiously. But in here, occasionally, Jimmie Bee's great hour approaches.

With tremendous flourishes he jumps up to the stage, looping the flex of the hand microphone around. He tries to sing like Jim Reeves, like Johnny Cash. When he tries to sing like Elvis Presley, a piece of hair falls from his lengthening forehead to droop beside his face.

Jimmie Bee sits down again and produces his wallet. He has copied out advice from a radio disc-jockey which he thinks may help him:

'Save ten per cent. of income. Let the imagination soar. Act the part of the person you would like to be. Knock and the door will be opened. My ambition. To be number one entertainer in Music City.'

– but late that night, as he sits at the restaurant counter, his shoulders are shaking.

Another bus comes in. Another boy with another guitar gets off and walks across, towards the lights.

The Foulk Brothers: Pop Promoting Blues

'Ronnie . . . ' Ronald Foulk's secretary broke into the conference. 'Will you accept a transfer call from America?'

The Pop promoter who, in 1969, inveigled Bod Dylan out of
retirement, across the Atlantic and on to the Isle of Wight's
innocent foothills, is a chubby youth with bushy blond hair
and a semblance – totally misleading – of great caution and
nervousness.

'No,' he answered his secretary's question politely.

It was the eve of the Foulk brothers' latest promotion: a
concert featuring the American Rock star Frank Zappa and
the English psychedelic group Hawkwind. The venue was one
which only the Foulks could have dreamed up – that hallowed
London landmark, the Oval cricket ground.

The conference was about publicity. Before the Foulks' last
big concert – the Wembley Rock and Roll spectacular, with
Chuck Berry and Little Richard – they had sent a naked girl
wandering up Downing Street to knock on the Prime Minis-
ter's door. For the Zappa and Hawkwind concert, it was felt,
the device would seem a little familiar.

Peter Harrigan, the press officer, said, 'We could
announce that the stage has collapsed.'

'Then no one will come to the wretched concert,' Ronnie
pointed out. He turned to his secretary, still holding up the
telephone receiver.

'We never accept transfer charge calls,' Ronnie said. 'Who
is it?'

'They don't say. They just say will you accept the charges?
And if you don't, they'll sue you.'

One publicity stunt involving Frank Zappa had already badly misfired. This was to be Zappa's first concert in Britain since being pulled by a girl fan's enraged fiancé from the stage of the Rainbow Theatre, and sustaining a broken leg. Peter Harrigan had arranged for Zappa, still on crutches, to give a press conference at which his attacker's girl friend was propelled forward to hand him a consoling bunch of flowers. Zappa's manager was currently looking for Peter Harrigan in order to break his back.

'Or . . .' Harrigan said, unabashed. 'We could get someone screwing on the wicket.'

The thought of people screwing on the Oval wicket made Ronnie gasp in horror, push his blond hair out of his eyes and look down at his plum coloured slippers. 'No – it's rude,' he whispered. 'The Duchy of Cornwall' [the Oval landlords] 'would freak its head.' Then, sidling up to Harrigan, he whispered, 'Who would we get to do the screwing?'

Two names were mentioned of his many part-time helpers.

'No.' Ronnie said, aghast. 'They're married!'

It was suggested that the same girl who had given Zappa his flowers might be prevailed on to undertake this new service. They could offer her £50 to be ravished at the wicket of the Oval, coinciding with the pre-concert visit of inspection by the Greater London Council.

'Michael,' Ronnie said, 'what time do the GLC go down there?'

'Two-thirty,' Michael Baxter said.

'Do you do armoured vehicles?' Ronnie said into his telephone. 'For hire? We're wanting to hire an armoured vehicle.

'So . . .' he mused. 'We get them to screw after the GLC's been down there.'

'Before,' said Peter Harrigan.

'That's rude,' Ronnie whispered.

'No,' Harrigan explained. 'We go in and pull them apart.'

'But what are they going to screw on?'

Ronnie said, 'Peter Bull, you can get a bed together down at the Oval, please, with sheets and all?'

'What are the Oval people going to say, though, when they

259

see a bed going up?'

'Tell 'em,' Ronnie said, 'it's for Frank Zappa's leg.'

The marvel is not that Ronnie survived the Isle of Wight but that it does not haunt him. The final of his three Pop festivals, in 1970, lost him £100,000; he was afterwards hounded off by the gentle Island ratepayers; yet to Ronnie it is a dream that he never fully grasped. All those people together and no-one killed. 'It was a proud affair,' Ronnie murmurs looking at the photographs, at the thousands of faces stretching towards the sea.

His organisation survived, as any group must that has withstood a siege. Most of them are qualified for more spiritual work. Peter Bull is a film maker, Nick Wright an art teacher, Peter Harrigan alternates his publicist duties, somewhat implausibly, with teaching in Nigeria. This is their strength in the music industry: immunity from it. They even speak a private language, based on Ronnie's own North Country olde-English, in which for instance nobody goes, he 'repairs'. Peter Bull is never addressed by any but his full name. Thanks also to Ronnie, the fatigue and litter of Pop's counting-houses is continually assuaged by tuck, by cream cakes or masses of sandwiches. As his concert now moves towards fresh difficulties, his wife Bunny entered with soup in large gold-rimmed plates.

'Which would you prefer?' Ronnie inquired. 'Tomato, mushroom or Royal Game?'

But he seemed depressed. The trouble is that as an impresario his great moments came too quickly; since the Isle of Wight everything else has seemed a little flat. This concert, for a piffling 15,000, was being put on largely to introduce another two weeks later, but Ronnie was still worried by it. In a Rock show, he has learned, one must offer 'a legend and something current'. Frank Zappa, for all his disabled leg, and the supporting band, Hawkwind, did not seem to Ronnie's eye to be sufficient of either; although, as is the way of musicians, they had impressed themselves exceedingly. Both at the same time were demanding the privilege of playing last on the programme.

260

Then Ray Foulk, small behind his large desk, announced, 'There isn't any money in the bank.'

Ray Foulk is as small, slender and intense as his elder brother is chubby and expansive. It was Ronnie who, in the first place, persuaded Bob Dylan to come to the Isle of Wight, by telling him that Tennyson had once lived there. But it was Ray – making his first trip abroad – who went to New York to arrange the contract.

'You've got to raise a grand in cash by tonight,' Ray said sombrely.

Ronnie pushed his hair over his eyes.

'All right,' he said. 'Which of the cheques we've paid out haven't been presented yet?'

Distractions multiplied with evening. There were now fingermarks on Ronnie's hair. Ray had opposed the idea of copulation at the Oval – Ronnie is boss but sometimes the intensity of Ray carries a decision. Coconut matting was to be laid instead; however, the friend who promised to deliver it had not done so. On a Radio Luxembourg publicity banner, 'Luxembourg' had been spelled wrong; Peter Bull, in repairing too energetically round the office, had stubbed his toe and broken it; and Rikki Farr was with them once more.

The precise value of Rikki Farr to the re-assembling team is never immediately clear. Since the Dylan Festival he has been present at most of their concerts: almost equivalent measures of the glory and blame thereof attach to his portly frame. Rikki Farr is very large, gingerbearded, with a habit of holding out both arms as if to embrace all Mankind. His eye alights satirically on Peter Harrigan, the Press officer, dressed in an unlikely combination of dark blue blazer and Oriental beads. 'He – look at him!' Rikki Farr cries. 'Looks like an Oxford export-reject. Can't make up his mind whether he wants to join the rowing-club or become a follower of the Maharishi.'

The brothers had by now received an ultimatum from the management of Frank Zappa and of Hawkwind. Both must appear last in the concert or both would be withdrawn. Somehow, this fearful threat caused little consternation.

'You can only treat it as a joke,' Ray said. 'The whole music business is a joke.'

An emissary came from one of their financiers, and, with a blessed flutter of cheques, the deficiency in the petty-cash at least was made good.

Ronnie said to Ray, 'So what do we do about Zappa and Hawkwind?'

'Blast Hawkwind off the bill.'

'Then they'll only give a free concert somewhere else to take our audience away.'

An inquiry had already been received about the car to take Zappa to the airport on Sunday morning.

'Sunday morning,' Ronnie said, 'it's a dead cert we won't want to know him.'

On the morning of the concert, Ronnie telephones his mother in the Isle of Wight. 'Hello, Mother dear – yes, everything's fine, Mother dear. A few clouds in the sky, Mother dear, but the sun's peeping through.'

The gates into the Oval are open but barred by tough faces. 'Security' once more lies with the West Ken Mob, a group of youths of frightening aspect, to their employers no less than the general public. Once the West Ken Mob hold a gate, nothing can get through. Indeed, the great concert-morning arrival, of ice-cream, of ambulances and odd, chalky bread rolls, lasts far into the day owing to the reluctance of the West Ken Mob to admit anyone to the ground at all. When Ronnie arrived, the West Ken Mob even turned him away.

The stage grows out from the seats of the Vauxhall Stand. Whatever Ronnie's worries, the stage is never among them. It is built by his youngest brother, Bill, a graduate of the Royal College of Art, as quiet and shy as Ray is tenacious and shy, and Ronnie sociable but shy. The sight of it seemed to act as a restorative on Ronnie, as any construction of wood must reassure a world of uncertainties. 'Lovely venue, though, isn't it?' Ronnie said. He surveyed the green floor, the shuttered scoreboard, the gasometer above the yellow circle of the wall. He thought of the Isle of Wight, the fences all torn down, and feelingly added, 'Lovely wall, that.'

Beyond the wall is the world, piling from the rhythms of the Northern Line. A thin bulwark of Ronnie and Ray's friends and relations awaits them in the turnstile-huts. Peter Bull holds one, Bill's wife, Linda, another; it is impossible to over-rate the value of an honest turnstile-keeper. The feeling of siege is not unpleasant, mixed with one of reunion. Ronnie's sister, whom he calls Dearie-O, is there, and Ronnie's wife, Bunny, and her sister and a friend's baby, asleep. Harry Garood is back doing the electrical work; a small shopkeeper from Carisbrooke, Isle of Wight, one of their most valued supporters, who stoops among the buzzing city of volts as if attending to a cat's whisker. And Nick Wright and Roger Cole and Lauri Say; and, with a commotion at the gate, Rikki Farr is there, too. He wears dark glasses, though the day is over-cast.

In the turnstile-huts, openings of light appear; the metal-work snickers; they begin to come in.

Slowly at first, forcing airbeds and baggage through, then surging forward in the exhilaration of being first, they are nothing yet but a crowd's patched atoms. All crowds are terrifying but each one the Foulks have confined has been somehow different of expression. There was the crowd at the *first* Isle of Wight Festival, which everybody has forgotten, and the Bob Dylan crowd that seemed to engender its own evening sun. There was that quarter of a million crowd in 1970 whose curious blend of apathy and belligerence was never quite comprehensible. Bill Foulk is the one most haunted by it. 'I think if that crowd had been a bit better organised,' he says, 'they might have killed one of us.'

Ronnie, standing by the Vauxhall Gate, was disappointed by this one. Zappa's people or Hawkwind's? Through the stands the greenness was overlaid by an almost uniform blue. 'There aren't so many freaks about as there were.' Ronnie said.

The progress of a Rock concert is much like that of a boil. When it has begun to take its course there is little that can be done apart from external application. The final Isle of Wight

Festival carried them along with it for five days before depositing them, spent, upon its infinite lawn of rubbish. Even today, at so much less of an event, the equation of it is too large for thought – the stadium, the crowd, the watching authorities, the sum to be earned or forfeit. You can only repair, as Ronnie does, ceaselessly to and from the turnstiles. You can only try to stop the little boys climbing in for nothing as they are, in little scrapes and flashes, all along the curve of the wall.

Outside the bowl of grandstands, one could almost forget the 15,000 people within. Great, beautiful things may have been astir among them but it was not written on the faces of those led forth to be bandaged or sedated; there was a dullness in the air as if a crowd can swallow the very passage of time. The music was background music, for all its uproar, nor did the eye jump as one band followed another: the same hair, the same pointed hats and skinny, stamping legs, the same clueless guitars held high in a belief of brilliance. From beside them, behind them, or far off in the cricketers' Pavilion, the effect was the same; a Punch and Judy show endlessly repeated. So eight hours passed.

A man without trousers walked a little apart from the crowd, his shirt-tails barely covering his defiant genitalia. He lay down on the coconut-matting in a Roman attitude, then he turned over. 'I can't keep this up much longer,' he remarked.

Of the three brothers, only Bill Foulk is actually happy at a Rock concert. Bill is perfectly contented standing about in the open air. Before their mother was widowed they lived in a big house in Derbyshire with grounds laid out by Capability Brown. If that gave Ronnie his notions of space and size, it made Bill want to be a landscape gardener. The stage completed, he was up at 5.30 a.m. this morning with a squad of volunteers laying the mats over the wicket. The remainder of the concert he spends in an umpire's white coat at the Vauxhall Gate, telling people he'd like to let them in but there's nothing he can do.

As for Ronnie, his repairing seldom takes him near the stage. This is Ray's domain: Ray stands alone in the noise-torn walkways, his thumbs in his hipster-pockets, his thin, pale face set hard. From time to time, someone comes up and screams a question at him, or a threat. Ray shakes his lank hair firmly.

'He loves aggravation,' Ronnie says.

'– thrives on it,' concurs Bill.

The stage is Ray's but a more gorgeous personage usurps the microphone.

'Testing,' Rikki Farr booms, 'on Channel 31.'

'Testing,' he repeats, 'on Channel 31.'

Behind the stage Bill Foulk smiles.

'We don't have 31 channels,' he explains.

It is with darkness that a concert enters the critical phase. In daylight the crowd is perfectly occupied with being a crowd; it grows dangerous, like many beasts, when its vision is reduced. Already a fight is beginning in the ghastly shadows around the popcorn concession. 'I couldn't stand it,' Ronnie says, repairing wide of the incident. And little girls are now climbing over the wall.

The dispute had been settled as to which act played last. Frank Zappa had agreed to go onstage first, thus appeasing the vanity of Hawkwind and enabling the whole concert to finish, as prescribed by the GLC licence, at 10 p.m., The Foulks could feel confident of being able to present their second Oval concert in a fortnight's time.

Zappa's fee was £12,000. Of this, half had been paid in advance; the remainder would be handed to him before he struck a note, in cash. But Ronnie's doubts as to his drawing-power had been realised. The day's gate-takings were not sufficient for the balance to be paid in cash: such a matter must therefore be broached as will make any promoter fearful. Would Zappa take a cheque?

At the Vauxhall Gate, Roger Cole espied a human pyramid forming against the outside of the wall. Roger Cole is mysteriously adjutant both to the West Ken Mob and to the sceptical-looking commissionaires who support them. He has the aspect of a pirate – beard and bare chest and wrist-thongs – with the polite voice of an estate-agent. He hurled himself, coat-tails flying from his naked torso, struck the pyramid in the centre, toppled sideways with it.

Since Zappa's manager had threatened to break his back, Peter Harrigan took no part in the negotiations now proceeding – indeed, he could only approach the backstage area by ducking along car-bodies like a Resistance fighter. Zappa would accept a cheque, but the meeting was not cordial. With Ray was the Foulks' company solicitor, who happened to be wearing plimsolls. This led Zappa's manager brusquely to question his powers-of-attorney. Ray returned from the meeting pale with anger.

'I just looked at him. I said, "What are you doing, calling me a con-man or something?"'

'The trouble is,' Michael Baxter said drily, 'they've sussed out that we've got other money in here.'

The money counted, the incarnation might become complete. Yet the coming of Frank Zappa was of a vividness unequal to the bargaining for it. He was, after all, a man of normal size, with a prominent nose, swinging on a crutch. The nose was visible from time to time over the parapet of the stage while Zappa delivered an electronic symphony, like the disputing of many xylophones, to a largely expressionless night. By the time he had finished, it was 10 o'clock. The GLC licence had expired. Hawkwind were still to play.

Ronnie telephoned his mother again.

'Hello, Mother dear . . . Yes, all going well, Mother dear. Fine weather, yes, Mother dear, nice night . . .'

Behind the Vauxhall stand, a large crowd had collected owing to the mixing-up of Zappa's followers with Hawkwind's. This annoyed the uniformed commissionaire, whose instructions were to permit nobody backstage. 'I may not earn the fabulous sums they do,' he complained, 'but I earn £40 a week as an upholsterer for London Transport on the Northern Line.' The commissionaire took an angry pinch of snuff. 'They're no better than I am.' he added, 'just because they get a bit of the other at night-times.'

As Zappa left the backstage enclosure, a girl shrieked something at him and was pushed aside by his black bodyguard. An admirer of the girl started to attack the roof of

Zappa's limousine with a wooden post. He was laid senseless by the black man. The same black man had also dealt with one of the West Ken Mob who now leaned at a drainpipe with a diagram in red where his lips ought to have been.

It became imperative to curtail the performance of Hawkwind. The point was emphasised by the ominous appearance of a senior policeman, Chief Superintendant Solway, twirling his keys round his fingers and asking to see 'an official of the company'. Ronnie and Ray put it to Hawkwind's manager, whose tam o'shanter was worn at the angle of an earmuff. He said that, if Hawkwind's power was suddenly cut off, there would be 'a riot'.

'I think you're being hysterical,' the solicitor in plimsolls crisply said.

'Look, man, I've being doing Hawkwind concerts for a year and I *know*.'

'They got to turn their own amps off,' Harry Garood the electrician said, 'otherwise they'll blow up.'

'– Look man, I've been doing Hawkwind concerts for a year and I *know*.'

Groups of people stood about, arguing noisily but with an underlying fatigue. Ronnie stood in one argument, Ray in another, Rikki Farr in another – even the voice of Rikki Farr was subdued. None of them now seemed connected with the stage, where Hawkwind leapt and adored themselves in a light-show of a type popular five years ago. All round the Oval windows angrily bloomed; twin beams from the lighting-tower hung like Zeppelins overhead. The doors, so vehemently closed all day, were open, and little boys ran everywhere. Nearby a water-main had burst.

It was agreed to turn the power down slowly, then to bring up the arc-lights from the Pavilion. Directly this was done, the crowd, so far from rioting, merely turned and began to drift, on the chink of its own arc-lit filth, away.

The groups behind the stage were reluctant to disperse, however, as if clinging still to some illusion of climax. Peter Bull said to Bill's wife, Linda, 'Remember when we put on the Who and the Faces here last year – that was the last time we really felt a part of something, that we were giving something out and getting it back. What we've all been through in the past four years is over, because we're not feeling anything come back any more.'

A naked boy was led past them. As he went he fondly kissed the St John Ambulance attendant.

'Depressing, isn't it?' said Bill's wife.

'Yes.'

'Aftermath,' said Bill's wife.

'Yes, real Monday morning feeling.'

'It's been like that,' she said, 'since nine o'clock this morning.'

Imagine that chaos spread over five days. After the last Isle of Wight Festival all of them collapsed. Even Ronnie, whose permanent faint agitation is an expression of stamina, dissolved into nervous shock – so Bunny, his wife, says – because it was claimed that a guard-dog had bitten somebody. Only Ray, so pale and small, endured it all and was back the next morning to face wreckage as far as the eye could see, just as he remained behind after the others had wearily left the Oval.

It did not seem so bad, however, after sleep. The horrors of the moment turned into anecdotes; of Chief Superintendant Solway, of Zappa's manager, of a mysterious and frightening member of the West Ken Mob named Toolbox who had been guarding a barricade. What worried Ronnie was that the GLC licence for their next concert might be revoked. When it was not, just as Ray had predicted, Ronnie insisted that the prices of the tickets must be halved. He also went on a diet.

Aside from Ray's second-hand Rolls Royce and Ronnie's semi-permanent table in the Polynesian Room at the London Hilton, neither of the Foulk brothers in any way resembles the juvenile millionaire their concert-promoting career is popularly supposed to have made of them. Ronnie, in particular, had seemed almost repelled by the piles of grubby pound notes that shuffled past him at his Oval concert. 'Funny thing – I can't stand counting money,' he said. 'If there's one thing I can't stand, it's counting money.'

There will be no more Isle of Wight festivals. Indeed, even the Foulks seem to recognise that the festivity has gone out of Rock in any venue. Their next promotion is a three-day anti-pollution festival, garbed as a medieval fair. The only big Rock name they still hunger to win is Elvis Presley. Ronnie is appalled by the enormity of the idea. Ray is working already on preliminary negotiations.

The second Oval concert two weeks later, featuring the avant-garde Rock trio Emerson, Lake and Palmer, was inevitably something of an anticlimax. This time, the Foulks had a co-promoter, one Michael Alfandary, a hairy young man, prone to bouts of nervous exhaustion. But the black moods of the Zappa concert had gone; the very turf-keepers seemed kindlier. The crowd, too, had changed. It was as if all their faces, away to the cricketing perimeters, formed one countenance, and that wore a pleasant expression. Rikki Farr stretched out his arms. 'Why don't you all sit down and enjoy the evening sun?' And, like the peaceful subsiding of one, they all did.

Michael Alfandary, the co-promoter, kept himself invisible until the concert's final hours. He explained that he was suffering from a boil on his bottom.

'The trouble is, ' Ronnie told him kindly, 'this concert is bigger than you normally do, Michael, and smaller than we normally do.'

He pushed his hair over his eyes and, with some exhilaration, added, 'I think I fancy a bag of chips from the fish-stall.'

One of the gate-keeping West Ken Mob came in to be paid, carrying a rolled-up Emerson, Lake and Palmer souvenir poster. The Foulks murmured approval at so mild a weapon. Grinning modestly, the youth unrolled the poster to reveal a wooden chair-leg.

Last thing of all, Ronnie telephoned his mother in the Isle of Wight.

'– Hello, Mother dear. Yes, everything went well, Mother dear, we copped some fine weather ... Yes, see you tomorrow, Mother dear ... 'Bye.'

SHOUT! THE TRUE STORY OF THE BEATLES
by Philip Norman

One of the greatest stories in the history of popular entertainment came to a brutal end when, in December 1980, a
hail of bullets ended the life of John Lennon, founder
member and wayward leader of the Beatles.

In *Shout!*, Philip Norman recreates the Beatle phenomenon – recalling how John, Paul, George and Ringo rose
to international fame and how the eventual collapse of
Apple Corps reduced a billion-dollar empire to squalor,
anger and suspicion.

'The definitive Beatles biography'
                                    The Sunday Times

'Conscientiously researched . . . his grasp of his material
is faultless'
                                    George Melly, The Observer

'Nothing less than thrilling . . . the definitive biography'
                                    New York Times

0 552 11961 X   £2.50